KURDISH DIASPORA MOBILISATION
IN DENMARK

Edinburgh Studies on Diasporas and Transnationalism

Series Editors: Bahar Baser and Mari Toivanen

Bringing together high-quality academic works written by diaspora and transnationalism scholars, this series adopts an interdisciplinary approach and is open to empirical and theoretical submissions alike, making meaningful contributions to contemporary debates in the field. While focusing on economic, political, social and cultural factors that shape and maintain transnational identities and diasporic attachments to the country of origin and residence, the series is also open to submissions on different aspects of transnational interactions from an arts and humanities perspective.

Published and forthcoming titles
Second-generation 'Return' Migration: The Turkish-German Experience
Nilay Kılınç and Russell King

Kurdish Diaspora Mobilisation in Denmark: Supporting the Struggle in Syria
Anne Sofie Schøtt

edinburghuniversitypress.com/series/esdt

KURDISH DIASPORA MOBILISATION IN DENMARK

Supporting the Struggle in Syria

Anne Sofie Schøtt

EDINBURGH
University Press

Edinburgh University Press is one of the leading university presses in the UK. We publish academic books and journals in our selected subject areas across the humanities and social sciences, combining cutting-edge scholarship with high editorial and production values to produce academic works of lasting importance. For more information visit our website: edinburghuniversitypress.com

Edinburgh University Press Ltd
The Tun – Holyrood Road
12 (2f) Jackson's Entry
Edinburgh EH8 8PJ

Typeset in 11/15 Adobe Garamond by
IDSUK (DataConnection) Ltd, and
printed and bound by CPI Group (UK) Ltd,
Croydon, CR0 4YY

A CIP record for this book is available from the British Library

ISBN 978 1 4744 9170 9 (hardback)
ISBN 978 1 4744 9173 0 (webready PDF)
ISBN 978 1 4744 9172 3 (epub)

CONTENTS

Part IV Findings and Conclusions

ACKNOWLEDGEMENTS

First of all, I would like to express my gratitude to the Royal Danish Defence College, and especially to the Director of the Institute for Strategy, Anja Dalgaard-Nielsen, for providing me with the opportunity to embark on and complete the PhD research on which this book is based. Thanks also to my colleagues for precious discussions along the way, and to Natalia Thomsen, intern at the institute, for practical assistance when it was most needed.

I would also like to thank my doctoral adviser, Professor Jakob Skovgaard-Petersen at the Department of Cross-Cultural and Regional Studies, University of Copenhagen, for unwavering support and encouragement from an early stage of the research process. Huge thanks also to Associate Professor Ipek Demir, University of Leeds, and Associate Professor Nicole Dörr, University of Copenhagen, for inspiration and highly valuable input to various parts of this study.

Thanks to all those who urged me to turn my research into a book, and in particular to Emma Rees and the series editors, Bahar Baser and Mari Toivanen, at Edinburgh University Press, who made it possible. Thanks also to the reviewers for constructive comments to the manuscript. It should be noted that Chapter 4 is a revised and updated version of my article 'The Kurds of Syria: From the Forgotten People to World State Actors' (Schøtt 2017).

The present study could not have been completed without the participation of the people I met in the field. I am grateful to all of you for accepting my interview requests, inviting me to your events and allowing me to experience your world, which in turn allowed me to re-experience my own. This book also benefits from fruitful discussions with members of the Kurdish Studies community, whom I met at conferences and seminars. I owe Mustafa Topal and Özlem Has special thanks.

Finally, I would like to thank my friends and family, especially my husband and son. You deserve my deepest gratitude for love and support throughout this journey.

ABBREVIATIONS

DIAKURD	Kurdish Diaspora Confederation (Konfederasyona Kurdên Diyaspora)
ERNK	Kurdistan National Liberation Front (Eniya Rizgariya Neteweyî ya Kurdistanê)
FEY-KURD	Federation of Kurdish Associations in Denmark (Federasyona Komeleyên Kurdî li Danmarkê) (Danish: Sammenslutningen af Kurdiske Foreninger i Danmark)
FOKUS A	Association of Kurdish Students and Academics (Danish: Foreningen for Kurdiske Studerende og Akademikere)
HAK-PAR	Rights and Freedoms Party (Turkish: Hak ve Özgürlükler Partisi)
HNC	High Negotiations Committee
ISIS	Islamic State/Islamic State of Iraq and Syria (also called Daesh, Arabic: ad-Dawlah al-Islāmiyah fī 'l-ʿIrāq wa-ash-Shām)
KAD	Kurdish Alternative in Denmark (Danish: Kurdisk Alternativ i Danmark)
KCDK-E	Congress of Democratic Societies of Kurdistan in Europe (Kongreya Civakên Demokratîk a Kurdistaniyên Li Ewropa)
KCK	Kurdistan Communities Union (Koma Civakên Kurdistan)
KDP/PDK	Kurdistan Democratic Party (Partiya Demokrat a Kurdistanê)

KDPPS   Kurdish Democratic Progressive Party in Syria (Partiya Demokrat a Pêşverû a Kurdî li Sûriyê)
KDPS   Kurdish Democratic Party in Syria (Partiya Demokrat a Kurdî li Sûriyê)
KDP-S   Kurdistan Democratic Party of Syria (Partiya Demokrat a Kurdistanê li Sûriyê)
KNC/ENKS   Kurdish National Council (Encûmena Niştimanî ya Kurdî li Sûriyê)
KNK   Kurdistan National Congress (Kongra Netewiya Kurdistan)
KOMKAR   Association of Workers from Kurdistan (Komeleya Karkeran ji Kurdistanê)
KOMKAR-DK   Association of Workers from Kurdistan in Denmark (Komeleya Karkeran ji Kurdistanê-Danmarkê)
KON-KURD   Confederation of Kurdish Associations (Konfederasyona Komeleya Kurdî)
KRG   Kurdistan Regional Government
KRI   Kurdistan Region of Iraq
KSC   Kurdish Supreme Committee (Desteya Bilind a Kurd)
PAK   Kurdistan Freedom Party (Partiya Azadiya Kurdistanê)
PJAK   Free Life Party of Kurdistan (Partiya Jiyana Azad a Kurdistanê)
PKK   Kurdistan Workers' Party (Partiya Karkerên Kurdistanê)
PSK   Socialist Party of Kurdistan (Partiya Sosyalîst a Kurdistan)
PUK   Patriotic Union of Kurdistan (Yekîtiya Niştimanî Kurdistan)
PYD   Democratic Union Party (Partiya Yekîtiya Demokrat)
SDF   Syrian Democratic Forces
SKFD   Federation of Kurdish Associations in Denmark (Danish: Sammenslutningen af Kurdiske Foreninger i Danmark)
SNC   Syrian National Council
TAK   Freedom Falcons of Kurdistan (Teyrêbazên Azadiya Kurdistan)
TEV-DEM   Movement for a Democratic Society (Tevgera Civaka Demokratîk)
YPG   People's Protection Unit (Yekîneyên Parastina Gel)
YPJ   Women's Protection Unit (Yekîneyên Parastina Jin)

BRICOLAGE

'Exploration requires *bricolage*, the gathering and piecing together of clues, the following of tracks that lead back to the starting point, the recognition of signs that are instantly recognizable, and the discovery of other signs that were missed the first time around'

Alberto Melucci (1989, p. 13)

PART I

KURDISH DIASPORA MOBILISATION
AND IDENTITY FORMATION

1

INTRODUCTION

Introduction

The quiet revolution is no longer quiet

In August 2017, the Federation of Kurdish Associations in Denmark, FEY-KURD, hosted a public meeting in the Federation's community centre in the suburbs of Copenhagen. Under the title, 'The quiet revolution is no longer quiet', the organisers wanted to address the current developments in the Kurdish areas of northern Syria. Three speakers were invited to talk about the revolution and developments in Rojava. One was a Danish volunteer who had joined the YPG (the People's Protection Units), and the two others were members of a delegation who had recently returned from Rojava, representing a network of Kurdish doctors and nurses and an association promoting ecological agriculture in Rojava. Around forty people showed up to meet the YPG fighter and listen to the first-hand accounts of the two delegation members. Most of them were Kurds, but a few Danish supporters of the Kurdish cause also appeared. The YPG volunteer talked about his journey to become a YPG fighter and his experience of fighting Islamic State alongside dedicated Kurdish fighters. The two delegation members showed photos and talked passionately about the way in which Rojava society was getting back on its feet after the destruction wrought by Islamic State, thanks to the joint efforts of the population. The society was still in dire need of all kinds of material necessities in order to rebuild and develop its infrastructure. The atmosphere at the meeting was very intense. Everybody was delighted by the fact that a Kurdish democratic society was emerging from the ruins. The passionate discussion following the presentations, centred on the actions which the individual and the community could take to support the Kurds and to further the development in the Kurdish areas of Syria.

This study investigates Kurdish activism in Denmark in support of the Kurdish struggle in Syria. It analyses the various ways in which the Kurdish diaspora in Denmark mobilised in support of the Kurdish struggle playing out in the Syrian Civil War as well as against Islamic State, from the battle of Kobane (2014) to the battle of Afrin (2018). Moreover, it reflects on the impact of the Syrian crisis on the small but well-established Kurdish community in Denmark. Like the Kurds in Syria, the Kurds in Denmark would no longer be quiet, but would find new ways of expressing their engagement in the Kurdish cause. In doing so, I argue, they reformulated, and recommitted to, their Kurdish identity.

The Syrian crisis

In 2011, the so-called Arab Spring spread from one country to another in North Africa and the Middle East. Each country followed its own path. In Syria, the first protests took place in March 2011. After the initial peaceful demonstrations, the uprising gradually evolved into a civil war with a number of groups fighting against the Syrian security forces and with each other, following the violent response of the regime. In 2012, as government forces withdrew from the northern part of Syria to focus on the fight in the centre and the south of the country, Kurdish forces took control of the predominantly Kurdish areas. While the war raged in the other parts of Syria, the Kurdish areas enjoyed a relatively peaceful period. However, underneath the surface, a power struggle took place between the various political parties, in which the Democratic Union Party (PYD) proved to be the strongest player. The party took the lead in building up a new political system based on local self-governed administrative units in line with the ideology of the PKK leader Abdullah Öcalan. The party also benefitted from having a military branch, the People's Protection Unit (YPG), which could protect the Kurdish areas from external as well as internal threats. In the beginning of 2014, the Social

Contract of the peoples of Rojava was proclaimed, laying the constitutional ground for what became known as the Rojava Revolution. Thus, the Syrian Civil War paved the way for de facto autonomy in the Kurdish areas, covering the enclaves of Afrin, Kobane and Jazira at the Turkish border, in Kurdish called Rojava, i.e., the west (of Kurdistan).

In the beginning of 2014, another rebel group emerged, seizing the opportunity amongst the turmoil in Syria and the disability of the government to take control of the northern and eastern part of the country. Islamic State was originally an Iraqi movement, evolving from al-Qaeda in Iraq, which during the Syrian Civil War had joined forces with al-Qaeda affiliated groups in Syria. During the first half of 2014, the group seized control of a sizeable territory on both sides of the border between Syria and Iraq. Thus, in June 2014, when the caliphate was proclaimed from the great mosque in Mosul, Islamic State controlled a contiguous area spanning from Aleppo in the north-west to Baghdad in the south-east, with the Syrian city of Raqqa as the caliphate's capital. Two events, which took place in 2014, became defining moments both for the transnational Kurdish movement and for the international struggle against Islamic State. On 3 August 2014, Islamic State fighters attacked the city of Sinjar (Kurdish: Şingal) and the surrounding villages located west of Mosul and inhabited by Yezidi Kurds. During the attack, 9,000 women, children and men were killed or enslaved, while 50,000 managed to escape to the Sinjar Mountains (Serinci 2018, p. 344). The massacre shook the world when photos of fleeing individuals and families came out backed by witness reports of the atrocities committed by Islamic State. In Syria, Islamic State fighters reached Kobane in the middle of September and initiated a siege on the city. The Kurdish fighters of YPG and the female counterpart YPJ, the Women's Protection Units, endured heavy fighting that lasted for several months. Despite severe losses, the Kurdish fighters were able to lift the siege of the city on 26 January 2015. The paramount victory of the Kurdish fighters at Kobane was the first major defeat of the Islamic State fighters. The battle of Kobane also sowed the seeds of the tactical alliance between the YPG/J and the international coalition against Islamic State, which supported the Kurdish fighters in Kobane with intensive air support.

The international military intervention against Islamic State, called Operation Inherent Resolve (OIR), was initiated shortly after the attack by Islamic

State on the Yezidis in Sinjar. The US was the first country to respond to the international call for help to combat Islamic State, submitted by the Iraqi government through the UN Security Council, and the first US strike on Islamic State forces was launched on 8 August 2014. Later, a number of states followed suit and joined the US-led coalition. As stated by US president Barak Obama, the aim of the operation was 'to degrade, and ultimately destroy, ISIL' (Obama 2014). In contrast with the heavy presence of American ground forces in Iraq in the 2000s, this time the international intervention against Islamic State mainly consisted of airstrike capabilities to back the Iraqi and Kurdish forces on the ground and of military training programmes to strengthen the Iraqi and Kurdish armed forces against Islamic State. The operation was meant to support the fight of the government of Iraq against Islamic State, but very soon, it became evident that the organisation's ability to withdraw into Syria called for interventions in Syria as well. Thus, the coalition was already involved in airstrikes in Syria when Islamic State laid siege to Kobane in September 2014. In November 2015, the coalition established a tactical alliance with the Syrian Kurdish forces which emerged from the battle of Kobane, by sponsoring the formation of the Syrian Democratic Forces (SDF). As a multi-ethnic force encompassing the Kurdish forces of YPG and YPJ as well as non-Kurdish forces, the SDF was a very opportune collaborator for the coalition at the time as, in the summer of 2015, Turkey had hesitantly joined the coalition after a significant terror attack by Islamic State in Turkey. However, in joining, Turkey also wanted control over political developments in Rojava led by the PYD, which Turkey sees as a branch of the PKK and therefore as a terrorist organisation.

As a loyal partner of the US, Denmark joined the international coalition from the start of the intervention in August 2014. The Danish contribution was a result of a Danish foreign policy built on military activism which has evolved gradually since the Cold War. In this way, Denmark has gone further than what could be expected of a small state in the international system (Jakobsen and Møller 2012; Wæver 2016). The immediate reason for joining the operation was the threat of terrorism. Emphasising the urgency of the matter, the Danish Prime Minister Helle Thorning-Schmidt stated at a press conference that '[t]he terrorist organisation IS [. . .] poses a threat to Denmark and to our allies. If we do nothing, things will only get worse'

(Kongstad and Kaae 2014). To fortify the counter-terrorism efforts, the Danish parliament followed up by voting for two legal restrictions (in 2015 and 2016) that would prevent Danish citizens from travelling to conflict zones, without discriminating between fighters who wanted to join militant Islamist groups and volunteers for the Kurdish cause. These laws, however, turned out to be an obstacle for the Kurds and their supporters in Danish society who wanted to travel to the Kurdish controlled areas in Syria to fight on the same side as the Danish troops in the war against Islamic State.

The atrocities committed by Islamic State against the Yezidis in Sinjar and the siege of Kobane became huge mobilisation events among the Kurdish diaspora who felt solidarity with the sufferings of their fellow Kurds in the homeland. Thus, demonstrations were held in all major European cities to draw the attention of fellow Kurds, non-Kurdish citizens, and politicians in particular. Charity dinners and various other support activities were organised to raise money or collect clothes to send to the affected areas and to refugees who had fled the combat zone. At the same time, the heroic resistance and the victory of the Kurdish fighters in the battle of Kobane proved to the Kurdish transnational community that the Kurdish forces were able to do what no other forces had been capable of, namely to defeat Islamic State. Thus, the social media campaign #SaveKobane and similar activities mobilised Kurds from all political camps and Kurds without political affiliation as well as non-Kurds. The followers of the ideas of the PKK leader Abdullah Öcalan were also able to mobilise supporters for the political revolution of Rojava by stressing that the Syrian Kurds were able to build up and defend a democratic society in the midst of a war with a brutal enemy. In line with this, the Syrian Kurds were presented as spearheads for the democratic world against tyranny. Particularly, the female fighters in YPJ became symbols of moral superiority (liberal, secular and brave) and the complete opposite of the male Islamic State fighters (fascistic, fanatical and cowardly) (Toivanen and Baser 2016).

As was the case in all countries with Kurdish communities, the battle of Kobane made the Kurdish diaspora in Denmark immensely proud of being Kurdish as the Kurdish fighters were victorious and thereby defended Europe against the threat of terrorism. Besides the numerous humanitarian events aimed at raising money and collecting material necessities, public demonstrations were held and meetings with high-ranking politicians were arranged to capture the attention of the political decision-makers. However, as the news-worthiness of the Syrian Kurdish victories faded, and the Danish Parliament enforced the non-discriminatory restrictions on travels to Syria, the Kurdish activists felt increasingly disappointed and let down by the Danish public, and by the politicians in particular.

Then, in the beginning of 2018, Turkey and Turkish-backed militias captured the Kurdish region of Afrin. After Turkey joined the international military intervention against Islamic State in 2015, Turkey intervened directly in northern Syria in late summer 2016. Officially, Turkey launched the operation to support the Free Syrian Army against Islamic State, but more likely, the intervention was aimed at obstructing Kurdish military progress and ensuring that the Syrian Kurds did not seize control of territory west of Euphrates. After talks with the United States, Turkey withdrew from Syria, declaring the operation a success. In 2018, after the Islamic State was cornered in eastern Syria, the Americans were not prepared to spare the Kurds of Afrin. When US Secretary of State Rex Tillerson accepted the Turkish invasion, stating that Turkey has 'legitimate security concerns in northern Syria' (James 2018) and the Danish Foreign Minister repeated the message word for word (Staghøj 2018), it was a slap in the face for Kurdish activists in Denmark, who felt abandoned by the Danish politicians. To go against Turkey was a far more obscure cause for the Danish government than fighting Islamic State. For the Kurdish diaspora, the majority of whom originate from Turkey, it was a well-known, but not at all welcome battle. In 2019, Turkey had the upper hand, and the American troops were ordered to withdraw from northern Syria after Turkish President Erdoğan assured US President Trump that Turkey would handle the terrorist threat in the area. When Turkish forces and Turkish-backed rebel groups invaded Kurdish-held territory between Tell Abyad and Ras al-Ayn (Kurdish: Serê Kaniyê), the Kurdish-led Syrian Democratic Forces asked the Syrian armed forces to support them against the invasion. By the end of 2019, a deal was settled, based on the cooperation of Turkey and Russia, who had sided with the Syrian regime since the end of 2015.

Kurdish diaspora mobilisation and the Syrian Kurds

Prior to the Syrian uprising in 2011, little attention was paid to the Syrian Kurds and their struggles for recognition and political influence, outside of the Syrian Kurdish milieu. Overridden and repressed within the Syrian state, a self-declared Arab state since the late 1950s, the Syrian Kurds were a people with no official existence. This meant, among other things, that around 300,000 individuals of Kurdish origin did not hold Syrian citizenship (International Crisis Group 2013, p. 6). The low profile and the internal divisions among the Kurdish political parties in Syria meant that the Kurdish communities in the neighbouring countries did not pay much attention to the Syrian Kurdish struggle either, as they were preoccupied with their own political struggles (Sheikhmous 2013). Instead, Syrian Kurds who wanted to fight joined the Kurdish military struggle in Turkey and Iraq. This left Syria as a political refuge for high-ranking Kurdish politicians from Turkey and Iraq, useful for the Syrian regime as proxies in the regional power play. Thus, Jalal Talabani resided in Damascus in the 1970s and 1980s, as did Abdullah Öcalan in the 1980s and 1990s. Likewise, the Syrian Kurdish struggle was not a big issue for the Kurdish diaspora, which included few refugees originating from Syria. At the end of the 1960s, one of them, Ismet Cheriff Vanly, tried to mobilise against the Syrian repression of the Kurds, naming the Syrian Arabisation policies 'The Syrian "Mein Kampf" against the Kurds' (Vanly 1968b), with little success outside Kurdish circles. Likewise, among scholars, few studied the recent developments of the Kurdish political parties in Syria (e.g., Montgomery 2005; Yildiz 2005; Tejel 2009).

All this changed, when the Syrian Civil War broke out, and especially during the battle of Kobane when the Syrian Kurds proved to be the ones who could defeat Islamic State. Western media and politicians were asking who the Syrian Kurds were. A number of research papers and reports were published on the political factions and the military expansion (among them Gunter 2014; Gunes and Lowe 2015; Savelsberg 2016; Schøtt 2017; Schmidinger 2018), on the ideology of the Rojava revolution and its impact on society (Knapp and Jongerden 2016; Khalaf 2016) as well as on the representation of Syrian Kurds in European media (Toivanen and Baser 2016; Kardaş and Yesiltaş 2017).

Even though the struggle of the Syrian Kurds had a huge impact on the Kurdish diaspora, whose mobilisation also spread to non-Kurdish supporters, until then only few studies had focused on this issue (Eccarius-Kelly 2017; Weiss 2018; Toivanen, forthcoming). Clearly, there is a need for more studies on how the Syrian crisis has affected the activities of the Kurdish diaspora, how the military success of the Kurds in Syria has affected being Kurdish in a diasporic setting, and how this appeals to non-Kurdish activists.

This book will provide this overview, contributing to the literature on Kurdish diaspora and, particularly, to the literature on the diaspora mobilisation in support of the Kurdish struggle in Syria. In doing so, it will zoom in on the position of the Syrian Kurds among the other Kurdish diaspora groups. The Syrian Kurds often played the crucial role as mediators between the diaspora as a whole and the Kurdish political actors in Syria, but they have been overlooked in previous studies. Additionally, this study investigates how identifying with political entities in parts of the Kurdish homeland other than the area of origin affects the identification as a Kurd. This goes for the majority of the Kurds who originate from parts of Kurdistan other than Syria, and for the Syrian Kurds who seem alienated from the political development in Rojava and instead have plunged into activities in support of the Yezidis from Sinjar. To capture this way of identifying with the homeland, I will introduce the term *alter-territorial* identification which implies having a territorial connection to the homeland, but to a different area than the place of origin. I will elaborate on the term later in the book.

Danish military engagement

As the Syrian conflict progressed, more and more local, regional and international actors became engaged. These comprise states, regional and global powers as well as a variety of non-state actors, including local militias, political parties, humanitarian organisations, individuals and transnational movements. While the Kurdish diaspora in Denmark engaged in Syria, siding with the Syrian Kurds and their struggle against Islamic State, the Danish state engaged in Syria as a member of the international coalition against Islamic State. When in the battle of Kobane, the US sided with the Kurdish forces of YPG and YPJ to stop the advance of Islamic State, Denmark, as a loyal member of the US-led international coalition, also became an ally of the Syrian Kurds. Thus, the Kurdish diaspora and the Danish state happened to be on the same side in the conflict. They fought the same enemy, Islamic State, and they supported the same local ground forces, the Syrian Kurdish fighters, however, on very different terms. How did this affect the relationship between the Kurdish diaspora and the Danish authorities and how did it transform being Kurdish in a Danish setting?

This study investigates how an ethnic diaspora interacts with the host state while the state is militarily involved in the diaspora's homeland on the same side of the conflict as the diaspora. Denmark is an interesting case in this respect. The Kurdish diaspora in Denmark has easy access to streets and squares and enjoys the privilege of close relations to a number of national politicians who are sympathetic to the Kurdish cause. This leaves the Kurds with plenty of room for manoeuvre. This also applies to the supporters of the PKK, despite the EU listing the PKK as a terrorist organisation. The Kurdish diaspora groups work well together with the Danish politicians and authorities, even though this seldom leads to concrete political action in support of the Kurdish homeland politics. When Denmark engaged in the war against Islamic State, this ambiguous embrace became evident. As part of the international US-led coalition against Islamic State, which Danish decision-makers voted for without hesitation, Denmark sided with the Kurdish forces of YPG in Syria as well as the Kurdish forces in Iraq. At the same time, to contain the threat of terrorist attacks committed by foreign fighters, Danish politicians adopted laws that prohibit travel to certain war zones in Syria and Iraq, thereby criminalising Kurdish activists and foreign fighters supporting Islamic State without distinguishing between the two groups. This study investigates the interaction between the Kurdish diaspora and the Danish authorities in order to clarify the apparent inconsistency in Danish politics as well as the Kurdish response. In doing so, it contributes to the study of how 'the Kurdish diaspora develops an autonomous character that is not an exact reflection of the homeland political actors and inhabitants' as Bahar Baser, Ann-Catrin Emanuelsson and Mari Toivanen point out in their review article in the *Kurdish Studies* journal's special issue on Kurdish diaspora studies (2015, p. 142).

Diaspora mobilisation and conflict

This study also contributes to the study of diaspora mobilisation and war. Since the end of the Cold War, diasporas have played an important role in the study of violent conflicts, and the field has developed significantly (Koinova 2019). Recent studies have called for more empirical studies and better conceptual and theoretical tools to provide deeper insight into the nexus between diaspora mobilisation and conflict (Hall 2015; Koinova 2018; Féron and Lefort 2018). There is clearly a need for case studies that take the complexity of diaspora engagement into consideration. There is also a need for studies that rethink the theoretical base that led to previous simplistic generalisations. This study will provide both. It offers an in-depth analysis of the mobilisation of various players within the Kurdish diaspora in Denmark, vis-à-vis players in the homeland and vis-à-vis Danish authorities. It examines diaspora and civil war by using a micro-sociological approach based on a social constructionist framework.

The study of diaspora involvement in violent conflicts involves two sets of analysis. One set focuses on the process of diaspora mobilisation, and the other focuses on the impact of diaspora mobilisation on the course of conflict (Adamson 2013, p. 67). This study will centre on the first set of analysis, examining how the Kurdish diaspora as a transnational actor was mobilised by and engaged in the Syrian crisis. Other studies have focused on the mobilisation of the Kurdish diaspora vis-à-vis conflicts in the Kurdish homeland, for example emphasising the diffusion of homeland politics (Østergaard-Nielsen 2003), import of the homeland conflict (Baser 2015), or ways in which the diaspora translates the homeland conflict into the discourse of the hostland (Demir 2015). This study draws on social movement theory to conceptualise the process of diaspora mobilisation (Sökefeld 2006) and its interconnectedness with identity formation (Melucci 1989 and 1996). Especially, the study draws on the theory of strategic interactionism (Jasper and Duyvendak 2014; Duyvendak and Jasper 2015). The introduction of this novel approach of strategic interactionism into the study of the Kurdish diaspora mobilisation allows me to delve into the complexity of interaction between various players. This implies that the Kurdish diaspora will be analysed as a strategic player whose agenda will be aligned, reshaped or rejected by a number of other strategic players in Denmark as well as in Syria and Iraq. It also implies that the Kurdish diaspora mobilisation is perceived as an ongoing process underlining the dynamic aspect of mobilisation and identity formation as the players continuously confront or support each other's agendas. This approach also takes into account the interaction between rivalling groups within the Kurdish diaspora in Denmark which, to my knowledge, has not been given any particular attention in previous research on Kurdish diaspora mobilisation.

Kurds in Denmark

This study contributes to the widening of the geographical scope of the Kurdish diaspora studies by focusing on the Kurdish diaspora in Denmark. It responds to a demand by Baser, Emanuelsson and Toivanen who call for research on little-known diasporas for comparative purposes (2015, p. 143). While many of the investigations within diaspora studies have focused on the large diaspora communities in Europe, for example in Germany and Sweden, which constitute mobilisation centres for Kurdish politics and for Kurdish language and literature, the minor Kurdish communities on the diasporic periphery have more or less been left in the dark. Accordingly, only a few studies have looked specifically at the Kurdish migrant milieu in Denmark, even though Kurdish migrants in Denmark number 25,000–30,000 individuals, according to the latest update by Institut Kurde de Paris (Institut Kurde de Paris 2016) and thus, in terms of numbers, constitute one of the largest ethnic migrant communities in Denmark. More information on the history of the Kurds in Denmark will follow in Chapter 5, which delves into the emergence of the Kurdish diaspora in Denmark. I have discovered only three studies of relevance on the Kurdish mobilisation in Denmark prior to this study (Jørgensen 2009; Mikkelsen 2011 (in Danish); and Petersen 2011 (in Danish)). Martin Bak Jørgensen's PhD dissertation is a comparative study on how hostland political and discursive opportunity structures affect the identity formation and organisation processes of migrants from Turkey to Denmark, Sweden and Germany. In this study, Kurdishness is but one among several ethnic and religious markers for the migrants from Turkey. He concludes that the minority organisations adapt to the opportunities available, but also that these opportunities vary due to political decisions. In Denmark, the integration and citizenship regulations have been tightened, while in Germany, they have been relaxed. Over time, Sweden has upheld a regime with few restrictions. Flemming Mikkelsen studies the social, religious and political mobilisation of Danish immigrants. With regard to the Kurdish migrants, he traces the formation of organisations from around 1980, when the Kurds began to mobilise, separately from the Turkish migrant community. Like Jørgensen, he points to the opportunity structures as the main explanation. Mimi Petersen analyses identity formation among young migrants originating from Iraqi Kurdistan. She concludes that for young Kurds, especially girls, migration has proved an opportunity for liberation from what they perceive as undemocratic norms and values. She also concludes, however, that the experience of 'otherness' puts restraints on the young Kurds when interacting with the majority population. In addition, Jan Hjarnø did some research in the 1980s on Kurdish labour migrants from Turkey focusing on the employment and settlement of the first generation of migrants (Hjarnø 1988; Hjarnø 1991). None of these studies, however, focus specifically on the mobilisation of the Kurdish diaspora or investigate Kurdish activism as it unfolds in concrete interaction with other strategic players in Danish society. Nor do they address the mobilisation of the Kurds in an ongoing international conflict, in which the Danish state is militarily involved. Thus, this book will shed light on a neglected area.

Focus and Delimitations

These considerations lead to three main research questions, which this book seeks to answer: How does the war in Syria affect the activities of the Kurdish diaspora groups in Denmark? How do Danish authorities, decision-makers, other Kurds and opponents and supporters respond to these Kurdish activities? What is the outcome of the interaction between Kurdish activists and the other actors, and how does mobilisation in support of the Kurds in Syria form and transform Kurdish identities in Denmark? The questions will be answered with the following delimitations in mind, which relate to the time period and the Kurdish groups on which the study will focus.

The study focuses on the time period between 2014 and 2018. In 2014, the city of Kobane came under siege by Islamic State, who had conquered large areas of eastern and northern Syria, as well as large parts of Iraq, earlier that year. After four months under siege, the city was liberated. Even though the liberation took place with heavy close air support from the international coalition against Islamic State, the majority of diasporic Kurds viewed the Kurdish forces of YPG and YPJ as the brave and victorious fighters who were able to defeat Islamic State. Even the Kurds who did not approve of the political project of the Syrian Kurdish party PYD were proud that Kurdish forces were able to oust Islamic State forces. In the years that followed, while the PYD dominated the political process heading the so-called Rojava revolution, the YPG and YPJ were able to expand the autonomous territories. This ended at the beginning of 2018 when Turkey attacked Afrin and Turkish-backed militias captured the area, which marked the first major defeat of the Kurdish forces in Syria. While the victory in Kobane spurred Kurds worldwide into energetic action, the defeat in Afrin was a slap in the face, redirecting attention from the Kurdish struggle in Syria to other Kurdish battles. Thus, for most of the Kurdish diaspora community, the period from 2014 to 2018 marks a golden era and is characterised by a variety of activities in support of the Kurds in Syria. In addition, 2018 is the year I finalised my fieldwork.

This study investigates Kurdish mobilisation in Denmark in support of the Kurdish struggle in Syria. This implies an investigation revolving around activism promoting the Kurdish cause. The study will therefore focus on organisations and individuals who include the Kurdish cause in their agendas as well as commit themselves to activities that somehow promote the struggle of the Kurds. The Kurdish cause is not unanimously defined among the Kurds, and its political implications are perceived differently by different groups. The political end goals campaigned for by the two main Kurdish diaspora movements are an independent Kurdistan and democratic self-determination within the existing states. However, all the activities that focus on the Kurdish cause share the aim of mobilising Kurds in support of some kind of solution to the struggle of the ethno-national group, called the Kurds, in the homeland. This study will pay attention to Kurdish political lobbyism but will also analyse activism in other arenas, such as humanitarian activism and courtroom activism. The study will not pay particular attention to the cultural divisions among the Kurdish diaspora members, such as religion, language and traditions, since they represent secondary identifications among the Kurds when mobilised for the Kurdish cause. With regard to religious affiliation, there seems to be widespread acceptance of an individual's belief among the mobilised Kurds. However, secularism is a popular stance among Kurds, as I experienced at a family get-together that I attended, which was arranged by a Kurdish music association. Various artists among the guests, mainly from Iraqi Kurdistan, performed during the evening. One of the musicians was introduced by the toastmaster as an Arab from Baghdad, who had asked if he might participate. Initially, the answer was 'no'. Then he had said 'but we are all Arabs', but he was told 'no, we are Kurds'. Then he had said 'but we are all Muslims', but the reply was 'no, we are secular'. Finally, he had said 'but we are all human beings' and then he was accepted. The toast-master kept reminding everyone that 'we have come to have fun' (in Danish 'vi er her for at hygge os'). It should also be noted that, in contrast to the situation in Germany, no Kurdish mosque in Denmark is dedicated to Kurdish Muslims, cf. the project 'Mosques in Denmark' (Kühle and Larsen 2017, and confirmed in mail correspondence with the authors). This indicates that there is no collective Muslim identity among the Kurds in Denmark as the Kurds, if practising Muslims, are affiliated with Turkish, Iraqi or pan-Arab mosques. Besides adhering to secularism or Islam, Kurds in Denmark iden-tify as Alevis (from Turkey), Yezidis (from Turkey and Iraq) or Yarsanis (from Iran) (Fenger-Grøndahl 2016). The groups of Yezidis and Yarsanis count only few hundred individuals each. The diversity with regard to language (dialects) and cultural traditions are also of secondary significance for the politically mobilised Kurds.

The position of the Syrian Kurds will naturally play a major role in a study of the Kurdish mobilisation in Denmark in support of the Kurdish struggle in Syria. However, due to the conflict environment in Syria, the Syrian Kurds are facing different struggles. Thus, this study seeks to cover both the support for the Kurdish power-holders in northern Syria, that is, the Democratic Union Party (PYD), and the support for the Kurdish opposition, i.e., the Kurdish National Council (KNC). In addition, I will also pay attention to humanitar-ian support for the Kurdish refugees, who fled Syria into Iraq and Turkey.

With regard to the Kurds in Denmark, this study will encompass Kurds originating from all parts of the Kurdish region in the Middle East, since the major Kurdish federations do not consider the geographical background of their members as long as they all agree on their version of the Kurdish cause. As the Kurds originating from Turkey have maintained 'hegemonic presence in diaspora politics' (Hassanpour and Mojab 2005, p. 222), they have also become dominant voices in this study. However, the Syrian Kurds are also prominent in this study due to their strong personal involvement in the Kurdish struggle in Syria.

The study is based on fieldwork among Kurds in Denmark. It was mainly conducted in Copenhagen, the capital of Denmark, and surrounding areas, as this is where the national Kurdish organisations are located and their rep-resentatives easy to access. It is also where the main Kurdish activities take place as the national Danish political institutions are based here, including the parliament at Christiansborg, which the Kurds try to reach through lobbying and public events. In addition, most of the Kurdish population in Denmark live in the capital area or in the suburbs surrounding Copenhagen. However, other big Danish cities, such as Aarhus, Odense, Aalborg, Esbjerg, Holstebro, Roskilde, Hillerød and Næstved, are also home to significant Kurdish populations, who participated in some of my interviews and observations.

Outline of the Book

Part I establishes the topic and purpose as well as the theoretical and methodological framework of the book. Chapter 1 introduces the main themes and presents the research questions. Chapter 2 places the study within Kurdish diaspora studies, which has emerged as a sub-discipline of Kurdish studies over the last three decades. This chapter also discusses the concepts 'diaspora' and 'transnationalism' to create a conceptual base for the analysis of the Kurdish diaspora in Denmark. This is followed by a presentation of the theoretical framework, which draws on social movement theory and theories on identity formation. Chapter 3 addresses the methodological considerations of collecting the data for analysis. The investigation of the Kurdish diaspora is primarily based on ethnographic fieldwork, which is described and justified in the chapter. Chapter 3 also discusses the ethical challenges of conducting fieldwork among Kurdish diaspora members. The chapter concludes by outlining how the analysis of the subsequent chapters is structured.

Part II analyses the emergence of the main actors included in this study, that is, the Kurdish diaspora in Denmark and the Kurds of Syria. Chapter 4 presents the incidents that led to the mobilisation of the Kurds in Syria. The chapter explains how the Kurds in Syria became allies of the international coalition against Islamic State during the battle of Kobane in 2014 but were abandoned during the Turkish capture of Afrin in 2018. Chapter 5 traces the emergence of the Kurdish diaspora in Denmark from the arrival of the first guest workers in the late 1960s to the influx of Kurdish refugees from Syria during the Syrian Civil War. The chapter provides an overview of the actors in the Kurdish diaspora milieu in Denmark, identifying two main movements, being the Öcalan and the Kurdistan movements, and a few independent activists. The chapter also dedicates a section to the position of the Syrian Kurds in Denmark.

Part III comprises the main analytical chapters, which analyse the political lobbyism, courtroom activism and humanitarian activism of the Kurdish diaspora in Denmark. Chapter 6 investigates the political lobbyism as it unfolds in the public space (in the 'Square') and vis-à-vis political decision-makers (at the 'Castle'). The chapter identifies the main actors that the Kurds interact with and analyses the outcome of that interaction. The chapter also analyses the rivalry between the two main Kurdish diaspora movements and suggests four determinants for success. Finally, the chapter discusses how engaging in Kurdish lobbyism has changed how people identify as Kurds in Denmark. Chapter 7 delves into courtroom activism. It explains the rationale behind the Kurdish military activism in support of the Kurdish struggle against Islamic State, and investigates the strategies adopted to counter the legal restrictions on military support. The chapter also considers the political and public reactions as well as the response from Kurdish diaspora actors towards courtroom activism. Finally, the chapter discusses the ambiguous interplay between Kurdish diaspora actors and Danish politicians. Chapter 8 investigates Kurdish humanitarian action, focusing on both support events in Denmark and delivery of relief in the homeland. The chapter also looks at how the humanitarian principles upheld by the activists are challenged by other actors who wish to exclusively support Kurds. Finally, the chapter discusses how being involved in humanitarian activism pushes the Kurds in different directions with regard to identifying as a Kurd in a diasporic setting.

Part IV (Chapter 9) presents the findings of the present study and outlines the major conclusions on how Kurdish diaspora activism unfolds in a Danish setting, and how this activism changed during the period from Kobane to Afrin. The conclusion argues that the ways in which Kurds in Denmark identify as being Kurds changed during the period in response to events in the homeland, the approach of Danish authorities towards refugees and migrants, and internal rivalries.

2

CONCEPTUAL AND THEORETICAL FRAMEWORK

Kurdish Diaspora Studies

Brief overview

A European Kurdish diaspora came into being as a result of the immigration of Kurdish labourers from Turkey to Europe from the late 1960s
and the influx of Kurdish political refugees from all parts of Kurdistan from
the 1980s onwards. Soon the diaspora itself became the subject of academic
interest and, during the 1990s, the field of Kurdish diaspora studies emerged
as a subfield of Kurdish studies, predominantly drawing on academic disciplines such as anthropology, sociology and political science.

The first major study to address the Kurdish refugee and migrant communities in Europe as a diaspora was *Kurdish Diasporas: A Comparative Study
of Kurdish Refugee Communities* by Östen Wahlbeck (1999). Wahlbeck's study
introduced 'diaspora' as an analytical tool to understanding and dealing with
Kurdish migrant groups in Europe. 'Diaspora' has since then been a hegemonic concept in the study of the Kurdish communities in Europe, even
though the concept has repeatedly been criticised[1]. I will review the literature
on the concept of diaspora later in this chapter.

---

[1] At the Kurdish Migration Conference at the University of Middlesex in 2017, Östen Wahlbeck gave a keynote speech on the research on the Kurdish diaspora published within the
last 20 years. Anecdotally, he recalled that he only had one article on the Kurdish diaspora at
hand when he wrote his dissertation in the 1990s (namely Blaschke 1991).

Studies on the Kurdish diaspora can be divided into three relatively distinct groups with regard to research focus and scope (Baser et al. 2015, p. 134). One group of studies deals with integration and citizenship policies in migrant-receiving countries and focuses on how the Kurdish migrants integrate into these countries (Wahlbeck 1999; Khayati 2008, Jørgensen 2008; Baser 2015). These studies conduct comparative analyses to investigate the different opportunities for integration and citizenship offered to the Kurdish community in different national settings. Another group of studies deals with the sense of belonging and identity formation among the diasporic Kurds (Alinia 2004; Petersen 2011; Eliassi 2013 (dissertation 2010); Zettervall 2013; Toivanen 2014; Demir 2015). These studies concentrate on Kurds and Kurdish communities settled in one national setting (although Petersen includes Kurds repatriated to Iraqi Kurdistan) and focus on perceptions of home and otherness. The third group of studies deals with Kurdish nationalism and homeland politics as ways to understand the political activism and strategies of Kurdish actors in Europe (Østergaard-Nielsen 2003 (dissertation 2002); Eccarius-Kelly 2002; Emanuelsson 2005; Mügge 2010; Grojean 2011 (dissertation 2008); Casier 2011; Adamson 2013). These studies take the Kurdish struggle in Turkey as their point of departure and focus primarily on the transnational activism of the PKK within the framework of EU–Turkey relations; some of the studies do take other Kurdish political organisations into account, however (for example Emanuelsson 2005).

Yet another group of studies is emerging from communication and media studies. These studies focus on the role of the media in the development of Kurdish transnational communities and social networks. While the first generation of these studies focused on the role of Kurdish TV stations (e.g., Hassanpour 2003; Ayata 2011), more recent publications are dedicated to analysing the role of digital media (Sheyholislami 2011; Keles 2015; Mahmod 2016). A recent dissertation addresses the relationship between remittances, transnational ties and migration patterns, drawing on economic migration theories (Pelling 2013).

Inspiration and deficiencies

In the following, I will present the inspirations that I draw on from the literature on the Kurdish diaspora in order to contextualise my own research.

After that, I will point at the shortcomings I find in these studies. I will include the three works that I have drawn on the most: the works of Bahar Baser (2015), Minoo Alinia (2004) and Eva Østergaard-Nielsen (2003), all of which focus on the mobilisation of the Kurdish diaspora and strongly emphasise interaction. The three works also represent the three main groups of study mentioned above.

In 2015, Bahar Baser published *Diasporas and Homeland Conflicts: A Comparative Perspective*. This monograph is the most comprehensive piece of research to date on Kurdish mobilisation and identity formation in a European setting. As the title suggests, the study is comparative, and it covers Sweden and Germany, both of which have a relatively large community of Kurdish migrants. It focuses on second-generation inhabitants but also covers historical mobilisation since the 1970s. It includes both hostland policies and mobilisation policies of migrant organisations. What is new in Baser's study is the investigation of the spillover of a homeland conflict, in this case, the Turkish Kurdish conflict, to the transnational space. Using a constructivist approach, she argues that the friction between Turks and Kurds in Europe is not merely a reflection of the conflict in Turkey. The conflict is reframed and re-enacted due to a combination of numerous factors, including new opportunities and different power relations in the host country (the political and discursive opportunity structures). While the tensions between Kurds and Turks are visible and often played out violently in Germany, the tensions are invisible in Sweden, or rather, framed in a way that fits into a Swedish inclusive discourse. In line with Martin Sökefeld (Sökefeld 2006) and Rainer Bauböck (Bauböck 2010), Baser views a diaspora as a mobilised group that comes into being and whose identity is formed accordingly.

In 2004, Minoo Alinia introduced social movement theory to the analysis of the Kurdish diaspora in her *Spaces of Diasporas: Kurdish Identities, Experience of Otherness and Politics of Belonging* (2004). This perspective has mainly been applied to political protest movements, including the mobilisation of the PKK, in order to explain collective action. Drawing on Alberto Melucci's work on new social movements, including theories on diaspora formation by Paul Gilroy and James Clifford, Alinia argues that the Kurdish diasporic identity is the outcome of interaction, i.e., social processes and political activities. However, Kurdish migrants have to relate to both the formal policies of multiculturalism and the informal attitudes of discrimination and racism. She calls this 'the two faces of Sweden'. The study centres around the experience of home and homelessness among first-generation Kurds in Sweden (in the city of Gothenburg) expressed through their relations to their country of origin, Kurdish diasporic institutions and the broader diasporic movement. Alinia argues that the collective identity of being a member of the Kurdish diasporic community constitutes a new 'home'. Theoretically, she proposes replacing a '(re)territorial notion of diaspora' with a 'de-territorial notion of diaspora', that is, replacing the essentialist 'homing desire' of diasporas presented by Safran with a social constructed heterogenic diasporic identity.

The 2003 study *Transnational Politics: Turks and Kurds in Germany* by Eva Østergaard-Nielsen was the first study to address the transnational relations of the politically active Kurds in Europe. The focus of her research is outlined in the first sentences of the monograph:

> This book is about how the politics of one country plays itself out in another through the presence and agency of migrants and refugees. It is about *transnational mobilization and strategies* of migrants and refugees, and the way that such engagement is perceived by political actors in their country of settlement and origin. (Østergaard-Nielsen 2003, p. 1, emphasis added)

Claiming that this case is paradigmatic of transnational activism in a European context, Østergaard-Nielsen studies the situation of immigrants and refugees from Turkey in Germany. Her study covers both Kurds and Turks originating from Turkey. She analyses the transnational relations at three levels: transnational political mobilisation among groups and movements; transnational practices; and the perception and policy of both the homeland state and the receiving country, in this case Turkey and Germany respectively. Drawing on diaspora conceptualisations (Tölölyan. 1991, pp. 4–5; Levitt 2001, p. 203) she asserts that the political identity of immigrants and refugees arises from a complex interplay between the mobilising agenda of the sending country and the opportunity structures of the receiving country. She argues that the strategy of the diaspora groups in relation to their homeland has changed from a confrontational to a multi-layered approach as the groups seek to persuade German political actors to engage in or with Turkey rather than take direct action themselves (Østergaard-Nielsen 2003, p. 83). Despite the reservations in Germany about the migrant communities' engagement in homeland politics, these groups manage to uphold a political agenda of involvement in both homeland politics and lobbyism in Germany. By doing so, the study concludes, they manage to blur the distinction between domestic and international politics, forcing German politicians to (re)act accordingly. Østergaard-Nielsen thus points out that the mobilisation of diaspora groups in favour of de-territorial and transnational activism proves to be a strong and unpredictable political movement.

Even though I have been greatly inspired by these three researchers, their work does contain certain deficiencies, some of which I have briefly touched upon in the introduction of the book. Some relate to the authors' theoretical choices, while others relate to the scope of their research. Obviously, the studies also fail to touch upon conflicts that have emerged more recently.

As Baser (2015) and Østergaard-Nielsen (2003) rightly put it, diaspora politics is formed by the political context of the country of settlement. I want to take this argument further by rejecting the structural preconditions of their analyses and instead insisting on an interactionist approach that will bring the investigation closer to the actions that take place where Kurds act strategically vis-à-vis other strategic actors, e.g., at demonstrations in the streets and at meetings with decision-makers in the Danish Parliament. Thus, I will investigate the interactions between Kurdish groups and state authorities as well as political and other relevant actors, to whom the Kurdish groups have to respond and adjust their agendas. By doing so, I will arrive at a more nuanced picture of what is going on. While both Baser and Alinia find discrepancies between the official policies towards the migrants and the migrants' experiences in everyday life in the case of Sweden (Alinia's 'two faces of Sweden' (2004, pp. 162ff)), I will search for discrepancies in policies, in the public's views and in the strategies of various actors on Kurdish activism.

This also means that I will track Kurdish activism into various arenas. Østergaard-Nielsen studies political lobbyism (Østergaard-Nielsen 2003), but political lobbyism is one of many ways of supporting the Kurds back home; military and humanitarian support are other ways of supporting the Kurdish struggle in Syria. By studying various types of support, I will widen the scope of activism, recognising that other types of support may be just as vital as political lobbyism or may underpin political efforts. However, different types of support may also work against each other. Thus, this study will also look at the ambiguities of the Kurdish activist endeavour.

Few studies in Kurdish diaspora studies are specifically dedicated to the study of the spillover of a conflict to the host country. Baser's study on *Diaspora and Homeland Conflicts* (2015) is one of them. It focuses on the reframing and re-enactment of the conflicting relations between Turks and Kurds in a diasporic setting. Being a comparative study, it also investigates how the Turkish-Kurdish conflict is formed by the political opportunities in two countries of settlement. However, no study has so far addressed the 'importation of a conflict', which the Kurds and the host state take part in and participate in on the same side. My study will do that. I will address how the relation between the Kurds in Syria and the Danish state, who both fought on the same side in the war against Islamic State, is reframed and re-enacted in a Danish setting. It seeks to explain how the relation between the Kurds and the Danish authorities takes form in the various arenas in Denmark, far from the battlefield and the war against Islamic State.

This study will also investigate how the conflictual relations between the Syrian Kurds and other non-state groups manifest themselves in Denmark. First, there have been very few public incidents involving supporters of Islamic State. While the role of Islamic State has diminished during the course of war, Turkey has become increasingly involved in the military fight in Syria, reaching a temporary peak at the capture of Afrin. I will therefore also touch upon how the Turkish–Kurdish conflict has been re-interpreted in relation to the Syrian conflict. Second, the diasporic Kurds take very conflictual stances on the developments in Syria, as do their counterparts in Syria. Thus, this study will also cover the rivalry between the supporters of what I call the Öcalan movement and the Kurdistan movement, primarily as it unfolds in the political struggle for attention and support.

In the same way the Kurds living in Syria have been overlooked for a long period by academics as well as journalists (Yildiz 2005; Gunter 2014), the Syrian Kurds in Europe were almost invisible among the Kurdish diaspora groups up until the Syrian Civil War broke out in 2011. Ismet Cheriff Vanly (who lived in Switzerland) and Omar Sheikhmous (living in Sweden), both political activists and analysts, are some of the few exceptions. However, compared with the other Kurdish communities in Europe, the Syrian Kurds were few, and they had arrived individually. The establishment of an autonomous Kurdish region in northern Syria and the subsequent military success of the Kurdish militias at the battle of Kobane made the Syrian Kurds known to a wider global public. The Syrian Kurds in the diaspora became essential points of contact for both the Kurds in Syria and the Kurdish diaspora due to their social networks and ties to Syrian Kurdish political actors. The Syrian Kurds were able to communicate the need for all kinds of support from the Kurds in Syria to the Kurdish diaspora and also arrange meetings between leading diaspora members and Kurdish political actors from Syria.

This study will address the change in the focus of the Kurdish diaspora. While the Kurdish diaspora primarily focused on the Kurdish struggle in Turkey and Iraq prior to the Syrian Civil War, after the battle of Kobane, the Kurdish diaspora focused intensely on the struggle in Syria. The war also had implications for the distribution of roles within the Kurdish diaspora. This raises the question of whether this mobilisation in support of the Kurds in Syria has changed the perception of Kurdishness. I will investigate how being Kurdish in Denmark has been transformed by the involvement in the struggle of the Syrian Kurds. In line with the theoretical perspective applied by Alinia (2004), I will draw on social movement theory, claiming that Kurdish identity is formed and transformed through activism and collective mobilisation (see also Demir 2015, p. 20).

The increased focus on the Kurdish struggle in Syria and the mobilisation in support of the Syrian Kurds among Kurds from all parts of Kurdistan also raises the question of how the diasporic Kurds identify with the homeland and what they perceive as the homeland. Most often, Kurds identify with the homeland, meaning the place they or their ancestors have departed. For example, this is the case when Kurds originating from Turkey engage in the Kurdish struggle vis-à-vis the Turkish state. Sometimes, however, Kurds identify with parts of Kurdistan other than the place they come from and engage in the Kurdish struggle there. This is the case when Kurds with no personal relation or direct link to Syria get involved in the support for the struggle of the Syrian Kurds. This study will investigate how this identification with other parts of Kurdistan emerges and is shared within a community. Drawing on Alinia's distinction between (re)territorial and de-territorial orientation towards the homeland (Alinia 2006), this study will propose the term *alter-territorial* identification to capture the phenomenon. Alter-territoriality involves both an orientation towards the transnational community and a re-orientation towards the homeland, albeit another part of it.

While most of the studies on belonging and identity as well as studies on integration and citizenship involve fieldwork among Kurds settled in Sweden, most of the studies on Kurdish political mobilisation include fieldwork and interviews with Kurds in Germany in their analysis. The focus on Sweden, and to a lesser degree other Nordic countries such as Finland, reflects the public debate in the Nordic countries, building through the 1990s and the 2000s, on the responsibility of the welfare state to incorporate refugees and immigrants vis-à-vis their own obligations to integrate in the majority community. The general interest in the matter may have led to increased research funding in the field of diaspora studies as Bruinessen points out (Bruinessen 2014, p. 51). The interest in Sweden also reflects the fact that Sweden hosts a number of the leading Kurdish diaspora institutions and is therefore portrayed by some researchers as 'a center of gravity for Kurdish culture and Kurdish politics' (Khayati 2012, p. 16). Researchers' focus on Germany, on the other hand, and to a lesser degree other Western continental countries such as Belgium and the Netherlands, reflects the fact that these countries host large numbers of Kurdish migrants, who strongly support the struggle of the PKK. Thus, I will call Germany another centre of Kurdish mobilisation in Europe.

While a lot of research has been done on Kurdish mobilisation in these centres of the diaspora, less has been written about what is going on among the Kurds on the periphery of the diaspora. This study makes up for this by focusing on the Kurds in Denmark. This will add to our knowledge of this specific geographical setting, which only a few researchers have investigated. Among them, only one researcher has presented his findings to an international audience by writing in English (Jørgensen 2009). My study will also lay the ground for the comparative perspective called for by Baser et al. (2015, p. 143). Besides investigating the mobilisation of the Kurds in Denmark, I will also briefly relate the mobilisation in Denmark to the mobilisation in the Kurdish diasporic centres of Sweden and Germany.

In the following section, I will focus on the definition and usage of the concept 'diaspora' and related terms such as 'transnational' and 'transnationalism'.

I will start by tracing the concept through the literature before arriving at my own conceptual and theoretical framework.

Diaspora and Transnationalism: A Discussion of Terms

'Diaspora' has become a disputed term for a number of reasons. First of all, the concept itself has been criticised theoretically by scholars for having essentialist implications (Sökefeld 2006; Shain and Barth 2003). Second, scholars using the term have been criticised for applying it inappropriately and indiscriminately (Brubaker 2005) or for failing to take the development of the migrant communities and their changing ties to the homeland into consideration (Wahlbeck 2017). Finally, the term has been criticised for being politicised (Cohen 2008; Faist 2010). In the following, I will present and discuss the critique. It is important to discuss how the terms 'diaspora' and 'transnationalism' are related, so I have dedicated a section to this discussion. The two terms are often used interchangeably and sometimes even overlap, but they differ in terms of genealogy (Faist 2010, p. 9). I will argue that both 'diaspora' and 'transnationalism' are valid terms and applicable in the case of the mobilisation of the Kurdish migrant communities in Denmark.

Diaspora

The term diaspora originates from ancient Greek (διασπορά, meaning dispersion). In the Jewish-Christian tradition it came to denote the situation of the exiled Jews after the Babylonian destruction of the temple of Jerusalem, and subsequently the exiled Jewish community itself. In the 1960s and 1970s, the use of the term broadened to include other groups, such as Africans, Armenians, the Irish and the Palestinians. These groups had been subjected to similar experiences of slavery, genocide, famine or denial, resulting in their being traumatically dispersed from their original place of living while still retaining memories of the homeland (Cohen 2008, pp. 1–4). From the 1980s, the term was subjected to broader scholarly discussion, creating a multidisciplinary field of research within migration studies, with journals dedicated to diaspora studies.

William Safran's definition of diaspora represents a watershed in the emerging field at the beginning of the 1990s. It was provided in the first volume of the new journal *Diaspora*, which was established in 1991. In Safran's own words, the concept of diaspora applies to:

> [. . .] expatriate minority communities whose members share several of the following characteristics: 1) they, or their ancestors, have been dispersed from a specific original 'center' to two or more 'peripheral', or foreign regions; 2) they retain a collective memory, vision, or myth about their original homeland – its physical location, history, and achievements; 3) they believe that they are not – and perhaps cannot be – fully accepted by their host society and therefore feel partly alienated and insulated from it; 4) they regard their ancestral homeland as their true, ideal home and as the place to which they or their descendants would (or should) eventually return – when conditions are appropriate; 5) they believe that they should, collectively, be committed to the maintenance or restoration of their original homeland and to its safety and prosperity; and 6) they continue to relate, personally or vicariously, to that homeland in one way or another, and their ethnocommunal consciousness and solidarity are importantly defined by the existence of such a relationship. (Safran 1991, pp. 83–4)

Safran's definition draws on the classical understanding of diaspora and also paves the way for new applications of the term. The classical elements are the dispersed group, the original homeland, the place of residence (the hostland), and the collective memory and identity that tie the group together and to the homeland. In this respect, there is a double alienation process at play. The group are alienated from the homeland, which remains their true home and to which they should return, but at the same time, they feel alienated from the place of residence precisely because they belong to another place. Identifying with a place is thus an either-or situation, that is, it is not possible to identify with both home- and hostland. What is new in Safran's definition is the perception of the diasporic community. The term does not distinguish between voluntary and forced migration, between guest workers and political refugees, nor between immigrants and ethnic or racial minorities. They could all be seen as belonging to a diaspora and even the same diaspora community.

In *Global Diasporas* (2nd edn. 2008), Robin Cohen approves the definition by Safran but proposes some additional features, the most relevant to this study being 'solidarity with co-ethnic members in other countries' (p. 7).

The diaspora is not only perceived to be linked to the homeland but also to other diasporic groups dispersed from the same homeland, thus making up a transnational community across the borders of the homeland and across the borders of various countries of settlement.

Theoretical critique

The most fundamental critique of the concept of diaspora as defined by Safran, Cohen and others (including Sheffer 2003) comes from the constructionist camp, who take the processes of diaspora formation and the interaction of the involved actors into account. Martin Sökefeld encapsulates the constructionist critique stating that, '[m]igrants do not necessarily form a diaspora but they may become a diaspora by developing a new imagination of community, even many years after the migration took place' (Sökefeld 2006, p. 267). Sökefeld draws on the anti-essentialist and constructionist concepts of ethnicity as he considers diaspora formation a special case of ethnic identity formation. In contrast to the primordialists, who claim that ethnic identity is naturally given within a community, the constructionists hold that ethnic identity 'is the result of processes of attribution'. Referring to Benedict Anderson, Sökefeld stresses that just because nations, including ethnic groups, are *imagined* communities, they are not unreal as they are perceived as being real and therefore have a real effect on social life. (Sökefeld 2006, p. 266). In line with this argument, he suggests defining diasporas as *imagined transnational communities*, i.e., 'imaginations of community that unite segments of people that live in territorial separated locations' (Sökefeld 2006, p. 267). If the diaspora identity is not a direct consequence of migration, it must be a result of social mobilisation, he argues, pointing to social movement theory (Sökefeld 2006, p. 268). Accordingly, diasporas must be seen as mobilised communities. The same argument is expressed by Rainer Bauböck, 'Diasporas have to be invented and mobilised in order to come into existence' (Bauböck 2010, p. 315). Taking interactionism into account, I will take this argument a little further by arguing that diasporas are not only formed by mobilisation processes but re-created through ongoing processes of negotiation among involved actors.

It is not only the diaspora formation processes that have been criticised but also the notion of the diaspora community as a homogeneous and uniform entity in accordance with the above argument of negotiable identities. Researchers have raised the red flag against the generalisation or 'groupism' (Brubaker 2005, p. 12) taking the heterogeneity or hybridity of identity into account (see the work of Stuart Hall, Paul Gilroy, Homi Bhabha and Richard Jenkins). As individuals are involved differently in diasporic activities, a first step could be to differentiate between diaspora members with different roles and interests (Baher 2015, p. 16). Yossi Shain and Aharon Barth divide the diaspora members into three categories: core members, passive members, and silent members, and elaborate on the division thus:

> Core members are the organizing elites, intensively active in diasporic affairs and in a position to appeal for mobilization of the larger diaspora. Passive members are likely to be available for mobilization when the active leadership calls upon them. Silent members are a larger pool of people who are generally uninvolved in diasporic affairs (in the discursive and political life of its institutions), but who may mobilize in times of crisis. (Shain and Barth 2003, p. 452)

A useful term?

The actual use of the term diaspora has also been criticised. Rogers Brubaker's 'The "diaspora" diaspora' (2005) is one of the most cited works in the discussion of the usefulness of the term diaspora. He argues that 'diaspora' has 'dispersed' to such an extent that the original meaning has been drained out of the term primarily because it has been applied to an ever-broadening set of cases. Thus, 'If everyone is diasporic, then no one is distinctively so' (Brubaker 2005, p. 3). While Brubaker is referring exclusively to studies on dispersed populations, Cohen covers even more 'dispersed' studies that look at more general experiences of alienation, i.e., 'queer diaspora' (Cohen 2008, p. 9). In order to reclaim the academic field of diaspora studies, Brubaker identifies three elements that are widely accepted as being constitutive: dispersion in space, orientation to a 'homeland', and boundary maintenance. (Brubaker 2005, p. 5). Additionally, he proposes altering the characterisation of diaspora from an 'entity' or a 'bounded group' to the notion of diasporic 'stances' and 'claims' (Brubaker 2005, p. 13), and calls for research on how claimed members of putative diasporas adopt the diasporic stance. By doing this, he joins the anti-essentialist critique of diaspora. However, in a retrospective article on the original article, Brubaker concludes that, '[a] field limited to the study of diaspora as project, claim and stance would be an impoverished field indeed', acknowledging 'the importance of studying the often deep significance of "then" and "there" in the shaping of subjectivities in the here and now' (Brubaker 2017, p. 1560). By this, Brubaker withdraws to a more moderate stance, recognising notions of migration history, homeland and diaspora community in the studies of diaspora.

As mentioned before, some of the works in Kurdish studies discuss the usefulness of diaspora in the specific case of the Kurdish migrant and refugee community in Europe. Östen Wahlbeck explained this in his keynote speech at the Kurdish Migration Conference in London in 2017.[2] He pointed to three interrelated developments in the Kurdish diaspora community of key relevance. First, the migration patterns have changed as Kurds have dispersed globally and settled in Japan, Australia and South America. At the same time, reasons for migrating have become more diverse and complex. Second, demographic constituents have changed primarily because the second-generation migrants increasingly dominate the Kurdish communities, forming new political and cultural identities. Third, the role of the homeland has changed as new generational experiences, for example the Kobane crisis, and new communication technologies, such as social media, create different relations to and a new conception of the homeland. He concluded that the above indicates that 'the communities will continue to be characterised by a diasporic consciousness and identity' though more diverse and more closely related to a symbolic understanding of Kurdistan (see also Wahlbeck 2019). I certainly agree, but I think he underestimates the consequences of the interventions of diasporic Kurds in the developments in the homeland. Both the Rojava revolution and autonomy in the Kurdistan Region of Iraq have made it possible for expatriate Kurds to participate directly in the rebuilding of the homeland and the creation of new political entities. This means that Kurdistan has become not only a symbol that ties the transnational Kurdish community together but also a concrete place in the Middle East for Kurds from everywhere. This process has contributed to the strengthening the sense

---

[2] The Kurdish Migration Conference 2017 (15–16 June) was organised by Dr Janroj Yilmaz Keles and Dr Alessio D'Angelo at Middlesex University, London.

of transnational indigeneity (Demir 2017) and through that a possible sense of affiliation with other parts of the Kurdish homeland than the place of origin, that is, *alter-territorial* identification.

Politicisation of 'diaspora'

While scholars continue to discuss how best to understand and define diaspora, the term was adopted more smoothly by the media (Brubaker 2005, p. 4) and by political actors (Cohen 2008, p. 8; Faist 2010, p. 11). By framing themselves as members of a diaspora, nationalist activists claimed to represent the migrant community as a whole, legitimising their diaspora politics vis-à-vis fellow nationals and host-country donors. In order to reach out to migrants and refugees who recognise their role in the development of their country of origin, NGOs also conduct 'diaspora programmes', for example The Danish Refugee Council's Diaspora Programme. In addition, migrant-producing countries in the Global South have used the term to reach out to expatriates in the hope that this may evoke sentiment for the homeland and subsequently result in repatriation, political support or financial investment. Today, diaspora organisations in Europe and the United States represent a variety of ethnic and national groups. Thus, framing migrant groups as diaspora has been convenient and advantageous for a number of actors. However, this should not discredit the term. Instead, if interested, researchers can dig into how the term diaspora is used in this context, and why it became opportune to apply it either to oneself as self-identification or to a potential addressee.[3] Interestingly, the Kurds in Europe have not yet, at the time of writing, referred to their organisations as diaspora organisations. This may be changing, though. In 2018, Kurdish representatives from a number of European countries gathered in order to establish a Kurdish European confederation. The initiative was named The Founding Committee of the Kurdish Diaspora Confederation (DIAKURD).

---

[3] See the Somali Diaspora Organisation (a Somali diaspora organisation in Denmark: http://somdias.dk/) and the Danish Refugee Council Diaspora Programme (a government-funded aid programme for diaspora organisations in Denmark aiming at relief and recovery activities in Somalia and Afghanistan: https://drc.ngo/relief-work/diaspora-programme).

Transnationalism

The new and broader perception of diaspora embraces the absorption of transnationalism in the studies on international migration and trans-border activities. Thus, the journal *Diaspora* carries the subtitle *A Journal of Transnational Studies*. In the preface to the first volume, which also contains Safran's definition of diaspora, the editor, Khachig Tölölyan, stresses that the two concepts will be given equal emphasis (Tölölyan 1991, p. 4). Tölölyan basically argues that 'diaspora' and 'transnationalism' are two sides of the same coin. He claims that new trans-border activities have emerged within the last decades, challenging the notion of the nation state as a legitimate space for collective identification. The various activities of this transnational moment, as he calls it, have led to a 'renewed confidence for ethnonations existing across the boundaries of established nation-states'. In his view, diasporas are 'the exemplary communities of the transnational moment' and the term diaspora is applicable to a wide range of transnational phenomena synonymous with 'immigrant, expatriate, refugee, guest-worker, exile community, overseas community, ethnic community' (Tölölyan 1991, pp. 4–5).

Although both terms refer to cross-border phenomena, they have been used to express different aspects of these phenomena. While diaspora has most often been used to denote culturally distinct communities scattered away from the homeland, transnationalism has been used to address the ties and activities across borders. In short, 'diaspora' refers to *groups* while 'transnationalism' refers to *processes* (Faist 2010, p. 13). This reflects the different intellectual genealogies of the terms, as Thomas Faist argues. Diaspora has primarily been used in studies on specific religious, ethnic and national communities often without the essentialist implications of identifying collective identity across generations being contested, as we can see in the critique above. Studies on transnationalism, on the other hand, are rooted in social science ideas such as mobility and networks, thus stressing the fluid and dynamic aspects of social formations (Faist 2010, p. 15).

Transnational perspectives were introduced in migration studies at the beginning of the 1990s in what has been called the transnational turn in migration studies (Levitt and Nyberg-Sørensen 2004). Anthropologists such as Linda Basch, Nina Glick Schiller and Cristina Szanton Blanc define 'transnationalism' as 'the processes by which immigrants forge and sustain multi-stranded social relations that link together their societies of origin and settlement' (Basch et al. 1994, p. 7). Accordingly, they emphasise that migrants should not be viewed solely in the context of departure (emigrants) nor in the context of arrival (immigrants). Instead, migrants should be viewed as individuals with ties to two or more interconnected worlds (transmigrants).

Peggy Levitt goes a step further, in her study on Dominican migrants in the United States, by pointing out that the transnational practices were adopted not only by the migrants who left their home country but also by the non-migrants whose lives were transformed through input from abroad (Levitt 2001). Together, migrants and non-migrants form a transnational community upheld through processes that go both ways. Ties to the country of origin are maintained in exile through the formation of hometown associations and political and religious organisations, while social remittances, meaning ideas, behaviour and social capital, flow from the receiving to the sending country (Levitt 2001, p. 11). This loosely formed 'transnational village' inhabited by 'transnational villagers' is the base from which a diaspora may evolve. She thus argues that 'transnational communities are the building blocks of diaspora that may or may not take shape [. . .] If a fiction of congregation takes hold, then a diaspora emerges' (Levitt 2001, p. 15). To be considered a diaspora, the members must uphold a sense of collectivity or mutual recognition, in other words, a collective identity that both connects them to the homeland and dissociates them from there.

Perspectives for this study

The review of the literature on Kurdish diaspora studies combined with the discussion on the concepts of diaspora and transnationalism have led me to three defining assumptions about diaspora, which I will elaborate below. I will also explain how I intend to apply the concept of diaspora to the Kurdish migrant community in Denmark, emphasising that diaspora and transnationalism are valid terms in the case of the mobilisation of the Kurds in Denmark. As indicated before, the conceptual framework is based on a social constructionist stance. Thus, when applying the concept diaspora, I draw on the following constituent characteristics.

A dispersed community

A diaspora is a transnational community whose members have been dispersed from their country of origin. I embrace the broad definition by Safran and others. There may be different reasons for migration, such as political or economic, and the migration may be forced or voluntary; regardless of the reasons, the migrants may form a communal diaspora at the place of residence. I will argue that the first constituent of a diaspora is the members' relation to an (imagined) homeland, rather than the reason for the dispersion. Thus, the diaspora member share 'a collective memory, vision, or myth' (Safran 1991, p. 83) about their homeland despite their different migration experiences.

This also applies to the different generations of a diaspora. There may be different generational experiences of both homeland and hostland, such as experiences of escape due to political activism or experiences of a childhood in a suburb of Copenhagen with occasional trips to the family back home (see, among others, Alinia (2004) and Zettervall (2013) focusing on identity formation among the first generation of diasporic Kurds, and Toivanen (2014), and Baser (2015), focusing on the second generation). Still people may identify with the same collectivity. They may not have individual memories, but they will make 'prosthetic memories' of the homeland through stories, photos and videos shared in different media. Due to the ability of 'prosthetic memories' to produce empathy, they go beyond individual ownership and become collective (Landsberg 2004, pp. 20–1). This does not mean that generational differences do not exist. As Karl Mannheim explains, generations are based upon shared memories of historical events among a group of people during their formative years. He distinguishes between 'personally required' and 'appropriated memories'. While the former form the basis of the generational consciousness, the latter are transmitted from generation to generation, securing the continuity of a cultural community (Mannheim 1923, p. 94). In relation to diasporas, this means that generational differences may exist and may transform the diasporic consciousness over time but may at the same time represent variations within the diaspora community. This leads to the next constitutive characteristic of diaspora.

In the case of the Kurdish migrant milieu in Denmark, the Kurds represent different migration backgrounds and also reflect generational and gender-related differences, but not at the expense of communal interests and collective identities. These shared interests and identities are celebrated at family evenings, Newroz festivals and major music events, such as the Şiwan Perwer concert. At such events the Kurdish diaspora comes into being.

A mobilised and mobilising community

Even though a diaspora should be seen as a dispersed community, it should not be seen as fixed over time, nor delimited in terms of group boundaries. On the contrary, a diaspora is a community that comes into being through ongoing internal and external social processes and is thus characterised by fluidity. I draw on Martin Sökefeld's notion of a diaspora as a mobilised community emerging around a communal imagination of a homeland (Sökefeld 2006, p. 267). This coincides with Peggy Levitt's notion of the 'fiction of congregation' (Levitt 2001, p. 15) as well as with Rainer Brubaker's notion of the diasporic stance (Brubaker 2005). This means that the consciousness of the diasporicness has to be awakened among the exiled for a diaspora to emerge. I will argue that the mobilisation process involves a number of actors and contexts of interaction. First, there is an ongoing process of negotiation among different members and organisations within the diasporic community on how to perceive the homeland and how to respond to homeland crises. Second, cooperation exists between diaspora communities in various countries of settlement as well as between diaspora communities and actors in the homeland in order to coordinate support initiatives. Third, the negotiations take place with external actors both in the homeland and in the countries of residence. In order to analyse the mobilisation processes, I will draw on social movement theory (Melucci 1989, 1996; Jasper 2014b) and theory on identity formation processes (Jenkins 1994 and 2014). These theories conceptualise mobilisation as a continuous process among a number of actors. I will elaborate on this in a section on social movement theory. Thus, being mobilised, and mobilising, is another constituent of diaspora.

With regard to the in-group interactions, I find the distinction between core, passive and silent members of a diaspora (Shain and Barth 2003, p. 452; Baser 2015, p. 16) fruitful, although I will stress that the categories should be understood as Weberian ideal types. This will help us understand different degrees of involvement in the diasporic cause. However, the boundaries between the different member groups become blurred when applied to real phenomena. The categories should rather be seen as stages of evocation from the silent and passive ranks in the mobilisation process. I will primarily use the distinction when it comes to selecting informants and interviewees as I will focus on the politically active (core) members.

Heterogeneity

The last constitutive characteristic of diaspora to be mentioned here is heterogeneity. As diaspora comes into being through mobilisation processes and ongoing negotiation among involved actors, the individual perceptions and strategies of these actors should be recognised. Although the purpose of this book is to uncover the support of a diaspora, I can only achieve this through understanding the diasporic activities of involved groups and individuals. Consequently, the collective identity of a diaspora should be understood as fluid and polyform and only reachable through presentation of the negotiation and communication among groups and individuals. Thus, instead of searching for the collective identity (singular) of the diaspora, I will examine the collective identities (plural) of the different individuals and diaspora groups. Of major relevance to this study is how the diaspora groups relate to host- and homeland, and which transnational strategies they pursue or, rather, what the transnational village should look like. Heterogeneity in this respect will also be a matter of contesting notions and strategies as the groups abide by different ideologies.

In order to grasp the special case of the diaspora members who embrace cosmopolitanism while still adhering to a diaspora identity, I would like to draw attention to a study by Jonathan I. Israel titled *Diasporas within a Diaspora: Jews, Crypto-Jews, and the World Maritime Empires (1540–1740)* (2002). Israel uses the expression 'diasporas within diasporas' to describe the 'uniquely extended maritime trading diaspora within the wider Jewish diaspora' that emerged after the Expulsion (Israel 2002, p. 3). Israel describes these maritime traders of Jewish descent as individuals drawing on their intercultural experiences and social networks, but at the same time utilising their personal skills as traders and businessmen to succeed in a non-Jewish world. In line with this, I will apply the notion 'diasporas within diasporas' to the group of Kurds who identify themselves as Kurds but dissociate from the traditional national Kurdish cause and instead connect with a global democratic discourse.

Heterogeneity also implies different ways of perceiving and identifying with the homeland. Thus, I coin the term *alter-territorial* identification to describe a way of identifying with another part of the homeland than the place of origin. The term represents a new way of understanding the relation between the diaspora and the country of origin that draws on both the re-territorial and the de-territorial notions of diaspora identification. The re-territorial notion implies that the diaspora, as a dispersed community, is defined by its relations to the homeland. The diaspora members' dream to return persists and is kept alive by collective memories. The de-territorial notion, on the other hand, implies that the diaspora is primarily defined by its association with the dispersed community. This notion stresses the diaspora's transnational identification with and detachment from the homeland as a physical place. Instead, home is a transnational construction among mobilised diaspora members. I have argued that a diaspora can be considered both a dispersed community related to the homeland (drawing on Safran) and a mobilised transnational community (drawing on Brubaker et al.). However, the alter-territorial way of relating to the homeland implies that the diaspora members' loyalty is dislocated from the place of origin to another part of the homeland, in this case another part of Kurdistan. Thus, the alter-territorial identification encompasses three elements: a de-territorial identification with the transnational Kurdish community, a re-territorial identification with the homeland, and a dislocation of the association from one part of Kurdistan to another by identification with the struggle of fellow Kurds within the transnational community.

To sum up, this characterisation of diaspora described above allows me to dig into what unites the Kurds in Denmark but also what separates them from each other. Thus, I will investigate how the Kurdish diaspora comes into being as a transnational community with adherence to the Kurdish cause. At the same time, I will uncover the dynamics of intergroup contention and rivalry through which the different Kurdish collective identities take form. The main divider within the Kurdish diaspora is shown to be cleavages regarding visions for Kurdistan and the strategies to reach the ultimate goal. These cleavages are instigated by conflicts in the homeland.

In the following, I will further introduce the theoretical framework, drawing on social movement theory and theories of identity formation. I take a social constructionist stance based on symbolic interactionism.

Theoretical Framework

In this section, I will present and discuss the theoretical framework of this book. I have chosen a social movement approach for the study of the Kurdish diaspora as I perceive the diaspora as a mobilised and mobilising community, as seen in the discussion of diaspora above. The core questions asked by social movement theory are *why* and *how* people mobilise or, *why* and *how* individuals participate in collective action and, by doing so, form a social movement with common agendas and shared identities. Applying an interactionist approach, as I have done, means focusing on the processual elements or the dynamics of social movement formation, that is, the *how* questions. The literature on social movements has focused on a number of other elements, including the movement's call for social or political changes, their challenges to the state, the social organisation of the social movement (network, group, institution), the economic foundation of the movement, and the diffusion of repertoire among groups (see for example Fominaya 2014, p. 8).

Social movement theory

Social movement theory has emerged as a sub-discipline of sociology although other disciplines, such as political science, social psychology and history, have contributed to the development of the field. A brief chronological sketch will outline the most influential schools and their respective characteristics. In the following, I draw on the works by Snow et al. (2007), Goodwind and Jasper (2009) and Martin (2015).

In the 1960s, researchers began viewing social movements as representatives of sound social behaviour rather than borderline phenomena of society. Before that, social movements had mainly been viewed as uncontrollable crowds evoking infantile emotions in the individual (Goodwin and Jasper 2009, p. 5). The change in the perception of crowds led to the introduction of new approaches into the field of social movement theory, including rational choice theory and social psychology theories.

In the 1970s, political and economic explanations pointing to societal structures as explanatory variables gained ground. The *political opportunity structure* approach became one of the dominant theories. It was based on the work of Charles Tilly, who explores state-formation processes and the development of social protest in Europe in modern times. According to this approach, social movements occur as a reaction to the state. The state can be more or less open or closed, and the political protesters will respond accordingly. Social movements are thus products of political opportunities (Eisinger 1973). A variant of this school, the *political process* approach, takes a broader perspective by including processes and strategic interaction (McAdam 1982). Another dominant approach was the *resource mobilisation* theory, which takes an economic perspective, claiming that social movements should be investigated according to the resources they are able to raise. The resource mobilisation approach thus analyses social movements as organisations formed by the resources at hand (McCarthy and Zald 1973). In Europe, a third structural approach inspired by the Marxist notion of historic stages took form. While the industrial society was dominated by struggles over material production and the emergence of, for example, the labour movement, the post-industrial society fostered *new social movements*, which fought for non-material goods, such as rights and identity (e.g., Touraine).

In the late 1980s, the so-called cultural approaches were formulated in response to the structuralist approaches. The cultural approaches focused on the construction of meaning within social movements, including *framing* processes and the formation of *collective identity*. Frame analysis draws on Erwin Goffman and focuses on how social movements frame, that is, assign meaning to, specific events and conditions in order to mobilise potential participants (Snow and Benford 1988, 2000). The studies on collective identity are based on an interactionist approach that focuses on how collective identity is constructed and negotiated through interaction (Melucci 1989 and 1996). *How* social movements emerge and develop became more urgent than *why*.

The establishment of cultural approaches paved the way for a general rejection of structuralism within social movement theory during the 1990s and the 2000s, a rejection that favoured agency-oriented and dynamic approaches. Charles Kurzman refers to this as 'The Poststructuralist Consensus in Social Movement Theory' (Kurzman 2004). The consensus covers a broad spectrum of approaches, ranging from 'conjunctural models' (Kurzman 2004, p. 113), characterised by interrelations of multiple explanatory factors (e.g., McAdam, Tarrow and Tilly 2001), to constructionist approaches based on interactionism (e.g., Jasper 2006). James M. Jasper later developed *strategic interactionism* by emphasising the strategic decision-making of the activist, as I will elaborate on below. New phenomena have since been included in social movement analysis, such as the role and use of media, cultural expressions (rituals, music and visual communication), religious movements and global activism (see Martin 2015).

Interactionism

The analysis in this book will be based on the theory of interactionism. Specifically, I will draw on the main tenets of symbolic interactionism (Blumer 1962) as well as on the social movement theories of Alberto Melucci (Melucci 1989, 1996) and James M. Jasper et al. (Jasper and Duyvendak 2014; Duyvendak and Jasper 2015). I will also address the identity issues of social movements, including the discussion of ethnicity and identity formation by Richard Jenkins (Jenkins 1994 2014).

I have chosen an interactionist approach for two main reasons. First, an interactionist approach recognises the complexity of social interaction without reducing the social processes to linear and causal mechanisms. In this way, I can explain both the fluidity and the heterogeneity of the diaspora as an outcome of continual interaction. This interaction takes place internally among Kurdish diaspora groups in Denmark. It also takes place externally among Danish Kurds and other players. An interactionist approach will also allow me to explain the ambiguous response of the Danish state toward the Kurds, since I assume that the Danish state is a heterogeneous actor comprising several authorities with different interests.

Second, I have chosen to adopt an interactionist approach because it will allow me to interconnect the analysis of diaspora activism with that of diaspora identity. In other studies, the two analyses tend to be only eclectically combined. As collective identity is perceived as the outcome of strategic interaction (Melucci 1996, p. 70), the analysis of diaspora activism and the analysis of identity formation are here considered theoretically interlinked.

The basic principles of interactionism are drawn from Herbert Blumer's notion of 'symbolic interactionism'. Blumer coined the term in 1937 in an article on social psychology (Blumer 1937, p. 153). In 1962, he elaborated on the implications of interaction for human society by summarising his understanding of the pragmatic philosopher George Herbert Mead. He defined symbolic interactionism as follows:

> The term 'symbolic interactionism' refers, of course, to the peculiar and distinctive character of interaction as it takes place between human beings. The peculiarity consists in the fact that human beings interpret or 'define' each other's actions instead of merely reacting to each other's actions. Their 'response' is not made directly to the actions of one another but instead based on the meaning which they attach to such actions. Thus, human interaction is mediated by the use of symbols, by interpretation, or by ascertaining the meaning of one another's actions. This mediation is equivalent to inserting a process of interpretation between stimulus and response in the case of human behaviour. (Blumer 1962, p. 242)

According to this interpretation of human behaviour, (1) human beings have selves that interpret their surroundings, including the action of other human beings; (2) individual action is a construction based on interpretation; and (3) collective action consists of alignment of individual action trough interpretation by the individuals of each other's action (Blumer 1962, p. 244). In other words, human society is essentially symbolic interaction. Moreover, the interactionist approach stresses the agency behind action.

When this interactionist approach is applied to social movements, individuals and groups are seen as agents who fight for whatever their goal might be in interaction with other agents with their own goals. Collective action occurs when individuals act as one group. This is the main point in Alberto Melucci's *Nomads of the Present: Social Movements and Individual Needs in Contemporary Society* (1989). He explains:

> Collective action is not a unitary empirical phenomenon. Whatever unity exists should be considered the result and not the starting point, a fact rather to be explained than assumed. [. . .] Individuals contribute to the formation of a more or less stable 'we' by rendering common and laboriously negotiating and adjusting at least three orientations: the *goals* of their action; the *means* to be utilized; and the *environment* within which their action takes place. (Melucci 1989, p. 26)

The social movement, the 'we', comes into being when the goals, means and environment are continually negotiated and renegotiated among the group members. In other words, a social movement 'constantly requires this 'social construction' in order to persist (Melucci 1989, p. 27).

Players and arenas

The theory of *strategic interactionism* as presented by James M. Jasper and Jan Willem Duyvendak (editors) in *Players and Arenas: The Interactive Dynamic of Protest* (2014) and *Breaking Down the State: Protestors Engaged* (2015) takes the interactionist approach a step further. While Melucci focuses on the interaction between members of a social movement, Jasper and Duyvendak include interaction with external actors. In fact, they stress that interaction takes place everywhere and all the time. In doing so, the two authors are close to denouncing the term social movement by emphasising the situatedness of interaction and thus the fluidity of collective actors. I still consider 'social movement' a valid term, as I will argue later. Disregarding the rather unnecessarily assertive presentation of strategic interactionism, mainly by Jasper vis-à-vis structuralism, I find two concepts useful for the analysis of how the Kurdish diaspora comes into being and mobilises in support of a homeland conflict. These are *players* and *arenas*.

Players are 'those who engage in strategic action with some goal in mind' (Jasper 2014b, p. 10). They are strategists who seek certain goals and have certain capabilities and resources at hand to fulfil their goals. As interaction is the core explanatory factor, the only constraints on the ability of players to accomplish their goals are the agendas imposed on them by other players. Interaction should here be understood as a dynamic interplay that covers all the different ways human beings engage with each other. Thus, the players participate in a back and forth process of moves, observations, considerations and response in which their agendas are aligned, bent or rejected. Jasper calls the players' negotiation 'strategic' to stress the efforts to impose agendas or views of the future on other players (Jasper 2014b, p. 19). These strategic considerations are influenced by emotions and should not be seen as rational in an objective sense (Jasper 2014, 13), like military and business planning. As the main aim of social movement research is to explain collective action, I prefer the term 'actors' over 'agents' and 'players' simply because 'actors' are the ones who act; 'agents' or 'players' stress the competitive aspect. I will be using the concepts interchangeably though. 'Activist' will be used when I want to stress the actors' long-term engagement and dedication to a cause.

Players can be individual actors ('simple players') or collective actors ('compound players') (Jasper 2014, 10). Individual actors are individuals with individual goals and agendas. Collective actors are groups of individuals who come into being when the individual goals are aligned, so that the group of individuals appear as one actor. Switching perspective, though, will allow us to look inside and see that 'a player that looks unified from the outside is still going to be an arena for contestation within'. This is called 'fractal division' (Mische 2014, p. 58), which refers to actors being perceived from one point of view as players interacting with other players, and as arenas for internal interaction from another. This division into smaller units may continue in fractal patterns (Jasper 2014b, p. 12). I will thus analyse the Kurdish diaspora both as a compound player interacting with other players, such as the Danish state, and as a heterogeneous arena of contestation and rivalry between different Kurdish groups. I will also look at the Danish state both as a compound player and as an arena comprised of different authorities with different agendas (Jasper 2015, p. 12).

Arenas are spaces where interaction takes place. They vary according to expected rules and means. If the rules are bent or the means changed, the actors have transformed the arena. For example, waving a political flag at a singer's concert changes the setting from a cultural to a political arena. Arenas also vary according to how many players are engaged, which roles they take on, and whether relations between them are formal or informal (Jasper 2014b, p. 15). A courtroom will thus prescribe specific and formal behaviour in contrast to, for example, the street. When actors enter an arena that suits their goals and capacities, they may appear stronger and become capable of dominating the situation. In other cases, they may be able to mobilise other players to participate, thereby becoming a stronger contestant vis-à-vis other actors (Duyvendak and Fillieule 2014, p. 307). Actors can connect different arenas strategically through their actions. Thus, military involvement in specific zones in Iraq and Syria is linked to the courtroom in Denmark by the adoption of a law, which prohibits travel to these specific war zones.

According to Jasper, arenas can be further explained when compared with the structuralist notion of 'structure' and with Pierre Bourdieu's notion of 'fields'. In contrast to structures, which are conceived as existing prior to the action they determine, arenas are result of the action that takes place.

Likewise, in contrast to 'fields', which are metaphorical constructions invented by the researcher, arenas are concrete physical places made by the actors. Thus, Duyvendak and Fillieule define arenas as spaces which are

> both concrete (that is, from a dramaturgical perspective, the place and time of the staging of interactions, for example, the street or a courtroom) and symbolic (that is from a rhetorical perspective, the site of the polemics or the controversy, of testimony, expertise, and deliberation) which brings together all the players, individual or complex, participating in the emergence, definition and resolution of a problem. (Duyvendak and Fillieule 2014, p. 306)

This means that arenas are fluid and changeable, just like actors, formed by mutual and unpredictable interaction. The aim of a strategic interactionist approach will therefore be to discover the processes of interaction, i.e., investigate how agendas are presented and negotiated in different arenas, and how they are either accomplished, denounced or transformed. As Jasper explains, 'By analysing interactions, and the choices various players make during them, we aim for a fully dynamic vision of how protest unfolds' (Jasper 2014b, p. 23). The mobilisation of the Kurdish diaspora in Denmark will be investigated from this perspective. I will identify Kurdish groups, their agendas and interplay with other actors in certain arenas in Denmark as well as transnationally in order to determine how their support for Kurds in Syria unfolds.

Historical and cultural patterns

The concept of interactionism should be modified or specified to avoid overestimating the fluidity of players. As indicated above, Jasper even goes as far as claiming that '[t]alking about players allows us to avoid the term "social movement"' (Jasper 2014b, p. 14). Thus, there is a built-in risk of ending up investigating a series of separate interactions if the researcher follows the dynamic and social constructionist conceptualisation of strategic interactionism. To avoid situationism and voluntarism, the researcher must admit that previous interaction forms or transforms a player and provides the player with dispositions for future action (Duyvendak and Fillieule 2014, p. 309). Human beings are more than free-floating individuals; they embody previous experiences and interpretations, both individual and collective perception. Thus, a player's decision-making may be influenced by both his or her personal biography and all forms of 'cultural constraint' (Polletta and Kretschmer 2014, p. 51). Accordingly, arenas are more than spontaneous situations in which action takes place. Over time, they are formed and transformed by actors who translate their historical and cultural backgrounds into new situations with new norms and rules.

When entering an arena, the strategic actor tends to choose certain actions based on previous experience. This is what Charles Tilly calls 'repertoire'. Thus, repertoire includes 'the whole set of means [an actor] has for making claims of different types on different individuals' (Tilly 1986, p. 2, quoted by della Porta 2013, p. 1081). By adhering to a well-known and well-rehearsed repertoire, the activists may know exactly what to do, but at the same time miss opportunities that stem from a fresh encounter with the other players. However, the repertoire may be disregarded and new actions introduced if the players choose to change their strategy, or new players enter the arena.

Accordingly, I will argue that 'social movement' is still a valid term, representing an actor who is formed over time by the engagement of individuals and by negotiation among groups within the movement on goals and repertoire. In other words, the social movement is both the outcome of mobilisation and still in a process of mobilisation.

Identity formation

In addition to uncovering the processes of Kurdish activism emanating from Denmark, I will also examine the impact of this activism on being a Kurd in a Danish setting. I will look at how Kurdish identity is expressed and how it is influenced by the various actions targeting the Kurdish homeland. I will not focus specifically on national identity as an ideological expression but on the everyday negotiations among decision-making individuals, who may or may not look to ideological answers to the questions: Who am I? And who are we?

According to the interactionist approach of Alberto Melucci, for which see above, collective identity is the outcome of collective action as a 'we' comes into being. In *Challenging Codes: Collective Action in the Information Age* (1996), he explicates further:

> I call *collective identity* the process of 'constructing' an action system [. . .] Collective identity is an interactive and shared definition produced by a number of individuals (or groups at a more complex level) concerning the

orientations of their action and the *field* of opportunities and constraints in which such action is to take place. By 'interactive and shared' I mean that these elements are constructed and negotiated through a recurrent process of activation of the relations that bind actors together. (Melucci 1996, p. 70)

Even though Melucci develops his thoughts on the interconnectedness of action and identity within the framework of new social movements, I will argue that his conceptualisation is applicable to all social actions, in line with the framework of interactionism. Viewing identity as an outcome of collective action is also proposed by Donatella della Porta (della Porta 2008). She argues that protest, meaning particular chains of events or campaigns, is 'a type of event that tends to produce effects not only (and possibly not even mainly) on the authorities or the public opinion but also on the movement actors themselves' (della Porta 2008, p. 48). Some protests have a high degree of 'eventfulness' as they have strong impact on the participants, which includes developing new identities or transforming existing ones. The activism unfolding during the autumn of 2014 in support of Kobane may be perceived as an eventful protest that strengthened the sense of belonging to a Kurdish transnational community among the Kurds in Denmark.

The formation of collective identity should not be seen solely as an internal process, however, as such actions never take place in a vacuum. External actors (or other players according to the conceptualisation of Jasper) need to be included to gain an adequate picture. In 'Rethinking ethnicity: identity, categorization and power' (1994), Richard Jenkins expounds an analytical framework of ethnic identity formation by drawing on the works of Fredrik Barth, who points to internal as well as external identification processes. Jenkins recognises Barth's older works, in which he applies an individualistic voluntaristic approach, as well as his later works, in which he recognises the importance of historical and cultural contextualisation of decision-making. However, the processes of identity formation that Jenkins describes are not just about ethnicity but are applicable to all forms of social identity (Jenkins 1994, p. 202).

The main argument is that social identity is socially constructed through processes of internal and external definitions as well as on individual and collective levels. This implies that identity is formed through a dialectic synthesis of internal and external identifications. It also implies that the individual processes of identification are embedded in the collective processes of identification and vice versa like fractal divisions (Jenkins 1994, p. 203). Thus, the 'self' is an arena for intrapersonal interplay, just as the 'group' is an arena for interpersonal negotiations. The group for their part responds to the categorisation of them by other groups. The distinctions of the analytical framework described above are primarily analytical to circumvent the complexity of real life. Likewise, all the processes take place synchronically but can be singled out and studied individually in an analytical approach (Schøtt 2014, pp. 14–15).

Drawing on Melucci and Jenkins in my analysis of the Kurdish diaspora, the Kurdish diaspora identity will be perceived as the outcome of strategic interaction at several levels or in several arenas: between the Kurdish groups and external actors, and among and within the Kurdish groups. As the negotiations of goals and agendas are ongoing, the formation of Kurdish identity will be perceived as fluid and heterogeneous (Jasper et al. 2015, p. 29). Thus, it will be more appropriate to talk about Kurdish diaspora identities in plural form.

3

METHODOLOGY AND FIELDWORK

Methodology

The research questions of this book are answered through a theoretical contextualisation of data collected primarily during ethnographic fieldwork. The fieldwork included a set of qualitative methods, the main ones being participant observations and semi-structured interviews. Participant observation was chosen because the goal of this book is to investigate action as it unfolds in various arenas. Semi-structured interviews with activists were included in order to add to the study a comprehensive understanding of the motivations and strategic considerations that lie behind the activities observed. Thus, employing participant observations and semi-structured interviews enabled me to produce the data required by the interactionist approach (explained in Chapter 2). The study also draws on other sources of information, including TV newscasts, documentaries and written sources.

The fieldwork took place in Copenhagen from March 2016 to March 2019, covering the three years of my PhD programme in the Department of Cross-Cultural and Regional Studies, at the University of Copenhagen. The fieldwork was divided into three phases to reflect the process of information acquisition: entering the field, finding the desired information and departing the field with valid information.

During the first phase, I attended public events on the Kurdish issue and made contact to representatives of the Kurdish diaspora. The main aim was to introduce myself to the field and ask people for advice on the events it would be relevant for me to attend and the groups I needed to contact. The aim was also to identify potential interviewees, allowing for snowball recruitment of interviewees. The second phase included twenty-three semi-structured interviews with Kurdish activists as well as participant observations and brief conversions with attendees at innumerable events. The third phase was basically dedicated to a wrapping-up process, during which I terminated the fieldwork and made sure I had sufficient data to conclude my analysis.

In practice, there were several overlaps between the phases. As a fieldworker, I repeatedly introduced myself to new informants and carefully evaluated the information I had collected numerous times throughout the process. The field is not a fixed space, nor is the researcher's realisation a linear process (see Melucci 1989, pp. 13–14). In addition, the fact that I did my fieldwork in Denmark where I live allowed for an overlap of the phases. I had the freedom to plan the fieldwork as a series of hit-and-run operations and thus allow myself some trial and error by following emerging tracks and opting out of others in order to be able to answer my research questions.

The Fieldwork

Participant observations

The participant observations took place at various events in the centre of Copenhagen and in the suburbs, in the public space and in the parliament building as well as in community centres and wedding halls. I participated in numerous events, such as Newroz celebrations, demonstrations, marches, public meetings with Kurdish politicians from abroad, seminars and panel debates on the situation in the Kurdish areas, memorial events commemorating crucial incidents in the Kurdish history, support events for Rojava, Kurdish film festivals, celebrations on Kurdish Flag Day and private family feasts. Thus, I conducted what Bahar Baser calls 'moderate participation' (Baser 2015, p. 269) by participating in selected events rather than undertaking extended, embedded fieldwork in the Malinowskian tradition.

The participant observations followed a fixed format. Thus, while attending the meetings, I observed who was participating, which role they played in the event (organiser, invited speaker, moderator or attendee) and which repertoire they performed. I also listened to the speeches and slogans to grasp the message and determine which audience the speakers were addressing. Flags and posters were also important, signalling the political affiliation of the demonstrators. In order to learn about the motivation of the attendees, I had numerous brief conversations with people in the field about the reasons for their participation and how they were engaged in the Kurdish cause. The participation part of the participant observations involved dancing, shouting, listening, walking and getting cold from demonstrating during the Scandinavian winter. Drawing on Erving Goffman, Ruth Wodak distinguishes between 'frontstage' and 'backstage' in relation to performing politics (Wodak 2009, pp. 9–10). I focused on the frontstage activities of the Kurdish activism, that is, the activities that took place in public or semi-public (open for registration) spaces, rather than the backstage activities, i.e., the closed meetings where strategic decisions were made. I chose this particular focus, as I wanted to zoom in on the Kurdish action, including the interaction between the Kurdish players and their allies and opponents. The interviews therefore became my primary source of information about the strategic considerations behind the action.

Interviews

During my fieldwork, I conducted twenty-three interviews with members of the Kurdish diaspora in Denmark (see the Appendix). The interviews were semi-structured interviews with activists representing the various groups within the Kurdish diaspora. The primary selection criterion was engagement in support of the Kurdish struggle in Syria. The group of Kurds that satisfied the criterion included Kurdish activists involved in mainly political lobbyism and humanitarian activism, as well as Syrian Kurdish rights activists and military volunteers. Within this group, I tried to reach the driving forces of the mobilising segment of the Kurdish diaspora, i.e., the 'core members'. By using this term, I follow the distinction of Yossi Shain and Aharon Barth who divide members of a mobilised group into three categories: 'core members, passive members, and silent members' (Shain and Barth 2003, p. 452; Baser 2015, p. 16). I also aimed for a sample of interviewees based on different political affiliations (pro-Öcalan groups, other political parties as well as independent activists), migration experience (refugee and labour migrants (or descendants)) as well as gender. Religious belief was not included. As I have pointed out in the introductory chapter, I wanted to focus on supporters of the Kurdish cause, meaning activists who perceive the Kurds as an ethno-national diaspora group. It turned out that most of my interviewees originated from Turkey or Syria, which reflects that these two groups dominated the activities in support of the Kurdish struggle in Syria. While the Kurds of Turkey prevailed due their 'hegemonic presence in diaspora politics' (Hassanpour and Mojab 2005, p. 222), the Kurds of Syria naturally prevailed due to their specific interests in the developments in Syria.

Most of the interviews were individual interviews, but a few were group interviews. Individual interviews were my primary choice as I wanted to elicit individual stories from which I could draw common features. However, the group interviews proved to be most convenient on a couple of occasions, such as when I was referred to a group of newly arrived Kurds from Syria. As they spoke only a few words of Danish, they were accompanied by one of their fellow activists, who acted as a translator. At other times, I met with groups of people who would complement each other in providing information about certain activities.

I conducted the interviews by means of a semi-structured path and elements of the life story interview. In the semi-structured interviews, it was my responsibility to focus on the interviewees' activism and engagement in politically conscious milieus and organisations (della Porta 2014a, p. 228). The life story interview allowed the interviewees to talk more freely about themselves and their background in a narrative form that fed the analysis of the intersection between the individual agency and the social interaction perfectly (della Porta 2014b, p. 264). The initial question was: 'Tell me how you got involved in this organisation/these support activities?'

The interviews were conducted in Danish as almost everyone I met spoke Danish. One was conducted in English, as this was the language that the interviewee preferred. Another was conducted in Danish and assisted by a translator, as we could not find a common language (see above). Most of the interviews were recorded and transcribed. A few were documented in my own personal notebook since this was what the interviewee preferred. In order to be able to include quotations in the study, I have translated the excerpts to English.

In addition, I interviewed a handful of politicians and Danish supporters of the Kurdish cause.

Other sources

The analyses in this book are also based on other sources of information which I identified along the way. These include various written sources, such as laws, bills, blogs, pamphlets and public strategy papers as well as TV newscasts and documentaries featuring Kurdish activists. I have incorporated these sources for three reasons. First, the Kurdish activists often respond to players who are not physically present at the event and who therefore evade my observations. I thus had to resort to other ways of ascertaining the stance of these players. For example, the political decision-makers may not be present in the arena, but they may have shared their opinions in the media. Second, I include activities that took place before I entered the field. For example, and as explained, I will cover the period starting with the battle of Kobane in 2014–15. Documenting this historical moment requires more than fieldwork methodology, so I draw on newspaper articles and other studies. Third, written sources, films and comments on social media may contribute to the contextualisation of the fieldwork. However, comments on social media will rarely be included as a social media analysis demands another methodological setup. I thus adhere to the distinction between viewing social media as a source of information and as an object of study (Mosca 2014, p. 397). Drawing on the former perception, I will only include social media such as Facebook and Twitter when they refer to upcoming events or contribute to the understanding of activities which I have otherwise come across. Obviously, I will only include the public comments.

In March 2017, halfway through the fieldwork, I took a one-week trip to Stockholm, Sweden, where I interviewed a number of leading Kurdish activists, participated in a demonstration on International Women's Day and visited the Kurdish Library. The purpose of the trip was to gather background information on Kurdish diaspora mobilisation and to get an outside view on the Danish Kurdish milieu.

Ethical Considerations

All interviewees were guaranteed anonymity. Some of the interviewees were unconcerned about this, as they had earlier spoken to the media about their activism. These activists were already acting strategically, which meant that they would only share with me what they would say publicly. Others were proud of their work and seemed eager to share it with a wider audience. However, I chose to insist on anonymity and made this clear to them. There are two reasons for that. First, what is communicated to me in the interview is done so in private. The interviewee might feel comfortable being quoted by name at the beginning of the interview, but even the strategic communicator may have second thoughts later (Sanford 2000, p. 102). No matter what the intentions of the informants were, as a researcher I am obliged to guard the informants from exposure as they also shared elements of their personal life stories and identity-related issues with me (Toivanen and Baser 2019, xxi). Second, as I study social movements, I seek to understand collective action and collective interpretations rather than the individual involvement per se. When I refer to statements and actions from other sources, such as media appearances and the Kurds' own work (such as art productions and biographies), I quote the activists by name as what I am quoting is already public knowledge.

Nearly everybody I asked for an interview accepted my invitation. The interest in participating touches upon the agency of the interviewees and the many reasons they may have for participating. For the researcher engaging with people in the field, this engagement entails the challenge of being instrumentalised (Sanford 2000, p. 103). During one of my first fieldwork encounters, a core member of one of the Kurdish movements explicitly stated: 'It is good that we now have our own researcher'. The statement indicates that some people sought to take advantage of my fieldwork and utilise my research to have their voices heard. Other activists explicitly tried to engage me in their political struggle either by asking me to host certain events or by asking for my advice about how to access Danish media. Apparently, I was contacted out of sheer frustration 'as nobody else seems to care', but I was also contacted for strategic reasons as a way to reach the non-Kurdish community.

In order to steer clear of being associated with one or more particular group(s), I positioned myself as sympathetic to their struggle, but dismissive of taking a stand on the various political solutions to the Kurdish issue. As a human being I am concerned about the same human questions as they are; questions related to human security and social and political justice. In that sense, I am sympathetic to their struggle against the repression and atrocities committed against Kurds in the Middle East. As a researcher, on the other hand, I declined to take a stand. By not getting politically involved, I earned the trust of various Kurdish groups who opened the doors for me to different Kurdish milieus. In the end, this allowed me to represent different and sometimes opposing voices, which is a prerequisite for presenting a trustworthy picture of the heterogeneous field of the Kurdish diaspora.

The Way Ahead

The analytical approach employed in the following chapters is derived from the theoretical framework on strategic interactionism and identity formation, as explained in Chapter 2. It also reflects the methodological framework for ethnographic fieldwork and the inclusion of other sources, considered in this chapter. The analysis of the mobilisation of the Kurdish diaspora in Denmark in support of the Kurdish struggle in Syria will be structured as follows.

First, I will analyse how the main actors, that is, the Kurds in Syria and the Kurdish diaspora in Denmark, emerged as transnational players (Chapters 4 and 5). The analysis of the Syrian Kurds will focus on how Kurdish players reacted to the various repressive policies of the French Mandate and later the authorities of the Syrian Republic, and how they took advantage of the opportunities that presented themselves in the wake of the Syrian Civil War. In Denmark, the Kurds mobilised and evolved into a diaspora through the interaction between labour migrants and political refugees who had fled political persecution in the Middle East. The diaspora was also formed by interaction with state authorities and as a reaction to crises and developments in the countries of origin. The analysis of the becoming of the Syrian Kurds and the Kurdish diaspora in Denmark will mainly be based on written sources as the analyses cover historical developments, but it will also include social media in order to cover current events. In addition, I will draw on my interviews with Kurds who experienced the developments first-hand in either Syria or Denmark.

Following the analysis of the main actors, I will zoom in on the Kurdish diaspora groups in Denmark and analyse their response to what they perceive as the needs of the Kurds in Syria (Chapters 6, 7 and 8). I will trace the activism in various arenas in Denmark. By means of ethnographic fieldwork I have identified three arenas of relevance for this study. These are the political arena, the courtroom arena and the humanitarian arena. These arenas will be broken down into sub-arenas, which are both concrete places and symbolic spaces of interaction (Duyvendak and Fillieule 2014, p. 306). Political activism takes place in the centre of Copenhagen, in the squares and at the castle of Christiansborg, while humanitarian activism unfolds in the periphery of the city, in the suburbs, and in the field of the homeland. Courtroom activism takes place in and around the courtroom, which becomes both a place for judicial struggle and a rostrum for political mobilisation. The courtroom activism involves only few activists. In fact, only one Kurd has flung herself into this form of activism in support of the Kurds in Syria, namely Joanna Palani, who fought with Kurdish forces in Syria and Iraq and later had the administrative decision to nullify her passport tried in court. I have chosen to include an analysis of courtroom activism in this book, despite only one Kurdish player being involved. As my investigation discloses, Kurdish political actors take advantage of ambiguous national policies by adopting ambiguous strategies. This appears to be a defining feature of Kurdish activism in Denmark and, thus, relevant to this study.

In each of the three arenas, the Kurdish diaspora activists employ different strategies to reach a certain outcome. These different strategies will be analysed in three separate chapters, each paying special attention to the motivation, the goals and the means of reaching the goals, that is, the repertoires of action embraced by the Kurdish activists. I will include supplementary concepts and research areas to grasp the specificity of the activism in the respective arenas. However, Kurdish activism does not take place in a vacuum, as explained in the theoretical chapter. The main analysis will focus on the interaction with crucial actors. In each chapter, I will identify the defining players and their agendas and analyse how the agendas of Kurdish activists are countered or accepted through a back-and-forth process of interaction. Each chapter will conclude with an assessment of the outcome of the Kurdish activism. The assessment will cover the outcome of the activism related to the goals of political lobbyism, courtroom activism and humanitarian action. It will also cover the implications of Kurdish mobilisation in the three arenas for the formation and transformation of Kurdish diaspora identity.

The analysis of political lobbyism (Chapter 6) will be primarily based on the participant observations I made when joining Kurdish political activists in the squares and at Christiansborg castle. The interviews I conducted will provide a comprehensive understanding of the rationale behind the activities. The analysis of courtroom activism (Chapter 7) will be based on a number of sources besides my own participant observations and interviews, including law texts, courtroom documents, bills, blogs, posts on social media, documentaries and public newspaper interviews. Each group of sources represents different players in the public debate on military activism, players who either support, ignore or counter the agenda of the courtroom activists. For a number of reasons, the analysis of humanitarian activism (Chapter 8) is largely based on interviews and only to a lesser extent on participant observation. First, most of the fundraising was done electronically and on social media. Second, many of the charity events I have included took place in 2014 during the battle of Kobane, before I began my fieldwork. Finally, the humanitarian action seeks to provide relief for the Kurds who are still in the conflict zone. This means that most of the activities unfolded in the field, in the Kurdish areas of the Middle East. From the very beginning, I made the choice to exclusively cover the activities in Denmark as my focus is on diaspora mobilisation, which took me into different locations in the suburbs.

Finally, I will gather the threads from the various analyses and draw an overall conclusion that includes the findings of my investigations and points to the major conclusions regarding Kurdish activism in support of the Kurdish struggle in Syria (Chapter 9). I will also substantiate the contributions of this book to the fields of Kurdish diaspora studies and social movement research.

PART II

THE EMERGENCE OF KURDISH ACTIVISTS IN SYRIA AND IN DENMARK

4

THE KURDS OF SYRIA: FROM THE FORGOTTEN PEOPLE TO WORLD-STAGE ACTORS

Introduction

Before 2011, the Syrian Kurds were referred to as the 'forgotten Kurds' (Yildiz 2005; Gunter 2014) since they attracted very little attention from researchers and public media prior to the civil war in Syria.

The Syrian Civil War placed the Syrian Kurds on the regional map as they managed to occupy and control some of the northern parts of the country. They even sparked global interest when they proved to be the most effective and loyal Middle Eastern allies to the American-led coalition against Islamic State on the Syrian front of the battle (IISS 2016, p. 310).

How did the Kurds of Syria mobilise around a Syrian Kurdish identity worth taking up arms and fighting for? In other words, how did the 'forgotten Kurds' suddenly become 'memorable'?

This chapter will trace the development of a Syrian Kurdish political identity and point to at least three factors crucial to understanding the mobilisation of the Syrian Kurds. First, the territory which became the state of Syria after the great wars of the twentieth century hosts many ethnic (Arabs, Kurds, Turkmen and Assyrians) and religious groups (Muslims, Christians, Alawites, Ismailis and Druze). The Kurds themselves do not form a homogeneous group either, but rather are fragmented along territorial and demographic cleavages. Second, these fragmentations have inspired different regimes in Syria to pursue a policy of ambiguous repression of the Kurds. This regime strategy has meant that the Kurds of Syria have been deprived of essential rights, while at the same time Kurds from neighbouring countries have been given special privileges as they were utilised as proxies against neighbouring states, primarily Turkey. Third, the Syrian Kurds have mainly employed a strategy of peaceful action and moderate policy (Tejel 2009, p. 5). The politically engaged Kurds have chosen complicity with the regime rather than rebellion, contrary to other parts of the Kurdish homeland (that is, in Turkey, Iraq and Iran). Thus, it is noteworthy that Syrian forces in connection with the current crisis in Syria withdrew from Kurdish areas in 2012 before the YPG took control. It is also worth noting that the main enemy of the YPG is not the regime, but Islamic State and other rebel groups. To clarify the strategic action of the Kurds in Syria, this chapter draws on the concept of *complicity* originating from Lisa Wedeen's study *Ambiguities of Domination*, which examines Syrian politics under the former president Hafez Al-Assad (Wedeen 1999). Accordingly, complicity should be understood as subjection of the citizens under a ubiquitous and ambiguous autocrat.

Becoming the 'Syrian Kurds'

The French mandate and the cradle of Kurdish nationalism

The collapse of the Ottoman Empire in the wake of World War I into a number of new states and mandate areas left the Kurdish population divided as inhabitants of different Middle Eastern states, mainly Turkey, Iran, Iraq and Syria. The Kurds of Syria have historically lived in the northern part of the country, along the borders with Turkey and Iraq. The Kurdish areas of Syria are fragmented into three principal parts, which form territorial outgrowths of the larger Kurdish territory in the neighbouring countries. The three areas are Kurd Dagh (i.e., the 'Kurdish Mountains') in the north-western corner of Syria, which delivers most of Syria's olive production; the area around the town of Kobane located by the Baghdad railway; and the Jazira area in north-eastern Syria in upper Mesopotamia. The Jazira underwent a considerable transformation from the end of the nineteenth century and throughout the first half of the twentieth, as nomads settled and became farmers, turning the area into the 'granary of Syria'. At the same time, the area received a large number of Kurdish migrants from the turmoil that emerged in the wake of the creation of the new Turkish republic. Kurds also live in the big cities, including Damascus, Aleppo and Homs. In Damascus, the Kurdish population is said to date back to the twelfth century invasion by Salah al-Din Ayubi, himself a Kurd. In Aleppo and the other cities, the Kurdish population consists mainly of immigrants from the rural Kurdish areas. Overall, at the time of the French Mandate the Kurds made up 250,000 of the total Syrian population of 2,950,000, about 8.5 per cent (Zisser 2014, p. 194). By 2011 the Kurdish-speaking population constituted about 10 per cent of the Syrian population or more than 2.2 million (Gunter 2014, p. 2).

In accordance with the principles of the Sykes–Picot Agreement, France was granted control over Syria by the League of Nations after the World War I; the agreement was ratified in 1923. According to Jordi Tejel, the mandate period paved the way for a certain 'political culture' among the Kurds of Syria, characterised by 'peaceful confrontation and accommodation of an ambiguous political scene' (Tejel 2009, p. 2). I find two events crucial in this respect: the formation in 1927 of the Khoybun League, which strived for Kurdish national awakening; and the adoption of the 1936 constitution, which through its favouring of the Arab population triggered a call for autonomy by the Jazira Kurds. This political culture translated into peaceful opposition within the country and even a degree of complicity with the incumbent regime, as mentioned above. In addition, Jazira was seen as a special case, culminating with around 120,000 Jaziran Kurds being deprived of their citizenship in 1962 (Tejel 2009, pp. 50–1; Allsopp 2015, p. 153).

Although the Kurdish presence in the Syrian region goes way back (Vanly 1992, p. 145), the Kurds were not unified as a national group before the time of the French Mandate (Tejel 2009, p. 3). Traditionally, the Kurdish identity was based on local tribal affiliation and loyalty towards local notables. This also applies to the other ethnic groups of the Ottoman Empire. The goal of the Khoybun was to break these vertical ties and mobilise the Kurds around the idea of a national Kurdish community bound together by horizontal ties. The Khoybun was inspired by the nationalistic awakening that struck the European countries during the nineteenth century and reached the Ottoman Empire at the beginning of the twentieth century. In the Syrian context the mobilisation of the Khoybun was an immediate reaction to the establishment of the new Republic of Turkey.

The Khoybun League was established in 1927 and included Kurdish intellectuals, ex-officers, sheikhs and tribal leaders (Tejel 2009, p. 17). Some of the founding members of the committee were refugees from Istanbul, where they had joined the Kurdish clubs. They had fled Turkey after the declaration of the Kemalist Turkish state or had been forced into exile after the failed Kurdish uprising in 1925. Among them were Memduh Selim, Ihsan Nouri and the Bedirkhan brothers (Tejel 2009, p. 144, n19). The Khoybun generally gained most support in the areas that received the most refugees from Turkey, that is, Jazira and Damascus. The main goal of the movement was to oppose the Kemalist regime in Turkey, and as such, it did not challenge the French Mandate in Syria. Relying on a divide-and-rule strategy, the French authorities even allowed the league to meet and mobilise within Syria as it could be utilised against Turkey. The border between Turkey and Syria had yet to be finally established, and this caused some tension between the two powers. The committee supported the Ararat Revolt (1927-30) and thereby became the core of the political and military leadership of the revolt. After the defeat in 1930 by the Turkish military, the Khoybun returned to the intellectual and cultural activities of the Ottoman period, the brothers Jaladet and Kamuran Bedirkhan playing leading roles. While the political project was elitist and short-term, the cultural initiatives had a broader and more permanent impact. Most important is the work of Jaladet Bedirkhan. He described and formalised the Kurmanji dialect and propagated the Kurdish alphabet based on Latin letters. The brothers also edited Kurdish journals and published studies on traditional music, history and Kurdish ethnography. The main purpose of these activities was to unite the Kurds. Kurdish clubs and societies emerged, where Kurds could meet to study the language and share the Kurdish history and heritage (Yildiz 2005, p. 29).

The old Kurdish elite of Jazira, in cooperation with Assyrian notables, aspired to more than cultural rights. They wanted a measure of autonomy like that granted to the Druze at Jabal Druze and the Alawites of Latakia at the beginning of the 1920s (Tejel 2009, p. 29). The area of Jazira was the last area within the Mandate territory to be subjugated to French authority, which did not gain full control of the region until 1927 (Tejel 2009, p. 27). Still, state presence was minimal, counting only a small number of officers and state functionaries, and the infrastructure was weak: poor roads, no hospitals and few public schools. Jazira definitely represented the periphery of Syria. The 1936 Franco-Syrian agreement, which entrusted power to the Arab majority of Syria, was the straw that broke the camel's back. A revolt broke out in 1937, but it was suppressed immediately. The autonomous claims rested on loyalty to local notables and tribal leaders, but after 1937, a growing distrust between the Kurds and the Assyrians arose. The mutual distrust between Jazira and Damascus persisted.

Thus, the legacy of the French Mandate was a divided society. The French authorities had used a traditional divide-and-rule tactic, which created tension between the rural and urban populations, between centre and periphery and between the different minorities and the Arab majority (Tejel 2009, p. 41; Yildiz 2005, pp. 28–9).

The post-mandate period and the rise of the Kurdish parties

The Syrian Republic became independent in 1946, following the end of World War II. Soon after this the country 'fell into a period of great political instability and was swung between martial and parliamentary rule by successive coups' (Allsopp 2015, p. 20). New urban elites emerged in post-mandatory Syria, shaping the authoritarian development of years to come. Two of the authoritarian presidents during the first decade of independence were Kurdish. Both were urban and Arabic-speaking and took no interest in specific Kurdish political issues. As a matter of fact, president Adib al-Shishakli attempted to exclude minorities from the political sphere by promoting a Syrian national identity (Tejel 2009, p. 41). Other political actors attempted to unify the population of Syria around Arab nationalism. Shishakli considered the Druze the foremost enemy of the state as they did not waive autonomy, but as Arab nationalism gained ground, the Kurds, as the largest non-Arab minority, came to be seen as the biggest threat to Syrian unity.

Arab nationalism became the most influential ideology of the period, often in conjunction with Pan-Arabism and Arab socialism influenced by regional and global events, such as the Arab-Israeli war in 1948, the Suez War in 1956 and the Cold War (Tejel 2009, p. 40; Yildiz 2005, pp. 30–1). In 1958, Syria formed the United Arab Republic with Egypt under the presidency of Gamal Abdul Nasser. Following a military coup in 1961, as a reaction to the Egyptian dominance of the United Arab Republic, the union was dissolved. Nationalisation of land, which was a major part of the Nasserist Arab socialism, also caused huge discontent among the Syrian elite. The ideas of Pan-Arabism and Arab socialism were not abandoned by the Syrian Arabs, though, but expressed in other ways, for example by the Ba'ath party.

The agricultural development in Jazira during the 1950s strengthened the local power of upcoming landowners, providing ever-more fertile political ground for Kurdish nationalism (Tejel 2009, p. 39). The Khoybun leaders had already left the political scene or joined non-Kurdish parties, mainly the Syrian Communist Party (Arabic: *Hizb al-Shuyu'i al-Suri*), which in the north of the country became known as the 'Kurdish Party' (McDowall 2004, p. 472; Tejel 2009, p. 43). Some Kurdish organisations existed, but in 1957, the first Kurdish party seeking to represent the interests of all Kurds in Syria, namely the Kurdish Democratic Party in Syria (KDPS) (Kurdish: *Partiya Demokrat a Kurdî li Sûriyê*) was formed. At the time of its creation, the party committee included Kurds from all the Kurdish regions of Syria, and it succeeded in bringing together Kurds of different political convictions. Among the founding fathers were Osman Sabri (secretary) and Nur al-Din Zaza (president). Most of the party leaders were leftist or at least did not object to this inclination (Allsopp 2015, p. 76). The party was affiliated to the Kurdistan Democratic Party of Iraq (KDP) (Kurdish: *Partiya Demokrat a Kurdistanê*) created in 1946 by Mustafa Barzani, although the Syrian branch from 1958 refrained from using the proper name Kurdistan to avoid the suggestion that the Kurdish enclaves belonged to an independent Kurdistan (Tejel 2009, p. 49). There is some contention regarding the original name of the party, as the accounts of the founding fathers differ (Allsopp 2015, p. 75). Some hold that 'Kurdistan' was used in the first year, others that it was added later on. One account claims that it was added in 1960 on the insistence of Jalal Talabani, who had also supervised the creation of the Syrian branch of the party while taking refuge in Syria in the 1950s. Regardless of the various claims, the party unravelled in 1960, and the leaders were jailed, accused of separatism (Tejel 2009, p. 49; Allsopp 2015, p. 78). While the leaders were imprisoned, two factions evolved within the party: one around Zaza, who asserted that the Kurds of Syria were a minority rather than a nation; the other around Sabri, who insisted that the Kurdish nation was the core ideal of the movement. In 1970 Mustafa Barzani tried to mediate, but the factions could not reach common ground. Instead, the original party divided into three parties.

Mustafa Barzani's mediating position came to be known as KDPS el-Partî (Allsopp 2015, p. 82). The leader of this central and conservative party was Daham Miro. The right-leaning wing, which followed the line of Zaza, was led by Abdulhamid Darwish. This party, which later took the name the Kurdish Democratic Progressive Party in Syria (KDPPS), had close ties to the Patriotic Union of Kurdistan (PUK) formed in Iraq in 1974 by KDP dissidents and led by Jalal Talabani. The connection was based mainly on personal relations between the party leaders. The left-leaning wing of the party, called the Left Party (Kurdish: *Partiya Çep*), pursued the policy of Osman Sabri, who also became the party's first leader. The party also aligned with the PUK, but for more ideological reasons, as both parties adopted a Marxist-Leninist approach. These three main branches still exist in a somewhat diluted version today, although the branches themselves have been subject to numerous internal divisions. Today the majority of Kurdish parties in Syria originate from the original KDPS (Allsopp 2015, p. 17).

The formation of the Kurdish parties took place in a political environment dominated by Arab nationalism. After the dissolution of the United Arab Republic, Syria resurrected as an Arab republic, and oppression of the Kurds intensified. This culminated in 1962 when 120,000 Jaziran Kurds, around 20 per cent of Syria's Kurdish population, were deprived of their citizenship (Tejel 2009, pp. 50–1; Allsopp 2015, p. 153). This can be seen as an attempt by the Syrian regime to further dominate Jazira. Two factors explain the increased interest of the regime in controlling the Kurds. First, Mustafa Barzani had led a successful revolt in Iraqi Kurdistan and controlled most of the highlands between the Iranian and Syrian borders. This made Damascus fear similar unrest in Syrian Kurdistan (Tejel 2009, p. 51). Second, Damascus had economic interests in the region due to its large grain production and the recent discovery of oil (Allsopp 2015, p. 19).

Legislative Decree no. 93 of 23 August 1962 prescribed a census for the region to marginalise those who were perceived to have obtained Syrian citizenship illegally. Thus, the identity cards of those who were considered non-Syrians were withdrawn. To regain them, the Kurds had to prove they had Syrian residence prior to 1940. Failure to do so meant that a large group of

Kurds were registered as *ajanib* (singular *ajnabi/ajnabiyah*), i.e., foreigners. They were referred to as invaders from Turkey during the mandatory period and deprived of their rights to education, property ownership, political participation, legal marriage, etc. Kurds who did not participate in the census became known as *maktumin* (i.e., concealed or hidden). They were unregistered and, being legally non-existent, they had even lower status than the *ajanib* (Tejel 2009, p. 51; Allsopp 2015, p. 154).

It is worth noting that this happened in the wake of the dissolution of the United Arab Republic, which involved the nationalisation laws being reversed and land being handed back to former landowners. It also happened at a time when European and American companies began oil extraction, and this made the regime aware of the urgency of countering the 'conspiracy with the goal of establishing non-Arab ethnic groups within the Syrian crude-oil triangle' (in the words of the governor of al-Hasakah province) (KurdWatch 2010, p. 6). By depriving Kurdish landowners of their citizenship and rights to property, the land could instead be handed over to loyal Arabs. Thus, at the beginning of the 1970s, after the Tabqa dam on the Euphrates had been constructed, 4,000 Arab families, whose land had been flooded, were resettled (with arms) in model farms in the Jazira (Tejel 2009, p. 61).

The Ba'ath Era and the Silence of the Syrian Kurds

The old parties under Ba'ath rule

In 1963 the Ba'ath party came to power following a coup d'état on March 8. The coup was carried out one month after the Ba'athist coup in Iraq. The Ba'ath ideology became a powerful alternative to Nasserist Pan-Arabism. The Ba'ath party was founded in 1947 in Damascus by Michel Aflaq and Salah al-Din al-Bitar and was ideologically based on secularism, Pan-Arabism and Arab socialism. The subsequent coup on February 23, 1966, consolidated Ba'ath party power in Syria by eliminating other Pan-Arab and Arab nationalist groups. This caused the Ba'ath party in Syria and Iraq to split into two branches, each trying to convince the Arabs that they were the leading power of the Arab world.

After the Ba'ath party came to power, Arabisation, and thus suppression of the Kurds, was intensified. The study by Lieutenant Muhammad Talab al-Hilal is telling in this respect. Al-Hilal was a former secret security chief in the Hasakah province, who in 1963 delivered a security report on the solution to the Kurdish issue in Jazira. The study is renowned for its derogatory attitude towards the Kurds, and brutal prescriptions for them. The Kurds are perceived as 'our enemies', and the presence of Kurds in Jazira is presented as the 'Kurdish danger' and a 'malignant tumor which had developed in a part of the body of the Arab nation' (Yildiz 2005, p. 34; Tejel 2009, pp. 60–1). The proposed cure to restore Arabism in Jazira was primarily the creation of an Arab belt by deporting the Kurds along the Turkish borders. The al-Hilal plan also mentioned measures such as no education and employment opportunities and simply the annihilation of Kurdish identity by favouring Arabs in every aspect of life. Thus, these prescriptions were in line with the intentions of Decree no. 93 of 1962. Despite the seeming urgency of the Arab nationalists' desire to control the Jaziran Kurds, the plan was not implemented until the beginning of the 1970s (Tejel 2009, p. 61).

Other repressive measures were implemented in the late 1960s and during the 1970s and 1980s to 'Arabise' the Kurds. These included the ban on the use of the Kurdish language in schools and later in workplaces, the continued ban on publications in Kurdish and omission of the Kurds from history school books (International Crisis Group 2013, p. 6). In addition to this, Kurds were met with general distrust and discrimination by the public administration and subject to arbitrary arrests by the security forces (Tejel 2009, pp. 62–3).

In Europe, Ismet Cheriff Vanly, a Kurdish activist from Amouda who had settled in Switzerland (Tejel 2011), tried to draw international attention to the repression of the Syrian Kurds. He published a number of booklets to 'break the silence' on the Kurdish issue in Syria, drawing parallels between the al-Hilal plan and Hitler's 'Mein Kampf' (Vanly 1968a; Vanly 1968b), though this was to no immediate avail.

On 6 November 1970 Major General Hafez al-Assad seized power after leading a coup d'état. The new regime was referred to as the 'corrective movement', as the official aim was to 'correct' or, to a minor degree, adjust the preceding Ba'ath rule. Thus, according to the constitution of the Syrian Arab Republic, which was adopted in 1973, the Socialist Arab Ba'ath Party was the leading party (Article 8). However, in reality the ideological base of the Ba'ath party was abandoned or changed. Pan-Arabism became obsolete as a result of the increasing competition between the Arab states, and Arab nationalism was utilised as a mere power instrument to gain control of the Syrian people and territory. Instead of drawing on these ideologies, al-Assad (during his rule) built an autocratic regime centred around a myth about the Assad family with himself as the protective father of the Syrian Arab people. The political milieu in Syria under Hafez al-Assad has been analysed eminently by Lisa Wedeen in *The Ambiguity of Domination* (1999).

Through 'political ethnography' (Wedeen 1999, p. 25) she describes the social dynamics of the authoritarian rule of Hafez al-Assad, showing how the domination of the regime was enforced through two instruments of power. One was violent repression by the many security forces; detention, imprisonment, abduction and torture. The other was the symbolic power of myths and fictional narratives about the loving and caring paternal president. While repression was carried out secretly and far from public attention, the symbolic power was exercised in the public space through posters, statues, rituals and spectacular events. The strategy proved effective, as both instruments were used unwaveringly. The power of the regime thereby became ubiquitous and inescapable. If the Syrians chose to oppose the regime, they were eliminated or defused, as proved by the Hama massacre in 1982; and if they chose to comply with the fiction 'imposed' on them (Wedeen 1999, p. 73), they became part of the repressive play themselves. Syrians were not compelled to believe in the mythical, eternal paternity of Hafez al-Assad, but to act 'as if' they believed it in certain public situations. By acting 'as if' the myths were real (Wedeen 1999, p. 69), the Syrian citizen became not only an object of domination, but also a suppressing subject him- or herself. This kind of system does not allow for a neutral position towards the atrocities. A person is either out or part of the game. The division between ruler and the ruled, as Wedeen explains, quoting Václav Havel, 'runs de facto though each person, for everyone in his or her own way is both a victim and a supporter of the system' (Wedeen 1999, p. 81). This is what Wedeen calls the ambiguity of the domination of al-Assad's Syria; and this is what characterises the political context which the Kurdish parties tried to navigate.

The Kurdish parties that grew out of the KDPS claimed to pursue the same goal, that is, the protection of the Kurdish identity for the Syrian Kurds.

Achieving this involved repealing oppressive laws and securing the Kurds' political and cultural rights. What they could not agree on was how to reach these goals. They disagreed on two specific issues. The first concerned which political solution would best protect the Kurdish identity. This issue related to an ideological discussion of who the Kurds are: a nation or a minority (Allsopp 2015, p. 80). The second concerned how best to interact with the regime. This issue related to the parties' assessments of the options in the political environment either for complying with the regime or for adopting a confrontational position (Allsopp 2015, p. 84). The three parts of the Kurdish political spectrum, established after Barzani's attempt to mediate in 1970, represented three different positions. The so-called right-wing party (KDPPS) headed by Darwish sought inclusion of the Kurds as a minority in Syrian society. Accordingly, the KDPPS insisted on 'soft political pressure' on the Syrian regime. Darwish, who accepted the rules of the game drawn up by the regime, went as far as securing a seat in the Syrian parliament as an independent, which was allowed in the 1990s (The Syrian Observer 2014; Tejel 2009, p. 67). The two other groups of Kurdish parties claimed that the Kurds represented a unique nation. The left parties saw the Kurds as a national group entitled to constitutional recognition. They chose a non-confrontational approach, considering both political and violent opposition to be suicidal. The conservative centrists also defined the Kurds as a national group leaning more towards the nationalistic ideal of autonomy. In doing so, they followed the line of the KDP in Iraq. But failing to gain support from the mother party in Iraq for the internal Syrian struggle, they also chose the submissive opposition. The ambiguous domination of the regime proved efficient at silencing the Kurds. It even made them cooperate from time to time with *mukhabarat*, the secret security service, to avoid annihilation. During the 1970s, the left party was ravaged by internal division due to ideological disagreements about Marxism-Leninism, resulting in an internal split in the Kurdish movement itself (Allsopp 2015, p. 82). The other splits within the Kurdish parties were primarily the result of personal and leadership issues, which is why some parties have the same name. By the end of 2012, seventeen of twenty Syrian Kurdish parties could trace their origins to the first Kurdish Democratic Party in Syria (KDPS), according to an estimate by Harriet Allsopp (Allsopp 2015, p. 17).

The arrival of the PKK in Syria

In 1978 the Kurdish Worker's Party (PKK) was founded in Turkey. Ideologically based on Marxism-Leninism and influenced by Kurdish nationalism, the PKK strove for the liberation of the Kurdish people and the establishment of an independent Kurdistan. After the military coup in Turkey in 1980, Syria offered refuge to the PKK leadership as part of a balancing strategy against Turkey. There were several reasons why Syria wanted to keep Turkey in check: first, there was the old resentment of having lost Alexandretta in 1939; second, Syria wanted to counter Turkey's influence on the water supply through the Euphrates (Enab Baladi 2017); and third, Syria felt encircled by the upcoming alliance between Israel and Turkey (McDowall 2004, p. 480). The PKK presence in Syria changed the conditions for the political struggle of the Syrian Kurds once more.

The PKK became very popular, especially among young Kurds, who considered the PKK more potent than the old parties (Allsopp 2015, p. 103). The competition was unequal, though, as the PKK could mobilise openly in the Kurdish areas in Syria, while the restrictions on the old parties were upheld. This was part of the deal with the PKK leader Abdullah Öcalan, which meant that the PKK could act freely and enrol new party members, as long as the Kurdish fight was directed towards Turkey. Consequently, around 7,000 young Syrian Kurds disappeared and presumably died in the PKK insurgency in Turkey in the 1980s. In an interview Öcalan even expressed, or saw strategic reasons to share, the perception of the Syrian Kurds as refugees from Turkey, who would gladly return (McDowall 2004, p. 479). Support for the PKK was strongest in Kurd Dagh and in Kobane (Allsopp 2015, p. 103), as the other parties still had a stronghold in Jazira.

The PKK presence had a significant impact on Kurdish culture, as 'the PKK took over the cultural framing of the Syrian Kurds' by politicising cultural expression according to the ideological base of the PKK (Tejel 2009, pp. 104–5). While the Kurds had celebrated Newroz (i.e., the Kurdish New Year on March 21) privately in the past, the PKK organised public events in order to make the festival a collective and political act and to foster a sense of cultural awakening. Similarly, Kurdish dance and music was performed in Kurdish colours (red, green, yellow and white) to infuse the Kurdish community with political unity. The PKK's activities revealed the powerlessness of the other parties. Even though they tried to imitate the politicisation of Kurdish culture, they neither managed to continue the Kurdish awakening after the rejection of Öcalan nor succeeded in recruiting young followers. In 1998, Turkey's patience ran out, and Syrian fear of a Turkish invasion ended the PKK presence in Syria. In early 1999, Öcalan was captured in Kenya and taken to Turkey.

Public mobilisation in the 2000s

The departure of the PKK, combined with the distrust in the old Kurdish parties, primarily among young Kurds, left a space open for new contending parties and independent activists at the beginning of the 2000s. Two major events constitute important landmarks in this development, namely the so-called Damascus Spring and the Qamishlo Revolt. The former led to a new kind of activism by the Yekîtî party, which, although elitist, put the Kurdish issue on the agenda of the underground opposition. The latter mobilised the Kurdish community on a broader scale, and young people in Kurdish areas as well as in Damascus and Aleppo became particularly involved in collective action. In addition, the Qamishlo Revolt exposed the ambiguous submission of the Kurdish parties to the regime as being out of touch with the Kurdish population.

In June 2000 Hafez al-Assad died, paving the way for the Damascus Spring. After the death of his father, Bashar al-Assad became president. Bashar al-Assad had trained as an ophthalmologist in London before returning to Syria to take up the position as heir apparent in 1994 after the death of his brother Basil. The Syrian opposition had some hope that the new president, Bashar al-Assad, would usher in political changes. In the first few months of rule, the new regime did allow some critical political debate. Political salons were established, and groups of intellectuals released documents asking for the state of emergency to be repealed and political pluralism to be established (Carnegie Middle East Center 2012, April 1). But in September of the following year the patience of the regime ran out. Ten prominent intellectuals and activists were arrested, marking the end of the Damascus Spring (Allsopp 2015, p. 110). For the Kurdish Union Party in Syria, called Yekîtî (Kurdish for 'Union'), there was no turning back, although repressive measures were implemented, for example a ban on the possession and distribution of all opposition publications including those in Kurdish. The Yekîtî party was founded in 1992 by representatives from both the left and conservative wings of the Kurdish political spectrum. They had adopted a strategy of territorial demands for Syrian Kurdistan and greater visibility of the Kurdish struggle through public campaigns and demonstration. The party was mainly rooted in urban areas and succeeded in mobilising young Kurds. Yekîtî benefitted from the power vacuum left by the PKK as well as the political opening of the Damascus Spring. Thus, in the following years party members pushed on with political activism, arranging protests and demonstrations in Damascus advocating Kurdish rights. Some of the demonstrations were supported by other Kurdish parties as well as other parts of the Syrian opposition. In 2003 the Democratic Union Party (called the PYD, Kurdish: *Partiya Yekîtî ya Dêmokrat*) was established as a successor to the Syrian part of the PKK. However, the PYD was not protected by the regime. Three coalitions of Kurdish parties emerged to stand against the regime. Yekîtî and the PYD, among others, formed the Coordinating Committee, which took the most confrontational stance, while the Kurdish Alliance headed by the KDPPS leader Darwish was the most conceding. The Kurdish Democratic Front took a middle position on the question (Kajjo and Sinclair 2011).

In 2004, a football match in Qamishlo escalated into a Kurdish revolt against the regime. The Qamishlo football team played a home game against the visiting team from Deir al-Zor. There are divergent witness reports on how it all started, but at some point during the match the fans from Deir al-Zor displayed posters of Saddam Hussein and chanted slogans insulting the Iraqi Kurdish leaders Masoud Barzani and Jalal Talabani. Traditionally, the Sunni Arabs of Deir al-Zor had been sympathetic to the regime of Saddam Hussein, who was ousted the year before by the US-led military intervention. The Qamishlo fans, on the other hand, responded with praise for the American president George Bush by exclaiming 'we will sacrifice our lives for Bush' (Tejel 2009, p. 115). A violent battle between the fans forced the security forces to open fire, killing seven Kurds. This sparked a popular uprising that spread across the Kurdish regions and even surfaced in the Syrian capital, Damascus, mobilising different social segments of Kurdish society (Allsopp 2015, pp. 33–6). The revolt, which lasted from 12 to 25 March, was eventually brutally defeated, resulting in '43 dead

(7 were Arabs), hundreds wounded, around 2.500 arrested, and more than 40 Kurdish students thrown out of Syrian Universities' (Tejel 2009, p. 116). The event sparked an assertive opposition among the Syrian Kurds, resulting in a new activist Kurdish identity. While the Yekîtî party and the PYD encouraged the resistance, the majority of the other Kurdish parties missed the opportunity to play a leading role in the Kurdish awakening. Instead, they once again found it more advantageous to comply with the regime. This made them expendable in the eyes of many Kurds. Syrian opposition groups, on the other hand, embraced the Kurdish struggle, and they even added the 'Kurdish issue' to their agenda in 2005 (Tejel 2009, p. 126). Thus, cooperation among human rights activists both within Syria and in the West was intensified.

One of the people who raised his voice after the Qamishlo Revolt and advocated for Kurdish rights was Ma'shouq al-Khaznawi. Prior to the revolt Sheikh Ma'shouq al-Khaznawi was a well-established religious authority from Upper Jazira accepted by the regime, as he promoted a liberal reading of the Koran (Tejel 2009, p. 101). It seems that the repression during and after the Qamishlo Revolt triggered his critique of the regime. After an interview with a Canadian daily in 2005, in which he opined that the Syrian regime should 'change or be terminated' (Tejel 2009, p. 101), he was kidnapped and later found dead; strong suspicion fell on the regime. His funeral mobilised around 10,000 visitors to the family's mourning tent (Allsopp 2015, p. 106).

In 2005, during the Kurdish awakening following the revolt, two new parties were founded: the Kurdish Freedom Party called Azadî (Kurdish for 'Freedom') and the Future Movement by Mashaal Tammo. Both parties joined the Coordinating Committee, the most oppositional and activist Kurdish bloc. In 2014 the Azadî party merged with the newly formed KDP-S (Rudaw 2014). KDP-S, *Partiya Demokrat a Kurdistanê – Sûriyê*, was a successor to KDPS formed in order to unite the efforts of a number of parties in opposition to PYD (Schmidinger 2018, p. 218).

By the end of the 2000s the regime had tightened its grip on the Kurdish parties, especially the Yekîtî party and the PYD. Yekîtî was monitored because of its increasingly oppositional stance, and the PYD because of pressure from Turkey to enact a zero-tolerance policy towards the PKK and Öcalan supporters (Kajjo and Sinclair 2011).

The awakening during the Qamishlo Revolt led to the emergence of a new and alternative Syrian Kurdish identity, which was more confrontational and venturesome than before.

The 2011 Uprising and the Birth of Kurdish Autonomy in Syria

The Syrian uprising

In March 2011, the Syrian Uprising erupted as part of the so-called Arab Spring in Tunisia, Egypt, Yemen, Bahrain and Libya. Triggered by the arrest and torture of a group of teenagers in Deraa and the violent reaction of the regime towards the demonstration that followed, the protests spread to other Syrian cities, including Damascus. As with the other uprisings, these demonstrations were headed by young people demanding democratic reforms and the resignation of the president.

Kurdish youths also took part in the protests from the beginning, both in the major cities of Syria and in the Kurdish areas in northern Syria calling for regime change. The Kurdish organisers coordinated their actions with the Syrian Arab opposition to the extent that one of the protest Fridays during the spring of 2011 was called Îna Azadî (i.e., 'Freedom Friday' in Kurdish) (Zisser 2014, p. 208; Allsopp 2015, p. 196; KB 2011).

However, most of the Kurdish political parties remained relatively quiet during the spring of 2011. This silence, combined with the lack of media attention on the participation of the Kurdish youths outside the Kurdish areas, led to discontent with the Kurds among parts of the Arab opposition, who denounced the Kurdish parties as being loyal to the regime. The Kurdish parties were suspicious of the rest of the opposition, anticipating that the Arab opposition would pursue an Arab or Islamist agenda, leaving the Kurdish issue behind, as seen before during the Qamishlo Revolt in 2004. The Syrian regime exploited the disunity of the opposition in an attempt to draw the Syrian Kurds closer by new decrees meeting the traditional Kurdish claims. Thus, in April 2011 the Syrian regime granted citizenship to more than 100,000 of the *ajanib* Kurds, whose number had grown to 300,000 by 2011 (International Crisis Group 2013, p. 6). It also annulled Legislative Decree 49 of 2008, which restricted ownership and sale of land in the Kurdish border areas (Tejel 2014, p. 226).

Some of the more radical Kurdish parties supported the demonstrations, though, and their leaders even participated as speakers at the demonstrations. These parties were the Future Movement and the Yekîtî and Azadî parties; the very parties that had persistently and explicitly criticised the regime since the mid-2000s (Allsopp 2015, p. 197).

After attempts to join the newly formed opposition group, the Syrian National Council (SNC), the Kurdish parties set up the Kurdish National Council (KNC) in October 2011, sponsored by Masoud Barzani, the president of the Kurdistan Regional Government of Iraq (Carnegie Middle East Center 2012, February 15). The Kurdish parties backed out of negotiations with the SNC primarily because members of the SNC insisted on Syria being an Arab state and part of the Arab nation (Allsopp 2015, p. 199). The KNC united the majority of the Syrian Kurdish parties for the first time. The first head of the council was Abdulhakim Bashar, leader of the KDPS. Only a few parties went their own way. Among them were The Future Movement, which for a period remained part of the SNC, and the PYD, which started to build up its own powerbase in the Kurdish areas, as the leader, Salih Muslim, returned from exile among the PKK in the Kurdistan Region of Iraq (Allsopp 2015, p. 208). The Future Movement explicitly pursued an agenda of regime change and continued its cooperation with the youths, whose vision for Syria was a pluralistic democracy. The leader, Mashaal Tammo, was later killed by the Assad regime. His funeral was attended by more than 50,000 people showing massive support for his claims (Al Arabiya 2012). After his death, the Future Movement joined the KNC. As the uprising became more and more violent and evolved into a civil war, the PYD benefitted from having a military branch on behalf of the other Kurdish factions. The People's Protection Units (called the YPG (Kurdish: *Yekîneyên Parastina Gel*)) was formed after the Qamishlo Revolt in 2004 (GlobalSecurity, n.d.) and backed by the PKK. As such, the YPG became the PYD's strongest asset. In 2012, a female brigade, The Women's Protection Units (called the YPJ (Kurdish: *Yekîneyên Parastina Jin*)), was included. When the Syrian armed forces withdrew from the northern part of Syria in August 2012 to concentrate troops in the centre and south of the country, the YPG took control of the predominantly Kurdish areas without fight. As the Kurdish militia gained ground, supported by the influx of PKK fighters (Allsopp 2017, p. 295), significant tensions arose between the PYD and the KNC. The leader of the Iraqi KDP once more intervened to reconcile Syrian Kurdish factions. Thus, in July 2012, the Kurdish Supreme Committee was founded by the two contentious groups and became the ruling body of the de facto autonomous Kurdish enclaves of northern Syria. During 2013, the Kurdish Supreme Committee became obsolete, though, as the PYD resolutely took the lead in the build-up of a new and alternative political system in line with the political ideas of the PKK leader Abdullah Öcalan (Gunes and Lowe 2015, p. 5). In November 2013, the PYD unitarily declared autonomy for the three cantons of Afrin, Kobane and Jazire (Rudaw 2013). The KNC was decisively outmanoeuvred. The Rojava Peshmerga, which was later formed as a military branch of the KDPS recruiting exiled Syrian Kurds in the Kurdistan Region, has never been strong enough nor even remotely close to threatening the hegemony of the YPG in the Syrian Kurdish regions, in Kurdish called *Rojava*, i.e., west(ern Kurdistan). Because of KNC's marginalised position within Syria, a number of Kurdish parties have left the council, among them the KDPPS, which instead has approached the PYD.

The Rojava revolution

In January 2014, the 'Social Contract' of Rojava (Self-Rule in Rojava 2014) was proclaimed. The charter laid the ground for the implementation of a federal political system based on local self-governed administrative units. The Social Contract complies ideologically with the concept of democratic confederalism developed by Öcalan in the early 2000s. Thus, the contract represents a rejection of state-centred democracy and of the nation state per se. This contradicts what the PKK originally worked for, namely Kurdish separatism followed by an independent Kurdish state (Gunter 2014, p. 65). Instead, the ideology of democratic confederalism promotes bottom-up democracy, i.e., a federal system based on engaged citizenship. Accordingly, the charter is called a social contract, as it is meant to regulate relations between individuals rather than between state and citizens.

During the winter of 2014–15, the YPG won a paramount victory in Kobane against Islamic State, which at the time proved to be the strongest challenger to PYD reign. The Kurds were supported by the US-led international coalition against Islamic State, as the ground forces of the YPG became the most important allies of the coalition on the Syrian front of the battle. It was a tactical alliance, though, as the PYD is related to the PKK, which is considered by the US and EU – not to mention Turkey – to be a terror organisation. Thus, the PYD has been excluded from all international peace negotiation initiatives related to Syria up until now. During the spring of 2015, the YPG succeeded in closing the territorial gap between the Kobane and Jazira cantons.

As the ideology of democratic confederalism does not promote nationalism or a specific ethnic agenda, but rather the opposite, it was important, to gain legitimacy, for the PYD to show both the inhabitants of Rojava and external allies that non-Kurdish groups were part of the revolution. This resulted in the creation of the Movement for a Democratic Society (TEV-DEM (Kurdish: *Tevgera Civaka Demokratîk*)) and, subsequently, in the formation of a multi-ethnic military force called the Syrian Democratic Forces (SDF) – an opportune move for the international coalition, which sponsored the creation of the SDF and thus tried to distance itself from the Kurdish cause in the struggle against Islamic State. In May 2017, the American president agreed to arm the YPG prior to the battle of Raqqa, revealing that the Americans in fact do not distinguish between the YPG and the SDF and consider the non-Kurdish elements insignificant contributions to the SDF (Stewart 2017). In line with the effort to represent itself as a multi-ethnic movement, TEV-DEM proclaimed the 'Federation of Northern Syria   Rojava' in January 2016, only to abandon the Kurdish term 'Rojava' in November 2016. At the same time, diplomatic representatives in several European capitals were set up to gain international attention and support. The Kurdish diaspora played a prominent role in connecting the PYD with European political actors. In September 2018, the Kurdish power-holders went even further by renaming the political entity the Autonomous Administration of North and East Syria. This signalled their willingness to be part of a federal Syria, but the name also hinted at their strength by making reference to the large area under their control – around one-third of Syrian territory.

While the PYD seems to have embraced non-Kurdish communities in political life in northern Syria, relations between the PYD and the KNC are still extremely tense (Khalaf 2016, p. 9). The KNC criticises the PYD for being totalitarian, which goes against its self-image of a pluralistic and inclusive alternative to the surrounding authoritarian regimes. Thus, the former head of the KNC, Ibrahim Biro, also the leader of Yekîtî, has denounced 'the "common practice" of intimidation of political activists and journalists in Rojava' (Rudaw 2016). As a matter of fact, leading members of the KNC have repeatedly been arrested by the Asayîş – the Rojava police forces – allegedly without clear reason. The critique of the PYD also centres on the idolisation of Öcalan and the prohibition of the Pan-Kurdish flag. The PYD rejects all claims and is accusing the KNC of frustrating the political developments in Rojava by obstructing the work of the self-administration (ARA News 2016). This internal Kurdish conflict is also partly the result of the influence of external actors, as the Kurds have always been forced to assess who will provide desperately needed support. Consequently, the KNC accuses the PYD of being lap dogs of the Assad regime, while the PYD accuses the KNC of being a helpless mouthpiece of the Barzani regime and, subsequently, in the pocket of Turkey. The Syrian regime did indeed withdraw from the Kurdish areas without a fight in 2012, and at the time, it undoubtedly considered other rebel groups stronger challengers to the power than the PYD. Still, there is a sort of tacit agreement between the PYD and the Syrian regime, which became clear during the battle of Aleppo in 2016, when the Kurdish area of the city escaped harsh bombings. In terms of the PYD's accusations, it is also true that the KDP supports the KNC against the PYD and the Federation of Northern Syria, and that the political leaders in Kurdistan Region seek to establish good relations with Turkey.

External threats to autonomy

Turkey has become increasingly concerned about the military and political success of Kurdish self-government in Syria. What the Turks want least of all is a Kurdish self-dependent state ruled by the PYD, which they perceive to be the Syrian branch of the PKK and, as such, an illegal terror organisation. For this reason, Turkey has gradually escalated its involvement in the Syrian Civil War. In the summer of 2015, Turkey joined the international coalition against Islamic State, only to break the ceasefire and attack the PKK and the PYD simultaneously. In the late summer of 2016, Turkish ground troops crossed the border – officially to support the Free Syrian Army against Islamic State, but more likely to stop Kurdish fighters from conquering the areas between Afrin and Kobane, which would give the PYD control of a contiguous stretch of land along almost the entire Turkish border. The operation was called Euphrates Shield to emphasise the Turkish interest in controlling the border area west of the Euphrates. At the beginning of 2017, Turkey called off the operation and declared it a success. However, the operation did not ease the Turkish concerns about the presence of a terrorist regime at their borders, and in January 2018, Turkish military forces launched an attack on Afrin. They called the operation Olive Branch, with reference to Afrin's vast olive groves. The Turkish attack and subsequent capture of Afrin in cooperation with groups of the Free Syrian Army was a slap in the face for the Kurdish power-holders as it made it clear that the great powers were willing to hand over the Kurds to Turkey. The US Secretary of State, Rex Tillerson, proclaimed that Turkey had 'legitimate security concerns' at the border (James 2018), and Russia allowed Turkish fighter jets to enter Syrian airspace. The Kurdish National Council issued a statement against the invasion, but it did not lead to further cooperation between YPG/YPJ and the Rojava Peshmerga (Schmidinger 2018, p. 259)

In the Syrian areas east of the Euphrates, 2,000 American troops continued to cooperate with Kurdish forces under the umbrella of the Syrian Democratic Forces. In October 2017, the capital of Islamic State, Raqqa, was liberated, and in March 2019, the SDF, supported by the coalition's airstrikes, captured the last remaining pockets of Islamic State territory around Baghouz at the Iraqi border. As mentioned above, the alliance between the USA and the Kurds was a tactical one, based on the common goal of defeating Islamic State. This became clear in December 2018 when president Trump announced the withdrawal of American troops from Syria, referring in a tweet to the US defeat of Islamic State in Syria (@realDonaldTrump 2018). President Erdoğan followed suit, declaring that Turkey was ready to take over and cleanse the area of terrorists (Erdoğan 2019). The American president then had to soften the statement as it was met with internal American criticism, but it was a harbinger of the inevitable, namely that US engagement in Syria would come to an end and the Syrian Kurds would have to look elsewhere for support. Half a year later, President Trump gave in to pressure from the Turkish leadership and renounced the SDF. Immediately after, on 9 October, Turkish forces and the Turkish-backed Free Syrian Army, now known as the

Syrian National Army, launched an offensive on the Kurdish area in northern Syria – officially in order to establish a safe zone for Syrian return refugees (O'Grady 2019). As American forces withdrew, the SDF saw no other option but to invite the Syrian regime to back them against the Turkish invasion. On 22 October, Russia and Turkey settled a deal to end the military confrontation. The agreement prescribed the pull back of Kurdish fighters to 30 km from the Turkish border installing Syrian and Russian forces to oversee the withdrawal, but the agreement also entrusted the border areas from Tell Abyad to Ras al-Ayn – which Turkish and Turkish-backed militias captured during the campaign – to Turkey. In addition, Russia and Turkey agreed on forming a joint Russian and Turkish border guard to patrol the border west and east of the Turkish controlled area.

Russia, which entered the Syrian Civil War in November 2015 in support of the Assad regime, has shown signs of being open to letting the Kurdish voice be heard. Thus, in 2016, Russia allowed PYD to open an administrative office in Moscow (Allsopp and Wilgenburg 2019, p. 194). Additionally, Russia explicitly supported the PYD on certain occasions, for example by promoting a federal solution to Syria at the negotiations in Astana in Kazakhstan in January 2017, and by pushing to include the PYD in the UN-led peace talks in Geneva. However, the Turks firmly denied this, and the Russians did not push further. To date, only representatives from the KNC have participated in the international negotiations. In January 2017, a delegation of leading members of the KNC were invited to Astana in Kazakhstan (Rudaw 2017, January 17), and in Geneva, March 2017, a delegation of KNC members formed part of the Syrian opposition group, the High Negotiations Committee. They were later accused by other KNC members of failing to promote the Kurdish questions among the Arab oppositional negotiators (Rudaw 2017, March 27). In 2018, Russia invited representatives of the Kurdish regime in northern Syria to the peace negotiations in Sochi, but as Russia did not oppose the Turkish attack on Afrin, which was ongoing, they refused to participate. KNC was not invited (Rudaw 2018).

Even though the Syrian regime as well as Russia has showed some interest in negotiating with the Kurds during the last years (Sheikhmous 2018, p. 6), neither provides a serious alternative to the USA in terms of being a safeguard against Turkey. Moreover, the battle for Idlib in 2020 reveals once again that the Syrian regime supported by Russia is willing to use any means necessary to crush all opposition in its effort to reunite the Syrian Arab Republic.

The Transformation of Syrian Kurdish Identity for the Future

How did the Kurds of Syria mobilise around a Syrian Kurdish identity worth taking up arms and fighting for?

First of all, the Syrian Kurds represent a small community, which was cut off from the greater Kurdish community by the borders of the new states emerging after World War I. However, they did have connections with the Kurdish movements in the neighbouring states,. The formation of the Syrian Kurdish parties can even be said to have been instigated by foreign Kurdish actors. This explains the formation of the Khoybun League, the 'old' Kurdish parties and the PYD. In line with this, the mobilisation of the Syrian Kurds was primarily aimed at the Kurdish revolts in Turkey and Iraq and only to a smaller degree at Kurdish politics in Syria and definitely not at military resistance against the Syrian regime. Hundreds of Syrian Kurds were recruited as Peshmerga fighters in Iraq in the 1970s and 1980s, mainly by the KDP (Tejel 2014, p. 73), and an estimated 7,000–10,000 Syrian Kurds were killed in Turkey, fighting as PKK guerrillas in the 1980s and 1990s (Tejel 2014, p. 76). All of this happened with the approval of the Syrian regime, the aim being to destabilise Iraq and Turkey in the regional power play. Apparently, the Syrian Kurds, in contrast, were too heterogeneous to form a proxy themselves.

By 2011, all of this changed. A more assertive opposition was formed in the wake of the Damascus Spring (2001) and the Qamishlo Revolt (2004), seeking a more confrontational approach to the Syrian regime. Thus, the new Kurdish opposition fought for Kurdish rights and influence in the Syrian society, leaving complicity with the regime behind. The civil war, which erupted as part of the Arab Spring (2011), focused more world attention on the Syrian Kurds. Two events during the civil war have greatly influenced the transformation of Syrian Kurdish identity. The first was the withdrawal of the Syrian regime from Kurdish areas, leaving the territories of northern Syria under the control of the YPG militia. The second event was the emergence of Islamic State, which proved to be an enemy of both the Kurds and the international community. This event provided the Kurdish YPG with an essential military ally, namely the international coalition fighting Islamic State. Fighting not only for Kurdish identity, the Kurds of Rojava embraced the international cause of fighting against Islamic State and for democracy, women's rights and pluralism, thus becoming a legitimate partner of the international coalition. Under the name of the Federation of Northern Syria, and latterly the Autonomous Administration of North and East Syria, they are pushing for an invitation to the international negotiations on the future of Syria and are presenting themselves as an integrated part of a new political reality of a future Syrian federation.

Turkey continues to pose a major threat to the autonomy of the Federation of North and East Syria, however. Since October 2019 when the American troops in Syria withdrew and Turkey captured the area between Tell Abyad and Ras al-Ayn, Turkey and Turkish-backed rebels, despite the ceasefire brokered with Russia, continue to attack Kurdish territory. The Syrian regime (supported by Russia) also poses a threat to the Kurds. Even though the agreement negotiated for northern Syria stipulates that Syrian forces cooperate with Kurdish authorities, it is unlikely that the regime will accept Kurdish autonomy in the long term.

In addition, major tensions among Kurdish groups and parties continue to represent one of the biggest challenges to Kurdish self-determination in Syria, as the tension between the PYD and the KNC is not only a local phenomenon, but also involves their regional and international allies. Furthermore, independent Syrian Kurdish activists have raised their voices. They advocate for liberal democracy and human rights, seeking support among Western intellectuals and governmental institutions. Due to the civil war, they have all sought refuge abroad, either in neighbouring countries or in the West.

5

BECOMING A DIASPORA: THE KURDS AND KURDISH ACTIVISTS IN DENMARK

Introduction

In January 2017, in the suburbs of Copenhagen, a group of Kurds celebrated the 50-year anniversary of Kurds arriving in Denmark. It was a get-together featuring Kurdish food, music and dance. A decade earlier, KOMKAR invited Kurds in Denmark to the 40-year anniversary of the arrival of Kurdish migrants from Turkey. In the invitation, the organisation encapsulated the experience of being a guest worker with the words '[h]ow time flies. It feels as if we arrived yesterday', alluding to those who came to Western Europe at the end of the 1960s and later settled there contrary to their original intentions. Wives and children were gradually reunited with the Kurdish immigrants through family reunification programmes. Since the 1980s, Kurdish refugees from all parts of Kurdistan have arrived and settled in Denmark and contributed to the formation of a Kurdish community in Denmark.

In this chapter, I will look at the emergence of a Kurdish diaspora in Denmark. First, I will outline the immigration waves from Kurdistan to Denmark. Then, I will explain how the Kurdish community became mobilised and draw comparisons to the mobilisation of the Kurdish diaspora in Germany and Sweden. Both of these countries constitute centres for Kurdish mobilisation in Europe. While Germany became a mobilisation centre for Kurdish political activism early on, mainly in support of the Kurdish struggle in Turkey, Sweden became a hub of Kurdish cultural mobilisation based on strong Kurdish cultural institutions, such as the Kurdish Library in Stockholm. Finally, I will provide an overview of the main (political) actors in the current Kurdish diaspora milieu in Denmark, identifying their organisational structures and networks as well as their political visions and strategies, including goals, tactics and assessments of opportunities and constraints. I will also focus on Syrian Kurds in order to draw attention to their specific position within the main Kurdish community in Denmark and to how their position has changed in the wake of the Syrian Civil War.

The Emergence of a Kurdish Diaspora in Denmark

Kurdish immigration waves to Denmark

Before the 1960s, only a small number of Kurdish students and exiled Kurds lived in Europe. The economic growth and increased demand for labour in Western Europe during the 1960s changed that, resulting in a large number of Kurds from Turkey migrating to Europe to work as 'guest workers'. West Germany was in most dire need of workers and signed bilateral agreements with a number of states, including Turkey in 1961 (Jørgensen 2009, p. 170). As many of the guest workers from Turkey were Kurds, Germany hosts the largest Kurdish population in Europe, estimated to number 850,000–959,000 people (Institute Kurde de Paris 2016). In Denmark, in contrast to West Germany, no bilateral agreement was signed. Instead, Danish employers invited workers primarily from Turkey, Yugoslavia and Pakistan to come and work. The workers easily obtained work permits due to the Danish Aliens Act of 1952, which was relatively liberal in this regard (Mikkelsen 2011, pp. 38–9). However, in 1969 and 1970, legislation was tightened, and in 1973, facing the oil crisis and increasing unemployment, the government placed a moratorium on the influx of labour migrants after agreeing with the employers' association and Danish employees to discontinue guest worker immigration (Bejder 2016). Between 1967 and 1973, about 20,000 guest workers came to work in unskilled positions in the textile and plastic industries and in iron foundries and shipyards (Schwartz 1985, p. 6). The immigration did not stop completely, though, due to an increase in family reunification in subsequent decades (Mikkelsen 2011, p. 37).

The majority of the Kurds who migrated from Turkey to Denmark to work as guest workers came from rural areas of the Konya province. They came primarily from the Kurdish villages Yeniceoba, Kuşça, Kütükuşagi, Bulduk and Kelsahan in the district of Cihanbeyli. Other Kurdish labour migrants came from Kurdish villages in neighbouring areas of Ankara province, that is, the districts of Haymana and Polatli. Yet other Kurdish migrants came from the province of Çorum. In contrast to the migrants from Konya and Ankara, who were Sunni Muslims, the migrants from Çorum were mainly Alevis. Most of the migrants from Çorum did not speak Kurdish due to Turkey's assimilation policies. The Kurds living in these provinces descend from Kurdish speaking tribes, who had departed the eastern part of present-day Turkey and settled in central Turkey, most at the beginning of the nineteenth century, but some as early as the sixteenth century.

Two older studies by Jan Hjarnø investigate the migration patterns of the Kurdish workers from the Konya province when arriving in Denmark, as well as their reasons for migration and their work and living conditions during their first years in Denmark (Hjarnø 1988; Hjarnø 1991). Hjarnø analyses how the migrants followed in the tracks of relatives and friends who had previously left. The formation of migration networks, also called chain migration (Tilly 1986), of guest workers meant that a large group of migrants from the district of Cihanbeyli headed for Denmark, while many migrants from the neighbouring district of Kulu moved to Sweden (Hjarnø 1988, pp. 15–16). Consequently, the majority of the Kurdish labour migrants and their reunified family members and descendants living in Denmark today stem from a handful of Kurdish villages, which are located less than 20 km from each other in the district of Cihanbeyli. The emigration also had a huge impact on the individual villages. In 1970, 300 men from Kuşça, equalling 75 per cent of Kuşça's male population aged between 18 and 50 years, worked in Denmark (Hjarnø 1991, p. 157). Rising unemployment rates in rural areas due to agricultural mechanisation as well as land reform introduced at the end of the 1950s, which, among other things, imposed a ban on cultivating previously uncultivated land, made many leave and seek job opportunities in Europe (Hjarnø 1991, pp. 28–9). In Denmark, many of the Kurdish workers settled in the Copenhagen metropolitan area. Initially, they settled close to the factories and foundries, where they were hired, but later they moved into newly built housing in the suburbs. Thus, a large group of Kurds originating from Konya settled in Ishøj, a suburban municipality southwest of Copenhagen (Hjarnø 1991, p. 158) which, in 2019, had the highest percentage of immigrants and descendants among the Danish municipalities, at 40 per cent (Danmarks Statistik 2019, p. 24). Other Kurdish migrants settled in other parts of Denmark, in the cities of Odense, Esbjerg, Aarhus, Aalborg, Holstebro, Hillerød and Næstved, among others.

From the end of the 1970s, political refugees from all four parts of Kurdistan arrived in Denmark. In Turkey, the political turmoil of the 1970s and the intensified repression of the political opposition following the coup in 1980 prompted many politically active Kurds to flee the country. In the 1990s, the escalation of the armed conflict between the Turkish state and the PKK, which destroyed more than 3,000 Kurdish villages and displaced more than 2 million Kurds, also made many Kurds seek refuge in Europe and Denmark (Hassanpour and Mojab 2005, p. 218). As Turkish society was generally characterised by insecurity due to the conflict in south-eastern Turkey, even Kurds with no direct connection to the Turkish–Kurdish conflict fled to Europe (Demir 2012, p. 817; Sirkeci 2006) either as refugees or as migrants under the family reunification programme. In Iraq, the Kurds were also subjected to repression by the state leading to a refugee influx in Europe. A small number of these many refugees ended up in Denmark. In the 1980s, during the Iran–Iraq war, villages in the Kurdish mountains in Northern Iraq were destroyed and people were gathered in detention camps in the lowlands. The persecution of the Kurds intensified in 1988, when chemical weapons were used to commit genocide during the Anfal Campaign. Between 50,000 and 100,000 Kurds were killed, 2,000 villages destroyed, and hundreds of thousands of villagers forcibly displaced (Human Rights Watch 1995). The Kurdish civil war (1994–7) led to more humanitarian and political refugees arriving in Europe. Iran also produced Kurdish refugees who ended up in Denmark. Some of these were individual political refugees, who fled the repression of the Islamic Republic from 1979; others were refugees and children of refugees, who fled the Iran–Iraq war in the 1980s and were later relocated from refugee camps in Iraq to Denmark as part of the UN programme of third country refugee resettlement (quota refugees). Until the Syrian conflict erupted in 2011, Syrian Kurds in Denmark numbered only a few hundred political refugees. Most of them had escaped the intensified repression against the Kurdish population following the Kurdish Uprising in 2004. From 2011, Kurdish refugees have been part of the large influx of Syrians fleeing the civil war. However, it is very difficult to tell how many of the 34,000 refugees from Syria who obtained a residence permit in Denmark between 2011 and 2017 (Statistics Denmark 2020b) are Kurdish.

According to the Kurdish Institute in Paris, 25,000–30,000 of the 1.5–1.7 million Kurds in Western Europe live in Denmark (Institut Kurde de Paris 2016). The figures are estimates but the most widely accepted, as European countries only register applicants for residence permits according to their state of origin, not their ethnic identification. In 2011, the Kurdish internet newspaper Jiyan.dk, which publishes in Danish, tried to trace the backgrounds of the Kurdish population in Denmark, estimated to number around 40,000 (Serinci 2011). Among other sources, the estimate was based on a survey indicating that 45 per cent of the migrants from Turkey, 25 per cent of the migrants from Iraq and 9 per cent of the migrants from Iran identified as Kurds (Bonnerup et al. 2007). As a result, the author found that the majority of the Kurds in Denmark, more than two-thirds, come from the Republic of Turkey. The Kurds from Iraq make up the second largest group – 7,500 people – while the Kurds from Iran and Syria comprise groups of around 1,500 people each. In addition, a few families originate from the former Soviet republics of Armenia and Georgia, and an unknown number come from Lebanon and Kuwait. However, this estimate predates the influx of refugees from the Syrian crisis, so the number of Syrian Kurds in Denmark must have increased considerably. Some Kurdish activists I met suggested that more than 10,000 Syrian Kurds are resident in Denmark at present, and that the total number of Kurds in Denmark is as high as 60,000.

While in the 1970s Kurdish immigrants were primarily hired to work in the manufacturing industry, today they hold a variety of job positions, mainly in the service sector. No detailed statistics on the occupations of the Kurdish population in Denmark are available, but the data on immigrants from Turkey represents most likely the migrants of both Turkish and Kurdish descent. Thus, a majority of the male immigrants are engaged in transport and trade and in the restaurant business. Among the female immigrants, a majority work in day care centres and in the fields of cleaning, health and education

(Statistics Denmark 2020a). Compared to people of Danish origin, however, Kurdish immigrants may suffer from disproportionate unemployment. Thus, the report 'Indvandrere i Danmark 2019' published by Statistics Denmark in 2019 states that the employment rates for migrants from Turkey are sixty-seven per cent for men and forty-six per cent for women, compared to eighty-four per cent for men and seventy-nine per cent for women of Danish origin (Danmarks Statistik 2019, p. 47). Presumably, this data covers the employment situation of Turkish and Kurdish immigrants alike. In addition, the report states that the difference between employment rates is evened when comparing the descendants of immigrants from Turkey to persons of Danish origin (Danmarks Statistisk 2019, p. 48). This may be due to the higher level of education among descendants of migrant communities compared with the educational background of the first generation of migrants. Consequently, the occupational profile of the Kurds is gradually becoming more diverse.

The mobilisation of the Kurdish diaspora

In the 1960s and 1970s, relatively few labour migrants from Turkey identified as Kurds. They attended the Turkish workers' associations and clubs, which often were established by friends and relatives from the same villages in Turkey, and they were generally perceived as Turks. This changed with the arrival of Kurdish political refugees from the late 1970s, who initiated the formation of Kurdish associations and networks. The coup in Turkey in 1980 and the subsequent repression of opposition groups led to an increased awareness of the Kurdish political struggle among Kurdish migrants in Denmark. This included attention to the struggle of the PKK, Kurdistan's Workers' Party, which was formed in 1978 and began armed resistance in 1984. In this respect, the development in Denmark is similar to that in other European countries hosting large groups of Kurdish guest workers and Kurdish political refugees (see, for example, Østergaard-Nielsen 2003; Baser 2015; and Bruinessen 1999).

Two Kurdish organisations came to dominate the diaspora milieu in Denmark. One was KOMKAR-DK, the Association of Workers from Kurdistan in Denmark, founded in 1986. The other was FEY-KURD, the Federation of Kurdish Associations in Denmark, founded in 1992 as an umbrella organisation for the Kurdish associations in Denmark, including the Danish-Kurdish

Culture Centre, founded in 1983. Both organisations had been established to unite the various Kurdish initiatives undertaken by Kurdish migrants in Denmark to strengthen the Kurdish mobilisation in the diaspora (Mikkelsen 2011, p. 111). Both organisations were Danish branches of European organisations, thus reflecting a European trend. KOMKAR was originally formed in Germany in 1979 as a federation of thirty Kurdish associations aligning with PSK, the Kurdistan Socialist Party. In the subsequent years, KOMKAR sprouted branches in Denmark but also in the Netherlands, Sweden, the United Kingdom, France, Switzerland and Austria (Baser 2015b, p. 118). Likewise, FEY-KURD, the Federation of Kurdish Associations in Denmark, was founded as a subdivision of the KON-KURD, the Confederation of Kurdish Associations, which was the PKK-supporting umbrella organisation in Europe headquartered in Belgium. KOMKAR and FEY-KURD subsequently became the main contributors to the mobilisation of the Kurdish diaspora in Denmark by organising cultural events, including Newroz celebrations, festivities and concerts, as well as political protests and meetings with high-profile Kurdish representatives from abroad. This activism was based on a 'dual agenda' (Østergaard-Nielsen 2003), which both federations followed in an attempt to improve the integration of the Kurds in Denmark and support the Kurdish struggle for political and social inequality, mainly in Turkey but also in the other parts of Kurdistan. The emphasis on integration also reflects how Kurdish activists seemed to accommodate to the governmen tal regulations on public funding, which favoured integration initiatives over religious and political activities. Thus, cultural, women's and youth associations more often received public funding than other immigration associations (Kurdish and others); 38 per cent compared to 22 per cent of the associations (Mikkelsen 2011, p. 160). Like the two mother organisations, the two Kurdish federations in Denmark competed for the attention and support of Kurdish migrants. While KOMKAR recruited mostly among political refugees, FEY-KURD succeeded in reaching the migrant community more broadly through various member associations, such as local culture associations, the Kurdish Women's Association, the Kurdish Youth Association and the Kurdish Conscientious Objector Association. In contrast to KOMKAR, whose members mainly were men in their 50s and 60s, FEY-KURD also managed to recruit many women, as well as second-generation Kurdish migrants. In that way, they built a relatively large base of active members, as well as passive members on whom the active members could call in time of crisis in the homeland. The prominence of the organisations allied with Kurdish parties in Turkey reflects what Amir Hassanpour and Shahrzad Mojab have called the 'hegemonic presence' of the Kurds from Turkey in diaspora politics (Hassanpour and Mojab 2005, p. 122) as a result of the numerical dominance of Kurdish migrants and refugees from Turkey. However, the prominence of FEY-KURD also reflects, as Hassanpour and Mojab point out, the strength of the PKK in mobilising the diaspora, which draws attention to the Kurdish struggle in Turkey rather than the struggle in other parts of Kurdistan.

In the 2000s, a number of new hometown associations were established connecting migrant communities in Denmark with Kurdish villages in Turkey (Christiansen 2008, p. 88). Some of the initiators stressed the social and cultural aim of meeting with fellow Kurds, others stressed economic support for the non-migrants in their hometowns in Turkey. As one association quickly recruited more than 1,000 members, this indicates that, for a large group of Kurdish migrants, village affiliation meant more to them than affiliating with the Kurdish cause in the political sense. However, it is also an indication of, as Connie Carøe Christiansen argues, 'transnational village solidarity in decline' as village solidarity no longer can be taken for granted and therefore, is institutionalised (Christiansen 2008, p. 100).

Denmark – in between Germany and Sweden

In many ways, the mobilisation of the Kurdish diaspora in Denmark in the 1980s and 1990s resembles that of the Kurdish diaspora in Germany as examined by Bahar Baser in her comparative study of the Kurdish diaspora in Germany and Sweden (Baser 2015). This is primarily due to similar migration patterns in the two countries – albeit on a different scale, as the Kurdish community in Germany is thirty times bigger than the Kurdish community in Denmark. When Kurdish guest workers arrived in Denmark and Germany, they settled in the same areas as the Turkish guest workers, and due to the assimilation policies of the Turkish Republic, many of them only spoke Turkish. When the Kurdish diaspora mobilised at the beginning of the 1980s as described above, the Kurds in Denmark and Germany were more likely to adopt a political Kurdish identity than a cultural identity that would lead to a dissociation from their Turkish affiliations. Thus, the political mobilisation of the Kurdish diaspora succeeded while, socially and economically, the interactions between Kurds and Turks 'more often than not prevailed' (Baser 2015, p. 226). The PKK benefitted greatly from this by focus on Kurdish identity as a political identity. However, idolisation of Öcalan became prominent in the movement, especially after his capture and imprisonment in 1999. A mobilised Kurd thus became an activist complying with the ideology of Öcalan rather than a person who recognises a relation to Kurdistan.

Although the mobilisation pattern of the Kurdish diaspora is similar in Denmark and Germany, one major difference exists: the extent of violence and contentious relations between Kurdish and Turkish migrants as well as contention between the Kurdish activists and the local and federal authorities. In Germany, Kurds have engaged in violent encounters with Turks while demonstrating; firebombs were thrown at Turkish mosques at the time of the Turkish attack on Afrin, and back in the 1990s, Kurdish groups occupied embassies and consulates and erected roadblocks. Kurdish activists in Germany accuse the German state of following the Turkish state's perception of Kurdish activists (Baser 2015). It is a fact that Germany and Turkey have had a strong economic relationship since the 1960s as a result of the bilateral agreement on guest workers. At any rate, both judicial and administrative restrictions on PKK-supporting activities have been implemented. In 1993, Germany was the first country in Europe to outlaw the PKK, and a number of Kurds have subsequently been sentenced for supporting the group. In 2002, following 9/11, the EU, including Denmark, followed suit by placing the PKK on the revised list of terrorist organisations. In addition, many Kurdish activists in Germany feel that their democratic rights of freedom of speech and assembly are restricted, claiming, as one German Kurdish student did when I talked to her, that the municipal authorities and the police deliberately divert their demonstrations and processions to the outskirts of the cities under the pretext of security concerns. In contrast, Kurdish groups in Denmark solely refer to the municipal authorities and the police as collaborating actors, who allow them to fulfil their agendas. Only on a few occasions and on a much smaller scale have the conflictual perception of the development in Turkey escalated into violent clashes between Kurds and Turks and Turkish interests in Denmark. It is worth remembering that while the immigration of guest workers from Turkey to Germany was based on a bilateral agreement between the two states, such an agreement did not exist between Turkey and Denmark.

In contrast to Germany, which became the mobilisation centre for the PKK in Europe, Sweden became a cultural and intellectual hub for the Kurdish diaspora (Khayati 2012; Ahmadzade 2003). Two main factors emphasised by the Kurds in Stockholm when I visited organisations there were the public funding of cultural initiatives for migrant communities and mother-tongue education of Kurdish children. These initiatives were in line with the Swedish multicultural policy on immigration since the mid-1970s (Baser 2015, p. 90), which stated that immigrant communities were expected to preserve and develop their heritage as equal members of the multicultural society. A lot of Kurdish literature was published in Sweden with the aim of revitalising and modernising the Kurdish language, especially the Kurmanji dialect, at a time when the language was suppressed in the homeland. While 402 Kurdish books were published in Sweden from 1971 to 1997, only 109 were published in Turkey in the same period (Ahmedzadeh 2003, p. 165). In 1997, the Kurdish Library in Stockholm was inaugurated. The library aims to become a national library for the Kurdish people. At the beginning, the library collected everything published in the Kurdish dialects, but this is not possible anymore, because of the number of Kurdish publications worldwide. In Denmark, politicians also dedicated public funding to immigration organisations. However, the funding was primarily directed at integration initiatives rather than cultural initiatives per se (Mikkelsen 2011, pp. 158–9). This was in line with the overall Danish approach to immigration, according to which immigrants should become integrated in Danish society (Jørgensen 2009, p. 121). Thus, Danish funding of immigrant organisations aimed to make immigrants knowledgeable about Danish society rather than maintain their homeland culture in a multicultural society. According to Martin Bak Jørgensen, this explains why two Kurdish associations, the Danish-Kurdish Culture Centre and the Kurdish Conscientious Objector Association, lost their public funding in the 1990s (Jørgensen 2009, p. 210). While the Kurdish Conscientious Objector Association faded, the Danish-Kurdish Culture Centre redefined its purpose in 2004 to comply with the official understanding of an appropriate purpose of an immigrant association. Interestingly, German politicians denied that Germany was a country of immigration right up until the turn of the century (Baser 2015, 109; Jørgensen 2009, p. 169). At this point, I want to stress that Swedish and Danish integration programmes encouraged the Kurdish associations to cooperate and comply with the authorities by means of an inclusive strategy towards the immigration organisations, especially in the 1980s, although their objectives differed. They did not push them into a contentious relationship, as was the case in Germany.

As in Denmark and other European countries, the Kurdish community in Sweden has emerged due to the arrival of labour migrants and political refugees. However, the Kurdish community in Sweden is unique as Sweden has welcomed a relatively large group of 'journalists, authors, academics, artists and directors' (Baser 2015, p. 133). The intelligentsia have taken advantage of the governmental funding and been a major contributor to the cultural development described above, which in turn has attracted even more Kurdish intellectuals fleeing repression in the Middle East. When I asked one of my informants, an academic, poet and refugee from Syria, why he settled in Denmark back in the 2000s, he said that he was heading for Sweden, but ended up in Denmark because he was short of money for the train ticket across Øresund (B, male, 20s). The prominent position of this group of refugees also fuelled the strong opposition to the Öcalan movement. Accordingly, young Kurds in Sweden have adopted a 'Kurdistani identity' (Baser 2015, p. 226), that is, a Kurdish identity connected to Kurdistan rather than the political ideology of Öcalan, which is most often the case among mobilised Kurds in Denmark and Germany.

Among the Kurds in Denmark, a few hundred are core members, such as board members and the main organisers of events (using the categorisation of the diaspora member into core members, passive members and silent members, as above) (Baher 2015, p. 16; Shain and Barth 2003, p. 452). At the big events, the organisations are able to mobilise one to two thousand of the passive members. This applies to the demonstrations in support of the Kurds in Kobane (2014) and Afrin (2018), the public meeting with Selahattin Demirtaş outside Christiansborg (2015), the Şivan Perwer concert in support of the independence referendum in Iraqi Kurdistan (2017), and the Newroz feasts (annual) held in a suburban music theatre. However, when the humanitarian aid campaigns were launched on social media in support of the victims of the battles of Kobane (2014) and Aleppo (2016), even more people were mobilised, donating different amounts of money to the various humanitarian organisations. The wish to support fellow Kurds in Syria was widespread even among silent members of the Kurdish diaspora. As a result, some Kurdish leaders felt it necessary to warn the newly mobilised members of the Kurdish diaspora as well as Danish supporters against Islamic humanitarian aid organisations, for example VIOMIS, which, they said, opposed Kurdish interests in Syria and supported the Islamists. Instead, they urged them to support Kurdish humanitarian aid organisations in line with their own political leaning, meaning the Sun of Mesopotamia and their international affiliate, Kurdistan's Red Crescent (Kurdish: Heyva Sor a Kurdistanê).

Kurdish Groupings in Denmark in the 2010s

The Syrian Civil War and the Syrian Kurds' success in fighting Islamic State and building an autonomous Kurdish entity in northern Syria also transformed the Kurdish diaspora. New organisations were created, and old ones changed their names or affiliations in order to adjust to the new situation. However, the main chasm between the PKK and non-PKK-supporting movement persists. In the following, I will provide an overview of the main actors in the current Kurdish diaspora milieu. I will analyse the Kurdish diaspora as an arena or a compound player (Jasper 2014b, p. 10) consisting of two rivalling movements constituted by a different vision and organisational structure, different allies and conflicting interests in the Syrian Civil War. The two movements comprise different associations and leading activists as well as different passive member bases. Thus, the two movements are themselves compound players, whose agendas are negotiated among their members (Melucci 1996, p. 70). I call the two movements the Öcalan movement and the Kurdistan movement depending on whether their pivot is Öcalan or Kurdistan. It is noteworthy that some of the organisations in the two movements have identical names. Even the names of the two umbrella federations are identical. Presumably, because they both claim to represent all the Kurds in Denmark. Additionally, a third heterogeneous group of Kurdish intellectuals, who distance themselves from the two main groupings and their political ideas, are trying to find their own position, also in support of the Syrian

Kurds. I call them independents as they seek independence from the two leading movements. In the end of this section, I will examine the specific position of the Syrian Kurds in Denmark vis-à-vis the Syrian war.

As I argued in the theoretical chapter, human beings are not free-floating individuals. They embody previous experiences and interpretations that may be both individual and collective. For the Kurds, these biographical and cultural dispositions also influence the individual's affiliation with associations and political parties. That means that the Kurds tend to end up as members or supporters of one or other of the political movements according to their migration experience, place of origin and family background. Therefore, I will also touch on the background of the Kurdish diaspora members to clarify the division between the Öcalan and the Kurdistan movement.

The Öcalan movement

Apo – the mobilising idea

What unites the members within the Öcalan movement is symbolic loyalty to 'Apo', the nickname for Abdullah Öcalan and Kurdish for 'uncle' (Jongerden, 2007, p. 57). Öcalan holds a very special position within the movement, which has only increased since his capture and imprisonment in 1999. He is the founder, leader and ideologist, and he inspires resistance. In sum, he is the symbol of Kurdish mobilisation. 'Öcalan is the key to peace in the Middle East', as a slogan says, referring to his centrality within the movement. This is also expressed in the campaign 'freedom for Öcalan, peace in Kurdistan', which includes recurrent demonstrations, protest marches and information stands at public places. One of my informants and a leading member of FOKUS-A, the Union of Kurdish Students and Academics, explained to me stating,

> The reason why we prioritise freedom for Öcalan and not freedom in Kurdistan is because we believe they are connected. The day the Turkish state releases Öcalan, they have changed their mentality towards the Kurdish people. They cannot imprison the person who is considered the people's leader, the leader of the people, and at the same time talk about peace. The day they release him, they can talk about peace because that means they sincerely want to solve this problem [. . .] So, that is why we prioritise freedom for Öcalan, because freedom for Öcalan will mean freedom for Kurdistan. (H, female, 20s)

The first step towards liberation of the Kurds is to become conscious of the repressive societal structures including capitalism, the nation state and patriarchy that led to an unfree humankind. FOKUS-A captures the essence of the mobilisation within the Öcalan movement, stating that the mission of the association is 'to organise the Kurdish youth through projects and events and thereby encourage a conscious Kurdish youth' (see FOKUS-A's mission statement on Facebook). In order to overcome the old world-order, the next step of mobilisation is to adopt the ideology of Öcalan, primarily the ideas of democratic confederalism, which is democracy by the people based on the right of self-determination (Öcalan 2013, p. 33). Becoming an activist trying to realise the ideas is the final step. Thus, yet another slogan hails Öcalan as the model activist by proclaiming, 'Abdullah Öcalan is fighting in jail. You must also fight'. For the Kurdish diaspora, this primarily means a political fight, but the wording also highlights the acceptance of armed resistance as a constitutive element of the Öcalan movement. Praising armed resistance against tyranny and fascism is deeply rooted within the movement. Overall, the mobilisation aims at what has been called 'a new "Kurdish Personality" developed under the cult of Öcalan' (Baser 2015, p. 226). Although the movement has grown out of the support for the PKK, which is still fully endorsed, the PKK leader has become even bigger than the party and attracts pure adoration.

Main organisations and allies

The spearhead of this movement is FEY-KURD, which is the umbrella organisation for the Öcalan-supporting associations in Denmark. The federation comprises a number of associations in Copenhagen as well as in other major cities in Denmark. The Copenhagen associations include the Danish-Kurdish Culture Centre, the Kurdish Women's Association and FOKUS-A. Other associations are based in Hillerød and Holstebro. While FEY-KURD coordinates all the external initiatives, including the relationships with other organisations and political actors, the member association organises the day-to-day activities aimed at the Kurdish followers. However, the member organisations also often initiate and plan public events, such as demonstrations and the annual Kurdish film festival. Although the member associations and the federation have different purposes and goals, the division of responsibility is often blurred and relies on the persons elected as representatives of the groups. Some overall directions can be observed, though.

The Danish-Kurdish Culture Centre has been the core of the movement since it was established in 1982. In 2016, the association was renamed the Democratic Kurdish People's Assembly in Denmark (The Democratic Kurdish People's Assembly in Denmark 2016) to stress the links to the self-administrative units in Syria as well as the units in south-eastern Turkey declared after the breakdown of peace negotiations between the Turkish state and the PKK in 2015. The association is a meeting place for the Kurds in Denmark and aims at integration of its members in Danish society as well as awareness of Kurdish culture and identity. The Kurdish Women's Association is a space for Kurdish women of the movement to socialise and organise events with a focus on the Kurdish women's position and the position of women in general. These include 8 March meetings and events featuring Kurdish heroines, such as the screening of a film about Sakine Cansız, one of the co-founders of the PKK, who was shot dead in Paris in 2013, and demonstrations to promote the Öcalan ideology, including the women's liberation. The women's association also deals with more traditional women's tasks, such as providing Kurdish food when required, for example at the Newroz celebration at Christiansborg and support events for Rojava. FOKUS-A, the Association of Kurdish Students and Academics, was founded in 2008. The union is the more ideological branch of the movement that organises reading groups where the members study the writings of Öcalan. They also organise concerts and the annual Film Festival in February, which has grown bigger every year since its introduction nearly a decade ago. The film festival presents Kurdish films to both Kurdish and Danish viewers and is a mobilising event for both groups, encouraged through interviews with instructors and panel debates about the situation in Kurdistan.

As mentioned earlier, FEY-KURD coordinates outreach activities. It is the main body that sends delegations to meetings in the parliament building and organises big events in cooperation with other groups in a time of crisis. Thus, the co-chairs of FEY-KURD function as a mouthpiece for the movement. FEY-KURD is also the link to the transnational Kurdish movement as a member of KCDK-E, The European Kurdish Democratic Societies Congress, until 2014 known as KON-KURD, the Confederation of Kurdish

Associations in Europe. Many of the campaigns are coordinated by KCDK-E, such as the demonstration in support of Afrin in January 2018 and the 'free Öcalan' initiatives, which are often conducted simultaneously in several European countries. KCDK-E has also encouraged its member associations to support HDP in connection with elections in Turkey. The movement is closely related to KNK, the Kurdish National Congress, successor to the Kurdish Parliament in Exile, which is the highest political transnational organ for the PKK/Öcalan-supporting parties and associations. Like KCDK-E, it is located in Brussels. For the time being, three members of the movement in Denmark are appointed members of KNK (Kurdistan National Congress 2017), which is a highly honourable position within the movement. The movement also supports the HDP in Turkey, and members of the movement are heading the HDP campaign around the time of elections in Turkey.

The federation and the associations gather in the movement's community centre in a suburb of Copenhagen. In 2014, the associations moved to the suburbs from the city centre, due to a lack of space. Lack of space is still an issue, one member told me, since they want to do more for young people. As a result, the association has moved to a new location in the suburbs of Copenhagen. Other associations are also invited to use the facilities at the community centre. Thus, PYD also resides there as do other parties within the KCK, The Kurdistan Communities Union, just as ERNK, the Kurdistan National Liberation Front – the political wing of the PKK – did in the 1980s and 1990s before the PKK was banned. Representatives of Gorran and PUK, I was told, also use the location. The Sun of Mesopotamia, which is a Danish Kurdish humanitarian aid organisation, also shares the address with the FEY-KURD and the other associations.

The Danish Öcalan movement cooperates with Kurdish Forum, founded in 2010, which functions as a mediating body between the Öcalan movement and left-wing politicians. Villo Sigurdsson, previous mayor of Copenhagen, is a leading figure. Kurdish Forum aims at raising the awareness of the Kurds and put pressure on the governments in the countries hosting them to improve their rights (Kurdisk Forum 2010). The annual Newroz reception at Christiansborg is a product of this cooperation. The movement is also allied with the left-wing party, the Red-Green Alliance, which holds a strong position in parliament. Many members of the movement are active politicians at district level, which has strengthened the ties between the movement and the party during the past two decades.

The mobilisation base of the Öcalan movement is mainly made up of Kurds from Turkey. For many Kurds originating from Turkey, the Öcalan movement seems the natural choice. The Kurdish issue in Turkey is the movement's focal point, despite the many activities in support of the Kurdish struggle in Syria. The members are political refugees and labour migrants as well as descendants of both groups. The mobilisation base also includes some Kurds from Syria and a few Kurds originating from Iraq and Iran. As the Kurdish revolution in northern Syria has progressed, the Kurds originating from Syria have become more and more visible within the movement. Like in other European branches of the movement (Schmidinger 2013, p. 327), the language spoken in the Öcalan movement in Denmark is primarily Turkish, as many members do not speak Kurdish. However, the Kurmanji dialect of Kurdish, which is the main dialect in Turkey and Syria, is also spoken, and Kurmanji language courses are offered at the cultural centre.

The Syrian war – mobilising events

The outbreak of the Syrian Civil War presented a great opportunity for the Öcalan movement, as its associates in PYD and YPG proved strong enough to assert autonomy and initiate a societal revolution in the midst of war. Although the many members of the Öcalan movement had followed the development in Rojava since the outbreak of the war, the battle of Kobane during the winter of 2014–15 became a huge mobilising event for the passive and even silent members of the diaspora. Great support was mobilised, and humanitarian aid undertaken, under the hashtag #SaveKobane. Very quickly, the Sun of Mesopotamia raised large amounts of money by way of MobilePay (instant mobile money transfer) donations. In 2016, a Danish branch of the Rojava committee was established. It became the initiator of a variety of political meetings and events in support of Rojava. These events included meetings with representatives from Rojava, political panel debates, and presentations about democratic confederalism or from volunteers who had worked at hospitals or joined the military forces. In Denmark, the Rojava committee had a significant number of Kurdish members, while in Sweden, the majority of the committee members were Swedish. In Denmark, the committee benefitted from the network of the leading figure, who was also a member of the international Kobane Reconstruction Board, formed in 2015 by the city council of Kobane to coordinate the reconstruction efforts. The board is composed of local people and members from Europe and other regions of the world (Peace in Kurdistan 2015). In addition, the Rojava committee hosted the annual World Kobane day on 1 November and translated three pamphlets containing writings by Öcalan. The Rojava Committee faded in 2017 but was resurrected as the Save Êfrin Platform at the time of the Turkish capture of the area of Afrin. Thus, 1 November 2018 was commemorated as Afrin Day in the People's House, a socialist community centre in Nørrebro, Copenhagen. This shows that many initiatives within the Kurdish movement are driven by individuals and fade if not pursued by other activists. At the beginning of 2019, yet another initiative was set up to support Rojava, namely the Rojava Alliance, which sought to unite the various socialist efforts in support of Rojava. The initiative is mainly supported by young non-Kurdish internationalists and socialists.

The Kurdistan movement

Kurdistan – the homeland

Independence for Kurdistan is the ultimate goal for a large group of Kurds in the diaspora as well as in the homeland. This became clear during the independence referendum campaign in the summer of 2017, when the leading Kurdish politicians in Iraqi Kurdistan succeeded in mobilising Kurds worldwide. Even Öcalan supporters declared their support, but their support was conditional as they emphasised the corruption of Barzani or claimed, 'it is not the right time'. For the passive and silent members of the Kurdistan movement, it was a diffuse dream that suddenly appeared as a real possibility. For active members of the Kurdistan movement, national independence has always been the political goal. One of the activists I interviewed substantiated the call for independence by referring to the majority populations in the four parts of Kurdistan and their position on the Kurds. 'They say we are brothers, but I do not need the brotherhood of the Turks, the Arabs and the Persians. We can be good neighbours. We can cooperate. But they will never respect me as a brother' (C, male, 50s). The call for independence is in line with the nationalistic idea of a nation state, which is based on the nation's self-determination within the boundaries of the homeland. Confronted with the reality of the division of the Kurdish-inhabited areas in the Middle East between Turkey, Syria, Iraq and Iran, the active members stress that the path to full Kurdish independence is a long one. They seem to agree on a step-by-step agenda. The first step will be to secure equal social and political rights within the existing states. The second will be to secure autonomy within federal states, and then, at some point, full independence for Kurdistan can be obtained. The end of World War I represents a dark moment in history for the Kurdistan movement, as the great power at the conference in Sevres promised the Kurds a state of their own but later withdrew the promise. The motivation of today's activists is to reverse this unjust decision, claiming the people's right to self-determination. On the day of the Kurdish independence referendum, the Kurdish online newspaper Jiyan.dk quoted Mustafa Barzani on the newspaper's Facebook wall, 'the wish for an independent Kurdistan lives in the heart of every Kurd'.

Main organisations and allies

The Kurdistan movement is less centralised and more heterogeneous than the Öcalan movement. This is primarily because the movement embraces a variety of Kurdish political parties, which have different agendas within the context of the existing states in the Middle East, despite all supporting the goal of an independent Kurdistan. These parties include parties in Turkey, that is, the PSK, PAK, HAK-PAR; the various branches and off-shoots of the KDP, including KDPS; the Kurdish Future Movement in Syria; and representatives of the PUK. The PUK supporters seem divided, as I have met some of them at Öcalan events and some at Kurdistan movement events. Some of the parties define themselves explicitly in opposition to the Öcalan movement and consequently denounce the use of violence as a political means. This is true for the parties originating from Turkey and Syria, which are marginalised by the hegemony of the PKK and PYD. Traditionally, the parties from Iraq and Iran support armed resistance. In order to coordinate their political activities and appear as a strong alternative to the political activists within the Öcalan movement, representatives of the Kurdish parties within the Kurdistan movement have worked together since the mid-1980s. The cooperation came to be known as the platform of Kurdish parties; in

Kurdish *Hevkarî*. In 2010, Hevkarî decided to establish an umbrella organisation in order to more smoothly coordinate the various cultural initiatives of the movement. The organisation was called the Federation of Kurdish Associations in Denmark, colloquially known as Federasyona in Kurdish. Thus, officially, there is an organisational division between the political parties and the cultural associations. The statute of the federation reads that '[t]he federation includes Kurdish associations in Denmark and is not affiliated with political or religious tendencies' (Statute of the Federation of Kurdish Associations in Denmark, Article 3). However, the federation and the platform often cooperate when, for example, organising Newroz celebrations and various other support events. The federation took over as the leading cultural association from KOMKAR-DK, which mainly included politically active Kurds from Turkey. In addition, KOMKAR-DK lost its position as the unifying force due to internal rivalry caused by the return of Kemal Burkay to Turkey from exile in Sweden, since he chose to support HAK-PAR and abandon the PSK. After that, HAK-PAR took control of KOMKAR. However, KOMKAR has invited the Kurdish singer and musician Şivan Perwer to Denmark several times over the years. In 2017, he played for 2,000 attendees at the Music Theatre in Albertslund. The event was organised as part of the independence referendum campaign, so the Kurdish national anthem, Ey Reqip, was played, and a big poster of President Masoud Barzani adorned the wall beside a poster of Kemal Burkay.

The federation encompasses the Kurdish Cultural Association (aimed at Kurds from Syria), the Yezidi Cultural Association, the Kurdish Women's Association, the Kurdish Initiative in Denmark, and other local cultural associations. KOMKAR-DK is also represented. The Yezidi Cultural Association has taken a leading role within the federation in relation to the conflict in Syria and the fight against Islamic State, although the association represents only 500–600 Yezidis living in Denmark. This is mainly thanks to the great efforts by the leaders of the association to call attention to the atrocities committed against the Yezidis by Islamic State . The public outrage at the humanitarian catastrophe on Mount Sinjar in August 2014 and the subsequent sexual enslavement of Yezidi women and girls (3,537 females were abducted by Islamic State (UNAMI 2016, p.7)) further enhanced the visibility of the Yezidi case and mobilised both Kurds and Danes to support the events arranged by the Yezidi Cultural Association. A group of young Kurds are trying to bridge the gap between young supporters of the Öcalan and the Kurdistan movement and have founded KAD, the Kurdish Alternative in Denmark. They dissociate themselves from specific political parties, aiming to create 'a Kurdish community in Denmark aware of its Kurdish identity'. The association is mainly attracting members of the Kurdistan movement, though.

The Kurdistan movement is part of the transnational Kurdish movement. The Kurdish political parties in Denmark are organisational branches of the Kurdish parties in the homeland. They refer to the politburos or the general assemblies of the parties like the local branches in the homeland. The federation has only recently become formally interlinked with organisations in the homeland and transnational organisations. Although, informally, the leadership of the federation has cooperated for years with similar associations in other European countries, for example, Sweden, Belgium and Russia. Thus, in 2018 at meetings in Stockholm, Moscow and Brussels, Kurds in Europe founded DIAKURD to unify the Kurdish initiatives aimed at politicians in European countries as well as in the European Parliament. DIAKURD, or the Kurdish Diaspora Confederation, is an assembly of the Kurdish federations in the diaspora. A number of Danish politicians are supportive of the demands made by the Kurdistan movement and accept invitations to speak at the Kurdish events. They represent a variety of parties, mainly left-wing parties, although politicians representing the Liberal Party and the Danish People's Party at district level also sometimes show up. However, the Kurdistan movement does not have the backing of a party organisation as the Öcalan movement does.

The mobilisation base of the Kurdistan movement is made up of Kurds originating from all parts of Kurdistan and with various backgrounds. As a result, it is a highly diverse group representing various religious beliefs, including Muslim, Yezidi, Alevi and secular, and various dialects spoken, primarily the two main Kurdish dialects, Kurmanji and Sorani. However, even though the Kurds often have a strong sentiment toward their place of origin, such as Sulaymaniyah, Afrin, Mardin and Sanandaj, and often gather according to family networks, the Kurdistan movement has brought together Kurds who share the idea of being a Kurd from Kurdistan, as mentioned above.

When, in the twentieth century, the Kurdish national movement introduced the idea of a Kurdish nation, their aim was to mobilise for a Kurdish national identity transcending tribal belonging and traditional political loyalties, as comprehensively studied by Martin van Bruinessen in *Agha, Shaikh and State* (Bruinessen 1978). Omar Sheikhmous, Kurdish analyst and activist from Amuda in Syria, describes an incident in 1959 when as a young man he and some friends went to a public Ottoman era bath in Aleppo. An older man overheard their conversation, and out of interest, he asked about their origin. While the older man asked for their tribal affiliation, Sheikhmous and his friends answered with their national identity, 'we are Kurds', in compliance with what they had learned as political activists. They knew their tribal affiliation, but were unwilling to be identified by it (Sheikhmous 2019, p. 2–3). Today, tribal affiliations are even more remote. As one of my informants said, 'I know my heritage, the tribe I belong to [. . .] It is like a tradition. My children, they don't know' (E, male, 40s).

The Syrian war and mobilising events

The outbreak of the Syrian Civil War and the success of the Rojava revolution in Kurdish areas made members of the Kurdistan movement feel a sense of powerlessness. However, the Kurdish resistance in Kobane, where the Kurds stopped the military progress of Islamic State, made the battle of Kobane a mobilising event even within the Kurdistan movement. The Kurdistan movement has focused more on the war against Islamic State than on developments in Rojava, making support of the Yezidis a top priority. In 2017, the independence referendum became a huge mobilising event for the Kurdistan movement. It did not help the fellow Kurds in Syria, though. In terms of the Syrian war, the Kurdistan movement has had more success raising money and doing humanitarian work than mobilising political support. In 2014–15, money and clothes were collected and sent to Kobane and Sinjar by individuals and organisations. The Federation of Kurdish Associations in Denmark has primarily cooperated with two Kurdish humanitarian organisations: the Red Sun, founded in 2011 by a group of Kurds in Odense, and the Azadi Rekxrawi, founded in 2014 by a group of young Kurds. In 2014, another humanitarian association, the Wings of the Peacock, was set up to support the Yezidis after 2014, both in the Middle East and as refugees in Europe.

The independent actors

During my fieldwork, I have met Kurds, primarily young Kurds, who are focused on Kurdish issues but do not align themselves with the two movements or any of the associations investigated. They are highly educated and seek cooperation with academics rather than politicians. Some are the children of political activists who have grown up with political activism as a way of living, but find their parents' endeavours futile. Instead, they seek to utilise their professional skills to raise awareness of Kurdish-related issues both in the Middle East and in Denmark. Among them are both children of high-profile Öcalan supporters and children of former Peshmerga fighters of the PUK or KDP, who denounce the political activism of their parents. Some are Kurdish migrants or refugees, who align with broader democratic movements in opposition to the autocracy or autocratic tendencies in their countries of origin. Among them are refugees from Syria, who were part of the Syrian democratic opposition while still in Syria, but who find this position difficult to maintain in exile as Kurdish issues are neglected within the opposition, who propagate an Arab discourse. Instead, they align more with a global class of young educated cosmopolitan people with democratic sentiments and an interest in human rights. Yet some are descendants of non-mobilised labour migrants from Turkey. They were engaged in humanitarian action during the Kobane crisis, but were unwilling to toe the line of the political parties and become members of one of the two movements. So far, they have only mobilised for this one time. In order to understand their position, which is alienated from the Kurdish diaspora and transgresses the national context of Denmark, I use the framework of a 'diaspora within a diaspora' for them (Israel 2002). By doing so, I emphasise their academic skills, professional networks and international focus, well aware that they are the most heterogeneous grouping among the Kurds in Denmark.

The Syrian Kurdish refugees

The Kurds from Syria, who arrived as refugees in Europe in the 1980s, 1990s and 2000s, appeared to be a vulnerable group as details about their political and socioeconomic position within the Syrian Arab Republic was unknown to the outside world. While some Kurdish refugees from Syria were granted residence permits in the 2000s due to political persecution for their activism in Syria (that is, as refugees according to the UN Convention on Refugees), others were deported due to their inability to prove that they were personally persecuted or persecuted as an ethnic group. The problem was that the Syrian regime would detain the refugees upon return regardless of whether the authorities had monitored them previously or not. Thus, a number of deported Kurds were detained on arrival in Damascus, as Christian Sinclair documents (Sinclair 2010), causing anxiety among Syrian Kurdish asylum seekers in Europe facing deportation or waiting for their application to be processed. To put pressure on the European authorities, they organised hunger strikes in a number of countries. In 2010, in front of the parliament building Christiansborg, a tent hosted twenty-eight hunger-striking Kurds, whose hunger strike lasted for about three weeks without success. A Turkish Kurd affiliated with FEY-KURD acted as their spokesman. Another Kurdish asylum seeker, Ramazan Hajji Ibrahim, committed suicide in an asylum centre, allegedly because he was terrified of what might happen if the Danish authorities deported him. FEY-KURD offered to organise his funeral and thus appeared to want to adopt the cause of the Syrian Kurds, who according to the spokesman had fled Syria due inhumane conditions 'deprived the possibility of a normal life' (Jensen 2010) rather than due to political activism. In 2010, the possibility of entering Europe had become more difficult than in the 1990s, when Kurds from Turkey migrated due to environmental insecurity (Sirkeci 2006). In the wake of the Syrian Civil War, all Syrians arriving in Denmark were granted 'Convention Status', as above, or 'General Temporary Protection Status' due to the critical situation in Syria.

Due to their relatively small number and late arrival, the Kurds from Syria arriving in the 2000s did not take a leading position within the Kurdish diaspora movements. Both the Öcalan movement and the Kurdistan movement were dominated by Kurds who had been in Denmark for several years. Some of them grew up there, and most had a background in Turkey, as mentioned with the 'hegemonic presence' of Kurds from Turkey (Hassanpour and Mojab 2005). They were fluent in Danish and had built up networks and close relationships with other Kurdish actors as well as with authorities and politicians. Thus, the Kurds from Syria came to play the role of the little brother within the movements, but the Syrian crisis changed that to some degree. In 2012, when the Syrian uprising turned into a civil war and the Kurds took control of the Kurdish areas in northern Syria, the Syrian Kurds in the diaspora community took on a new role as intermediaries between diaspora associations and central Kurdish actors in their homeland. However, the external positions within both movements seemed reserved for the old guard.

For the Öcalan movement, the Syrian Kurds, and particularly the members of PYD, became even more important as intermediaries, as the PYD took the lead in the political and social development of the autonomous Kurdish areas of Rojava. After the battle of Kobane, which made both the broader Kurdish diaspora and the Danish public turn their eyes to the Rojava revolution and the military progress of the Kurdish defence forces, the position of the diasporic Syrian Kurds stabilised. They were important witnesses to the developments in their homeland, when the Kurdish activists were granted audience in parliament. They were also important hosts when representatives from the autonomous region of northern Syria, for example the PYD co-chair Salih Muslim, visited Copenhagen. They played perhaps an even more important role in establishing contact with potential partners when the various support initiatives sparked by the battle of Kobane were going to be implemented and activists were heading to Rojava. However, until 2016, PYD was represented by a spokesperson originating from Turkey and from the inner circles of FEY-KURD. Officially, it was due to a lack of language skills among the PYD members, but it made the Syrian Kurds appear dependent on others. In 2018, during the Turkish attack on Afrin, PYD was the main organiser of the demonstrations and protest processions. Although the protests mobilised more people than in previous years, I felt that the strong position of the Syrian Kurds within the Öcalan movement was coming to an end. The anti-Turkey and anti-Erdoğan slogans made it sound as if the Kurds from Turkey were taking over the agenda, relegating the Syrian Kurds to the same marginalised position they had occupied prior to Syrian war.

Syrian Kurds within the Kurdistan movement had even less ability to reach a broader audience. They were facing the same glass ceiling within their own movement as the Syrian Kurds within the Öcalan movement were, but additionally, they were unable to persuade the Kurdistan movement to adopt the agenda of the Syrian Kurdish parties aligned with the KNC. The alliance between KNC and the Syrian opposition groups supported by Turkey made the Syrian Kurdish agenda hard for the Kurdish political activists of Turkish descent to adopt, although they share a strong aversion to the PKK and its subdivisions – an aversion that is widespread within the movement. When the Yezidi association took the lead in making the Yezidi genocide and the slavery of Yezidi girls and women their focus when supporting the victims of Islamic State, the Syrian Kurds followed suit. Later, in 2017, when the independence referendum in Iraqi Kurdistan was held, all the members' energy and hopes were thrown into the support for independence, a mission which failed before it even got started. The Turkish attack on Afrin in 2018 also proved to be a difficult political task, because of the role of Turkey (both an ally and an aggressor) and the position of YPG and YPJ (both a rival and the only defender of the Kurdish civilians). Therefore, the only thing that made sense in terms of protest slogan was condemnation of the attacks on civilians leaving the political situation untold. Thus, the Syrian Kurds within the Kurdistan movement have been marginalised twice, due to both their position within the movement, which includes their inability to make the other actors within the Kurdistan movement adopt the political agenda of KNC, and the marginalised position of the Kurdistan movement in general.

PART III

AMBIGUOUS INTERPLAYS

6

THE CASTLE AND THE SQUARE: POLITICAL LOBBYISM

Introduction

Kurdistan needs help now!

On a Friday afternoon, 8 August 2014, a protest demonstration took place in the square in front of Christiansborg, the Danish parliament building in the centre of Copenhagen. Between five hundred and thousand people gathered to support the Yezidi community, who were facing a humanitarian catastrophe during the military advance of Islamic State in northern Iraq. Five days before, on 3 August, Islamic State forces had entered the city of Sinjar. Over the days that followed, 9,000 women, children and men were killed or enslaved, while 50,000 escaped to Mount Sinjar. Hundreds among them died from lack of water and food (Serinci 2018, p. 344). The demonstrators gathered around the statue of King Frederik VII in the middle of the square, waving colourful flags of the Kurdish parties and associations. The protesters held signs reading 'Stop ISIS. Kurdistan needs help now!!!' and photos of victims, while listening to speeches by representatives of the Yezidi community and invited speakers, among them an MP from the Socialist People's Party. Other MPs showed up as the demonstration was taking place on their doorstep. It seemed as if the Kurdish diaspora was unified at the demonstration, addressing the atrocities committed by Islamic State on the Yezidi minority of the Kurdish people. The main message was one of condemnation of the Islamic State attack on Sinjar, and a call for help. As one of the organisers, Yilmaz Yildiz, proclaimed, '[w]e call out to the Danish society, the Danish government and the parliament. We call for humanitarian aid for the Yezidis and for a stop to the attacks of Islamic State on the Yezidis' (TV2 NEWS, 8 August 2014). A car suddenly appeared along the canal, the driver shouting slogans in support of Islamic State. As the traffic slowed down, some of the demonstrators ran to the car and tried to drag the driver out. Some of the guards at the demonstration ran ahead and stopped the confrontation, and the car drove off. Although the incident was dealt with, the police called off the demonstration shortly before it came to a natural end. The same day, President Obama announced that the US would enter the war against Islamic State by invitation of the Iraqi government. Subsequently, two bombing attacks were launched on Islamic State forces close to Erbil, and humanitarian aid was airdropped on Mount Sinjar for the distressed Yezidi refugees. A few weeks later, the Danish parliament followed suit and decided to join the American-led coalition in support of the Iraqi war against Islamic State.

Later that month, on 16 August 2014, another demonstration was held in Christiansborg Palace Square to raise awareness of the advances of Islamic State and the struggle of the Kurds. This time the demonstration started off as a procession from Vesterbro Square and moved through the centre of the city. Again, flags and posters were displayed in support of the Kurds and Kurdish associations, and left-wing politicians showed their support by delivering speeches. Later still, in September and October 2014, when Islamic State besieged the city of Kobane, an array of demonstrations and protest activities were held in front of the parliament building and around the capital and the country as a whole, calling for assistance to defend the city. Similar actions took place around Europe (Eccarius-Kelly 2017; Toivanen, forthcoming). At the same time, the #SaveKobane campaign spread globally on social media. During the following months and years, mobilised Kurds launched a multitude of activities in support of the Kurdish struggle against Islamic State. In order to influence Danish politicians more directly, Kurdish representatives and associations asked to be, and subsequently were, invited to meet the Foreign Affairs Committee of the Danish Parliament to present and discuss the situation of the Kurds in Syria and Iraq on the frontline against Islamic State.

What are the Kurdish associations trying to achieve when appealing to politicians and taking the Kurdish flags and slogans to the street? What repertoire do they perform and why? And how do other actors, who may either hinder or enable the Kurdish cause, seek to reach their own goals?

Kurdish activism in the political arena

In this chapter, I will analyse the political lobbyism of the Kurdish diaspora groups that aim to raise awareness of the Kurdish struggle in Syria. In doing so, I will focus on one strand of homeland politics, namely Kurdish politics directed at politicians and political institutions in the country of settlement (Østergaard-Nielsen 2003, p. 83). Political activism aimed at persuading the decision-makers to take action in favour of the Kurds in the homeland has become critical for the Kurdish movement, as taking direct action in support of the homeland has been seen as even more suspicious since the turn of the century. This is due to the toughening of the public integration debate, in which loyalty towards the homeland is discredited and perceived as a hindrance to loyalty to the country of residence (Østergaard-Nielsen 2003, p. 105). The recent situation involving the German professional footballer Mesut Özil playing for the Premier League club Arsenal is a perfect example of this (Schuetze 2018). In May 2018, during the Turkish presidential election campaign, Özil posed in a photo with Turkish president Recep Erdoğan. As Özil was born to Turkish parents, this was interpreted as political allegiance to the president at a time when Erdoğan was already being criticised for a suspicious mobilisation campaign aimed at the Turkish diaspora in Europe. The EU ban on the PKK (enforced in 2002) and the Danish laws criminalising travel and intent to travel to war zones (2015 and 2016) further complicate Kurdish homeland politics. It should be added that the settlement of Kurds in Europe has paved the way for a division of labour which allows the Kurdish activists to focus their efforts in their country of residence, as they have a better understanding of the political milieu in Denmark than Kurds residing in other countries, including the homeland.

The Kurdish agenda aimed at the political decision-makers is two-directional as the agenda addresses the politicians both directly and indirectly through the Danish public. The direct approach is partly based on long-term relations and alliances between Kurdish diaspora groups and

Danish politicians, and partly on ad hoc interactions, such as when a group of Kurds ask for a meeting with a member of the Danish Parliament. The indirect approach is based on the assumption that if awareness of the Kurdish cause is raised among a broader audience, the Kurds will be supported by advocates who may help call for action from the politicians.

While the direct approach takes the Kurdish activists into Christiansborg Palace, which houses the Danish Parliament 'Folketinget' and related parliament offices, the indirect approach takes the Kurdish activists to the streets and squares in an attempt to reach and mobilise the public. My analysis of the Kurdish lobbyism, which is the focus of this chapter, will be structured around these two arenas. I will analyse the interactions taking place in what I will be referring to as 'the Castle' and 'the Square'. As I have argued in the chapter on the theoretical framework, an arena is understood as a concrete place where people appear and act physically, but also as a symbolic space of negotiated meaning (Duyvendak and Fillieule 2014, p. 306). When mentioning 'the Castle' and 'the Square', I therefore refer to the physical places of Christiansborg and the main squares in Copenhagen, as well as to two sets of ascribed meaning.

While 'the Castle' represents the hidden and inaccessible, 'the Square' represents accessibility and visibility. The Castle, in Danish 'Borgen', is the short form of Christiansborg. Besides referring to the physical building, the Castle also informally refers to the parliament as well as to the political negotiations that take place within the building (as in the Danish TV series 'Borgen'). Being the place of national political negotiation, the Castle is perceived as the main political arena for the Kurdish lobbyists. However, like a medieval castle, protecting its residents by way of thick stone walls and tight security measures, the Castle is difficult to access. The only way to enter the building and gain access to the decision-makers is by invitation from within (Folketingets Administration, n.d.). As invitations are rare, the second-best option for the political activists is access to the square in front of the building, as if a political aura emanates through the walls from the hidden powers within. This also applies to the square in front of the City Hall. However, the squares are also chosen for political lobbyism for other reasons. In contrast to the hidden affairs of the castle, the square is an open and accessible place, and the activities are visible to everyone, attendees as well as passers-by. When the

Kurds take their political agendas to the public space, they become political actors. Occupying the squares and being physically present, they become plainly visible to the public audience. However, if they succeed in mobilising the masses, they become visible to the decision-makers as worthy political players, and may thus be able to push the politicians into desired action (Gambetti 2013; Arendt 1958). The two arenas, the Castle and the Square, are linked by the political agendas pursued by the Kurdish actors and are thus perceived as sub-arenas of the political arena where the Kurdish actors fight for their political goals. The success of the political lobbyism thus needs to be measured on the basis of analyses of the interactions in both arenas.

During the early stages of my fieldwork, when I tried to get an overview of the different Kurdish groups and associations, I noticed a peculiar similarity between the two main Kurdish umbrella organisations: they have the same name. Thus, the Federation of Kurdish Associations in Denmark (in Danish: Sammenslutningen af Kurdiske foreninger i Danmark) is the official name of these two organisations, which both claim to represent all the Kurdish associations in Denmark. Similarly, I noticed that the different Kurdish groups performed similar repertoires. Different Newroz celebrations were held on the same day in different squares in Copenhagen, and cultural events took place at the same suburban location, but with different political messages. Publicly, the two federations ignore each other, but internally, they compete to be the voice of the Kurdish diaspora, even though they recruit from quite different member bases as mentioned in Chapter 5.

In order to investigate how this competition unfolds, I will apply the concept of rivalry, which has been proposed by Mustafa Gürbüz as a way to interpret the relations between competing social movements in Turkey (Gürbüz 2016). He suggests that a third possibility of inter-movement relationship exists between being friends and enemies: *rivalry*. He has borrowed the term 'rival movements' from Charles Tilly (Tilly 1998, p. 268) and has developed it conceptually into meaning

> two or more social movements that are actively engaged in challenging the dominant power structure as well as one another. The rival movements neither try to exterminate each other as seen in opposing movements nor do they show elements of friendship in their relations. Instead, they engage in a fierce competition for material and symbolic resources. (Gürbüz 2016, p. 24)

Drawing on symbolic interactionism, he argues that former enmity between Kurdish movements in Turkey has transformed into rivalry, as the movements had to cope with a number of critical events from the capture of the PKK leader Abdullah Öcalan in 1999 to the electoral victory of the Justice and Development Party (AKP) in 2002. In a case study, he explores how the strategies of the PKK, Kurdish Hizbullah and the Gülen Movement have become more alike in the fight for symbolic resources such as prestige and legitimacy. The rivalry manifests itself in the social interaction as processes of *resemblance, niche building* and *strategic subversion* (Gürbüz 2016, p. 27). *Resemblance* refers to the development of similar organisations and civic initiatives since the rival movements are dragged into similar actions in search of the same opportunities. *Niche building* refers to the attempts of rival movements to specialise in certain fields, taking advantage of their specific benefits related to resources or identity. Although the two processes seem to contradict each other from a strategic perspective, Gürbüz argues that they are both expressions of strategic considerations. *Strategic subversion* refers to the efforts of rival activists to 'both strengthen their own prestige and harm the reputation of their competitors' (Gürbüz 2016, p. 28) by interpreting their own and others' acts from a normative perspective and thus 'building a moral authority' (Gürbüz 2016, p. 28).

Building on symbolic interactionism, Gürbüz claims that '[r]ival social movements are neither innately nor permanently "rivals"' (Gürbüz 2016, p. 24). This means that the relations between the movements are not fixed but develop and take new forms. I will therefore also analyse when the rivalry transforms into other forms of relationship and discuss which events lead to more friendly relations and which to more conflicting ones. After that, I will discuss the conditions for one group being able to dominate the other by gaining hegemonic status (Gunes 2012). Gürbüz uses the term 'rivalry' to explain the interaction between social movements. I will apply the term to the inner dynamics of the Kurdish diaspora to explain the interactions between the Öcalan movement and the Kurdistan movement. Initially, I will not distinguish between the movements but instead consider the Kurdish diaspora one (compound) player.

Gürbüz has been criticised for perceiving the three movements – the PKK, Kurdish Hizbullah and the Gülen Movement – as equal players in the Turkish Southeast, especially by equating the Islamist Gülen Movement with the Kurdish political movements (Gökalp 2017). In the following, I will solely adopt the conceptualisation of rivalry, including its manifestation in the social processes of resemblance, niche building and strategic subversion.

The Square

Repertoires

Taking political protests to the streets has become the default tactic for social movements who aim to raise political awareness among the public and simultaneously pressure the political decision-makers to take action. Like other actions in activists' repertoires , the public protest as an action form has developed over time due to the opportunities for public assembly (Tilly 1986, p. 2) and has thus become part of protest culture (Jasper 2014a, p. 36).

Kurdish activities in public space are organised on a variety of occasions. Some activities are recurrent and mark the anniversary of specific events. These include anniversaries of historic Kurdish events, such as commemoration of massacres and genocide – for example Halabja on 16 March 1988 – and the Kurdish national Flag Day on 17 December, introduced in 1999 by the Kurdistan Region parliament. The most significant annual event, however, is the Newroz celebration, which has become a major mobilising event of the Kurdish movement after the politicalisation of the Kawa myth by the PKK in the early 1980s (Gunes 2012, p. 96). Other activities are occurrence-driven, organised to raise awareness of current events of relevance to the Kurdish cause. Some of these events take place in the Kurdish homeland, such as the siege of Kobane by Islamic State in October 2014 and the Turkish attack on Afrin in January 2018, as well as the independence referendum held in the Kurdistan Region of Iraq in September 2017. Other current occurrences which trigger collective action in the public space do not take place in the Kurdish homeland but still relate to Kurdish interests. Examples include the capture of Öcalan in 1999 in Kenya, and the verdicts against ROJ TV and ten Kurdish individuals from 2012 to 2016 in Copenhagen. A third type of activity in the public space is launched to capture the attention of the European populations during periods when public attention on the Kurdish cause is waning. These activities are ad hoc cultural festivals promoting Kurdish music and food, and transnational campaigns launched to direct attention to general political issues, such as the march in February 2018 under the slogan 'Freedom for Öcalan – Peace in Kurdistan'.

Why take the Kurdish cause to the streets and squares?

First and foremost, the tactical utilisation of demonstrations and mass manifestations is a means to instigate political changes. That is the case when Kurdish associations demonstrate to push the political decision-makers to act in certain ways. When Turkey attacked Afrin, a leader of one of the organisations explained the rationale behind the demonstrations this way: 'The message is for the government. We will not leave the street until something happens. There need to be activists in the street continuously' (U, male, 40s). He argued that the constant pressure from groups of people would eventually make the politicians take action and change would happen. At the time of the Afrin attack, the goal of his organisation was to push the government to condemn Turkey within the NATO alliance, so that Turkey would be forced to withdraw from attacking the Syrian Kurds.

Another rationale behind Kurdish mass events in the public space is related to information and legitimisation of the Kurdish cause in general. Thus, demonstrations also aim at raising awareness of the Kurdish cause among a broader audience. Another Kurdish leader told me that '[w]hen we demonstrate, we demonstrate to draw the attention of the society to our situation. First and foremost, we want to reach the Danish population as we live in Denmark, and then the world society. Our goal is to be recognised and to gain support' (R, male, 40s). While the first-mentioned use of public gatherings aims to make political changes, the second is aimed at transformation at a more strategic level, the argument being that awareness will lead to recognition of the political cause and ultimately political action in support of the cause. Recognition of the political cause is also important to many of people I talked to as they equate recognition of the political cause with being recognised as an ethnic group in Denmark, which I will discuss in the end of this chapter. By being accepted as actors in the political arena, they feel included in the Danish community as full-fledged citizens. I will return to this idea when discussing the significance of being invited into the parliament building.

When demonstrations are planned, specific places and activities are chosen in accordance with the overall goal. The organisers have a strong sense of the potential and limitations of the various squares and choose locations carefully to reach certain audiences and achieve different purposes to maximise the effect. Interestingly, the different Kurdish actors assess the squares in the same way. Two squares are considered particularly valuable: Christiansborg Palace Square and City Hall Square. Both squares are located in the centre of Copenhagen and are visible to tourists and passers-by. They are also equally accessible to organisers and attendees from different parts of the city. Additionally, and equally importantly, the squares are located in front of two important political institutions, namely the Danish Parliament and City Hall, which adds to the symbolic significance of the squares. This centrality of the squares, the geographical placement in the centre of the capital as well as the proximity to key political institutions, is of utmost importance to the Kurdish activists. It is evidence of the centrality of the Kurdish cause and the political clout enjoyed by the Kurds and Kurdish associations as they are capable of getting hold of the public (political) space.

There is also a general consensus among the Kurdish organisers in terms of when the Christiansborg Palace Square is preferable to City Hall Square, and vice versa. One of the organisers, speaking on behalf of everyone else, points out that 'when we demonstrate at Christiansborg Square, we mostly address the politicians' and 'when we demonstrate at the City Hall Square, it is because there are a lot of people who provide us with the opportunity to talk about the cause' (R, male, 40s). Thus, Christiansborg Palace Square is preferred when the Kurds try to attract the attention of the political decision-makers and demand immediate action. As the demonstrations are held on the doorstep of the parliament, the decision-makers seem very close and within earshot. City Hall Square is preferred when they want to draw public attention to the Kurdish cause.

City Hall Square, which is located by the entrance to the main pedestrian street, Strøget, has added value as it is 'a place that people pass by' and thus perfect for a demonstration to catch the eye of passers-by. Another of my informants recounts that City Hall Square is perfect for large gatherings as

suddenly, an ethnic Dane passes by saying 'what is this?'. Then you have the opportunity to propagate Kurdish politics to the public and to show our colours [. . .] When you say 'I am a Kurd and we are celebrating Newroz', the person may go home and read about Newroz and learn more about the Kurds. (H, female, 20s)

She also addresses the opportunity of including the passers-by in the activities on the square as 'it is also about making people from the outside participate [. . .] It creates a great atmosphere, when people just arrive and you dance together just like that'. This also points to strategic efforts to hold the attention of the people passing by and encourage them to stop and join in. Apart from minor variations, the activities are generally very similar and seem to correspond to traditional protest repertoires (della Porta 2013). Like other protesters, the Kurds wave banners and flags to make the message visible at a distance, so, for instance, the Kurdish flag may be shown beside a banner pointing out that 'the Kurds do also have the right to self-determination'. Speeches are made by Kurdish representatives and invited Danish speakers to demonstrate the political backing of the protest. Kurdish musicians may play, and often attendees join in the *govend*, the traditional Kurdish dance. A few times, I have seen plays being performed, addressing an existing military or political crisis, such as the Turkish attack on Afrin. Some of the organisers favour processions, which make the protest even more visible in the public space. The procession will typically set off from a square in the periphery of the city, such as Vesterbro Square, and end up at one of the main squares, where it transforms into an ordinary demonstration with speeches, banners and flags. The public gathering of people is the main aim, as a big crowd is more visible and demonstrates the backing of the cause among both Kurds and Danes, thus confirming the strength of the association organising the event. This is a strong message addressing the decision-makers and the broader Danish audience as well as the transnational Kurdish community.

Access to the squares: Interaction with local authorities

While the Kurdish organisations find it difficult to hold the attention of the Danish national media, they find cooperation with the local authorities much smoother and more productive. They experience very few restrictions and rules when organising demonstrations and processions in the public space. A leader of one of the Kurdish associations (U, male, 40s) explained that if a demonstration has to be organised urgently in response to, for example, a massacre, all they have to do is submit an application to the police and the municipality a day ahead. They have never received a 'no'. Another informant confirms the friendly relations with the authorities and adds that occasionally they have been redirected to other locations if the requested square was booked or under reconstruction (R, male, 40s). This has been the case with Christiansborg Palace Square, which, as mentioned, is a favourite among the Kurdish activists. Until recently, the square was under reconstruction due to security concerns. According to the reconstruction plan, twenty-two large granite balls were placed in a semicircle to protect visitors on the square from drivers with malicious intent, thus preserving the square as 'a rallying ground for demonstrations and other events' (Folketinget Nyheder 2017).

What is the reason behind the authorities' endorsement of this public occupation of the squares in Copenhagen? In this section, I will look at Copenhagen municipality's strategies for urban life. When the Kurdish associations enter the public space, they have already interacted with the local authorities, who have approved their requests or adjusted them to make them compatible with the agenda of the municipality. Copenhagen municipality's strategy for urban life is described in their strategy reports. The first report, 'A Metropolis for People: Visions and goals for urban life in Copenhagen 2015', was published by the City of Copenhagen in 2009. The follow-up, 'Co-create Copenhagen: Vision for 2025', came out in 2015.

The strategies aim at making Copenhagen 'the world's most liveable city' (City of Copenhagen 2009, p. 2) or 'one of the top global cities' (City of Copenhagen 2015a, p. 2). Earning the title of 'liveable city' requires a vibrant urban life. The strategies stress that urban life is a must if Copenhagen is to be considered liveable by socioeconomically advantaged citizens and tourists. Urban life is defined as 'what happens when people walk around and hang out in public space' (City of Copenhagen 2009, p. 4). While the first strategy focuses more exclusively on the quantity of urban life, the second strategy includes qualities such as 'city with an edge' and 'a responsible city'. Nevertheless, in 2015 as in 2009, the first measurement of success mentioned is 'Copenhageners spend 20% more time in urban spaces' (City of Copenhagen 2015a, p. 19). This matches the aim of the Kurdish diaspora groups, who seek to reach the Danish politicians and public through the public space. Thus, I will argue that Kurdish protest activities contribute to the accomplishment of the primary aim of the strategies. In fact, the 'Urban Life Account' (City of Copenhagen 2015b) points out that the number of event permits – for events of all kinds – has increased by 216 per cent from 2010 to 2015.

However, there are other reasons why the local authorities welcome Kurdish events in the public space. I talked to one of the employees at the municipal administration, who processes the applications for demonstration permits. When I asked him how the Kurdish demonstrations contribute to urban life in Copenhagen and the city becoming a 'city with an edge', he simply stressed the right to peaceful assembly for all groups without discrimination. The administration has approved all applications from Kurdish groups in recent years since the police had no objections in terms of security. The employee merely said, 'you get what you ask for'. It is worth mentioning that in Denmark, freedom of expression includes freedom to express sympathy for any organisation. Demonstrators are thus allowed to bring PKK flags and pictures of Öcalan to the streets and squares, even though Denmark adopted the ban on the PKK at the same time as the EU back in 2002, when the PKK was added to the EU's list of terrorist organisations. In Germany, by contrast, the police and security forces are instructed that images of Öcalan and other flags associated with the PKK are prohibited (Gude 2017). A year after implementation of the police instruction, however, the ban on flags related to the Syrian organisations PYD and YPG was lifted due to a court decision (Shino 2018).

Even though those processing the applications are obliged to follow two different rationales, namely the strategy for becoming a 'liveable city' and the human rights enshrined in the constitution, there is no contradiction between the two regarding permission. The Kurdish demonstrations create urban life but are also a constitutional right. The local authorities embrace the Kurdish activities in the public space for both reasons.

Frustration and violence: Negotiating how to respond

When a demonstration takes place in the streets of Copenhagen, not everybody complies with the plan of action. This means that the organisers also need to handle obstructive actors amongst their own ranks. Most of the time, the demonstrations proceed according to plan, but sometimes unforeseen incidents occur and the frustration of some of the attendees spins out of control. This applies to situations where supporters of Islamic State or the Turkish attack on Afrin suddenly appear, fuelling the anger of some attendees. This also applies to demonstrations in front of the Turkish or Iranian embassies. The mere proximity of representatives of the enemy can trigger an emotional response in some demonstrators. In both cases, it is the presence of the enemy, even when only symbolic, that provokes attendees to respond aggressively. Every time this happens, the organisers and guards intervene, trying to regain control of the demonstration. These situations reveal two different perceptions of a suitable response to the enemy, or representative of the enemy, when demonstrating in a Danish setting. A closer look at the interaction between some of demonstrators reveals how an appropriate approach is negotiated in practice. One of my informants recounts, 'Some youths tried to attack the embassy [. . .] We made a human chain. We did not expect it as it had never happened before' (R, male, 40s). Another recounts an episode in front of the Turkish embassy when some of the attendees were about to set the Turkish flag on fire. He tried to dissuade them by telling them that in Denmark 'it is disrespectful [. . .] We are like them, if we do it [i.e. burn the flag]'. However, it was difficult to intervene in the situation, he explains, as the demonstrator 'freaked out' (U, male, 40s). Thus, the experienced activists resort to various responses when faced with actions they perceive to be inappropriate. Besides their attempts to isolate the troublemakers to defuse the tension, they resort to educational talks about democracy and democratic values and about how to conduct protests in a democracy.

The organisers are very keen to comply with police instructions. Their reasoning is straightforward. As one of the organisers puts it, '[w]e have the right to assemble and as long as we do not make problems and instead respect the rules and regulations, they will not intervene' (R, male, 40s). If they do not comply with the instructions, the police will call off the demonstration, and public attention will immediately shift to the aggressive behaviour that caused the cancellation. If the police detain the violent attendees, it will be even more damaging to the publicity. Most often, the troublemakers are considered to be on the periphery of the movement, so the organisers feel justified in correcting them. However, the organisers, who are most often mature men and women, seem to understand the frustration of the young attendees, many of whom are male refugees from the Kurdish areas of Syria. One of the Kurdish activists explains that '[m]any are young people. Their mother and father are in Syria. Their brothers are there. Some of their family members have died during the war, and some have died from bombardments. They are alone and when you are alone, you are dangerous' (U, male, 40s).

After Turkey attacked Afrin and engaged in direct confrontation with the Kurds in Syria, the main enemy of the Kurdish struggle in Syria became the Turkish state rather than Islamic State. This has had an impact on the protest demonstrations in Denmark and in Europe in general as Kurdish activists in support of the YPG and YPJ are now able to address their enemy directly, for example at the Turkish embassies. In addition, supporters of the political developments in Turkey and of the policies of president Erdoğan have become an integral part of European societies, as evidenced by the campaign around the Turkish constitution referendum in April 2017 and at the presidential and parliamentary elections in June 2018. Consequently, confrontations at Kurdish demonstrations have increased. Germany, for instance, has witnessed several violent confrontations between citizens of Kurdish and Turkish descent, as well as a number of arson attacks on Turkish mosques allegedly carried out by pro-Kurdish fractions (Degner, Diehl, Höhne, Peters, and Ziegler 2018). In Denmark, only a few minor incidents have taken place at protest events. On 24 March 2018, following a Kurdish demonstration yelling, 'Afrin is not alone', three men were arrested after chasing some of the Kurdish demonstrators at what was called a 'mass fight' involving twenty-five individuals (Bachmann 2018). One of the arrested was carrying a meat cleaver. Due to the police intervention, the violence did not escalate. One week earlier, a firebomb was thrown at the Turkish embassy in Copenhagen and four men, allegedly Kurds, were arrested (Ritzau 2018). As mentioned above, the senior activists feel the obligation to keep a tight rein on the young protesters, who, as noted, have not been brought up in a democratic tradition. This is precisely why 'you need a solution in Syria', as one activist puts it, as a political solution in Syria is needed to ease the sentiments of the Kurdish refugees in Europe (U, male, 40s).

To what avail?

Even though traditional tactics to reach the politicians and the public, such as demonstrations, seem to be part of the DNA of the Kurdish diaspora, criticism from other Kurds exists. One informant told me that she is sometimes asked 'why do you demonstrate? It is to no avail anyway', but she insists that she 'would rather demonstrate than stay at home doing nothing and feel powerless. Because, in the end, when I go to a demonstration, when I do something, I feel I accomplish something' (H, female, 20s). This shows how essential being active is for the activists. It also points to the centrality of demonstrations within the repertoire of Kurdish political activism. It reflects, I will argue, the process of creating and maintaining Kurdish identity in the diaspora. When acting collectively in support of the Kurdish cause, the activists become or renew their identity as Kurds. However, Kurdish activists sometimes question whether demonstrations are the most powerful tool for conveying the message, or whether it is time to adopt methods that are more progressive. Another informant (V, female, 30s) is lukewarm about demonstrations. She grew up with activist parents and, as a child, she experienced demonstrations regularly. She believes that other activities may be more effective at raising awareness of the Kurdish cause, and that both form and content should be reconsidered depending on who is being addressed. Instead, she has engaged herself in events aimed at more binding relations with the attendees and potential supporters, such as events that include talks, meetings with other activists, food and charity work.

Using demonstrations as the main action form indicates that the Kurdish diaspora groups consider it the most efficient way of reaching the Danish audience. The Kurds I met expressed despondence when I asked them about the willingness of Danish newspapers and broadcasting media to cover Kurdish issues. One interviewee (U, male, 40s) even claimed that the Danish media only broadcasts in accordance with Danish foreign policy, which is aligned with American foreign policy toward Turkey. At the time of the Turkish attack on Afrin, he pointed out that the Danish media did not publish Kurdish criticism of Turkey due to American compliance with Turkish policy toward the Kurds. Another interviewee (R, male, 40s) explained that the media is only interested in covering Kurdish demonstrations when things get heated, as in 2014 when demonstrators pounced on the Islamic State supporter in his car to silence him. He also referred to a recent online article in Jydske Vestkysten, a regional daily. The article covered a demonstration in the city of Sønderborg in support of the Kurds in Afrin at the time of the Turkish attack (Dürr 2018). The article focused specifically on a car that drove by the demonstration waving a red and white flag, which some demonstrators tried to grab. The flag was misinterpreted as being Danish, resulting in some readers writing nasty comments about the lack of Kurdish loyalty to Denmark and its democratic values. However, the flag was in fact Turkish, which explains the angry reaction on the part of the demonstrators. My informant recounted the story, stressing the indifference of the Danish media to the Kurdish cause and journalists' inappropriate focus on sensational episodes. The inaccessibility to Danish national media experienced by Kurdish organisations justifies the need for Kurdish-controlled media writing in Danish. Nûdem.dk and Jiyan.dk are the most read sources, with around 4,000 and 17,000 followers, respectively, on Facebook. While Kurdish organisations find it difficult to be heard in the national media, they have easy access to the Kurdish media, who are obviously interested in representing them. However, it is still difficult for the stories to reach a broader Danish audience.

The Castle

Political lobbyism is pressuring: 'I put pressure on you and you put pressure on the next one'

In contrast to mass protests, which are intended to mobilise the public and only indirectly influence the political decision-makers, political lobbyism inside political institutions is aimed directly at politicians to make them adopt the agenda of the lobbying actor. Kurdish activists try to reach the decision-makers directly by various means, ranging from meetings with individual members of parliament to seminars designed for politicians and political organisations. Some meetings are designed to evoke immediate political response, while others have long-term goals that involve building up networks for future cooperation. Like any other lobbyist, the Kurdish activist knows that lobbying involves a lot more than calling the Minister of Foreign Affairs and asking him to change Danish foreign policy or align it with a Kurdish agenda. Lobbying is a step-by-step process of creating advocates who can take the case in question to the next level of decision-making. One of my informants told me that, at a meeting at the Ministry of Foreign Affairs, he had explained the rationale to one of the civil servants from the Ministry in this way, 'I put pressure on you and you put pressure on the next one and so on. That is how it works' (U, male, 40s).

Repertoires

A first step in the process of influencing decision-making may involve the Kurdish organisation and representatives asking individual politicians for a meeting at which they will present their situation or cause, hoping to win the politicians over. The small Kurdish parties have had meetings with different members of parliament, primarily members with Kurdish backgrounds. Apparently, Kurdish activists presume that the Kurdish members of parliament, being Kurds, feel a strong allegiance to the Kurdish cause. The outcome of these meetings is very unpredictable as the politicians may have many other cases on their desk.

However, the Kurdish associations have been able to maintain the interest of a handful of politicians, who have accepted their invitations to speak on different occasions. During my fieldwork, I met the same politicians repeatedly. In order to coordinate efforts and formalise otherwise informal alliances between Kurdish and Danish politicians, various networks have been established over the years. In the 1990s, at the time of the intensification of the Turkish-Kurdish conflict and in the wake of the Gulf War and the liberation of the Kurdish areas in Iraq, the Danish-Kurdish Human Rights Committee was formed by Danish politicians representing most of the political spectrum in cooperation with members of a variety of Kurdish parties and associations. Also in the 1990s, the Danish-Kurdish Friendship Association was established by Danish and Kurdish activists, allegedly without conforming to political divides, but in reality left-leaning. Both networks faded as new generations of politicians took office. In 2010, a new network was formed, engaging both old activists and young Danish politicians with Kurdish backgrounds. Most of them are members of the left-wing parties, mainly the Red-Green Alliance, but also the Socialist People's Party and the Social Democratic Party. The Kurdish Forum, as it is called, aims to raise awareness of the Kurdish minorities in the Middle East among the Danish public and to put pressure on governments to improve the living and human rights conditions of the Kurdish people (Kurdisk Forum 2010, §2). The forum has entered the political arena in Denmark acting as a lobbying organisation for the supporters of the FEY-KURD and the Kurdistan National Congress (KNK).

Another important step is to access the meetings of the Foreign Affairs Committee of the parliament. As the tasks of the committee include processing bills within the field of foreign affairs and controlling the way the Minister of Foreign Affairs exercises his or her power (Folketinget, n.d.), convincing the committee to take over their cause is a high priority for the Kurdish lobbyists. The Kurdish representatives are typically summoned to a meeting within the walls of the Castle because one or more of the members of the committee want to address a certain issue, or they find that the Kurds can provide the committee with urgent information useful to parliamentary work. However, as roundtable-meetings attended by Kurdish representatives and associations are rare and the time is limited, a member of one of the Kurdish parties complains that '[w]hen you are there, you do not have much time. We were invited three times, and each time we had 15 minutes. You cannot deliver long speeches under such circumstances. We are asked, and we answer. It is brief' (K, male, 50s). When Kurdish representatives were invited to meetings with the committee during the period 2014–18, which is the period I have examined, two main questions were on the agenda (Udenrig-sudvalget, n.d.): the Yezidi genocide and the military and political struggle of the Syrian Kurds. These two questions also reflect the two main causes of the Kurdish diaspora in Denmark, if the short-lived mobilisation in support of the referendum in Iraqi Kurdistan is discounted. If the discussions in the Foreign Affairs Committee lead to the committee questioning the actions of the Foreign Minister, the committee can hold an open consultation with the minister. This happened in March 2018, during the Turkish attack on Afrin. The Danish Foreign Minister Anders Samuelsen had repeated the words of US Secretary of State Rex Tillerson, who had stated that Turkey had 'legitimate security concerns' in northern Syria. The committee was concerned because the minister had not criticised the acts of Turkey as he could have done within a NATO framework. Members from all the left-wing parties – the Red-Green Alliance, the Socialist People's Party, the Social Democratic Party and the Alternative – questioned the minister (Udenrig-sudvalget 2018). Interestingly, Kurdish representatives from PYD and KNK, who had been present at the open consultation, were invited to the Ministry of Foreign Affairs the following day for consultations on the situation in Afrin. This shows how political alliances, advocacy and persistent pressure can lead to the inner circles of political decision-making.

Yet another way to get hold of the politicians is by inviting them to cultural-political meetings at the Castle, like the event 'Newroz reception at the Castle' in 2016. The reception was organised by the Kurdish Forum and held on 21 March on the day of Newroz, the Kurdish New Year and main Kurdish cultural-political feast. Representatives of various Kurdish parties and organisations were invited to speak, such as KNK, Gorran, PYD and a Kurdish Women's Association. Danish national politicians from the left-wing parties also spoke at the event. In addition, Danish and Kurdish artists performed. The reception took place in one of the staterooms at the Christiansborg Palace, the 'Landstingssal', formerly the seat of the Upper Chamber and newly redecorated with outstanding paintings by living Danish artists. Besides the presentations, a Kurdish buffet was set out in the hall. The event required registration but was open to the public. Around 150 people participated in the event within the thick stone walls of the Castle while dusk settled outside the large windows. Apparently, the event was a success. The attendees were delighted to meet KNK representative Adem Uzun, a frequent guest and highly valued by the Öcalan supporters in Denmark, and listen to Nikolaj Villumsen, the enthusiastic supporter of the Rojava revolution and Member of Parliament for the Red-Green Alliance. Many felt honoured to be inside the Castle as they felt recognised both as Kurds and as full-fledged Danish citizens. However, one of the organisers (H, female, 20s) I spoke to was more hesitant, pointing out that 'the purpose is lobbying [. . .] Our goal is to invite organisations or politicians that we want to have a dialogue with, because, as you know, lobbyism in Denmark as well as in Europe is of utmost importance, right?'. She continued, 'We want to reach the politicians we otherwise have difficulties reaching as some of the parties, when it comes to Kurdish politics, are very heedful about the relations with Turkey'. She summed up by saying that 'it does not work, though, as the Kurds just want to make an appearance in parliament alongside a parliamentarian'. The following year, ordinary Kurds were no longer allowed access to the Newroz celebration at the Castle in order to make the networking with invited guest, including Danish decision-makers, more focused.

The Addressees of Political Activism

Danish political decision-makers

Why do politicians accept the invitations from Kurdish associations to speak at their demonstrations and cultural events or meet the Kurdish associations' request to be invited into the Castle? There are of course many reasons for wanting to support Kurdish engagement in the homeland depending on the individual politician. However, among the politicians engaged in the Kurdish cause I have identified three typical actors, who engage very differently with Kurdish activists. These are: the politician who speaks at Kurdish events because he or she, as a human being and a democrat, supports the Kurdish struggle for recognition in the homeland; the politician who is an ideological ally and collaborates closely with one of the Kurdish factions; and the politician with a Kurdish background, who identifies personally with the Kurdish cause.

The supportive politician

The politician who offers support for the Kurdish struggle in the homeland by speaking at Kurdish events most often represents the left-wing and centre-left parties. Historically, these parties have pursued a domestic policy of minority inclusion and also endorsed liberation of suppressed people when it comes to foreign policy. However, the struggle for personal freedom, human rights and self-determination seems to appeal more broadly across the political spectrum. Kurdish associations have in fact occasionally been able to attract politicians representing the liberal parties and also the Danish People's Party (a national conservative party). One of the politicians, Holger K. Nielsen, Member of Parliament for the Socialist People's Party and a former Foreign Minister, explained his support with reference to the division of the Middle East in the wake of World War I. When I spoke to him, he said that 'It is a great historical injustice that the Kurds were divided and subjected to four different states', stressing that '[t]hey have the right to have a Kurdish state'. Another politician answered, when asked about his contribution to the Kurdish cause, that he intends to persuade the Kurds to pursue a political agenda as he distances himself from terror, explicitly referring to TAK and their alleged relations with the PKK. He also mentioned that his support may legitimise their political struggle in Denmark as well as in their homelands. The supporters show very strong verbal support for the struggle for recognition of Kurdish identity and autonomy and openly criticise the violation of these rights. When it comes to political action, however, the support becomes vague. This is partly due to what is perceived as a lack of Danish ability to operate independently in the Middle East, as Danish foreign policy is closely tied to the strategic interests of the US. It is also due to the complexity of Kurdish politics and the various Kurdish parties. One of the politicians confided to me that 'at one time, I gave up finding out who is who. Damn, there are many events'. For this politician it is difficult to assess the consequences of attending one event over another and endorsing one political solution over another. This position is characterised by lot of sympathy for the Kurdish cause but seems to lack will and capability to act politically.

The political ally

The Red-Green Alliance is the only political party that has explicitly adopted the Kurdish struggle and allied with specific Kurdish groups. In 2015, the party formed the Kurdistan Solidarity Group in order to 'advance the knowledge of the Kurdish struggle [. . .] and strengthen the solidarity work' (Enhedslisten. Internationalt udvalg, n.d.). Søren Søndergaard, who is a member of parliament for the Red-Green Alliance and has been involved in Kurdish solidarity work since the 1990s, is the spokesperson for the group. The party supports the Kurdish struggle in all four countries in the Middle East, even though their solidarity work with Kurds in Turkey has attracted most attention for a number of reasons. First of all, most of the Kurds in Denmark originate from Turkey, so most of the political lobbyism of the Kurdish activists in Denmark is aimed at the conditions for the Kurds in Turkey. Danish politicians also have the ability to monitor and criticise the political repression through the Council of Europe, of which Denmark and Turkey are both members. The close relationship between the Red-Green Alliance and the Kurds from Turkey dates back to the case of Kemal Koç, as one of the party members told me. In 1996, a few years after the Red-Green Alliance was formed and elected to the Danish Parliament, Kemal Koç, a Danish citizen born in Turkey and a member of FEY-KURD, was arrested on his arrival in Ankara and accused of supporting the PKK (Søndergaard 1997, p. 152). Danish politicians, particularly members of the Red-Green Alliance, engaged actively in the case, thereby putting pressure on the Turkish state to free Koç. After 42 days, Turkey dropped the case and released Koç from jail. Koç later received 450,000 DKK due to charges of torture committed by the Turkish state in a settlement between Denmark and Turkey at the European Court of Human Rights (Berlingske 2004). The case brought members of the Red-Green Alliance and Kurdish activists from the milieu surrounding FEY-KURD closer together, which laid the ground for further cooperation. This has led to a number of initiatives showing the party's willingness to take action, besides delivering supportive speeches at events organised by Kurdish associations. In relation to the Kurds in Syria, the approach has been straightforward, as the party has clearly allied with the PYD. This means that the party has embraced the Rojava revolution and aligned itself with the ideological foundation of the revolution, that is, Öcalan's conceptualisation of democratic confederalism. The party has hosted a number of meetings with PYD representatives both at public meetings and at party meetings supporting their political lobbyism. The party has also provided financial support to the PYD. In 2014, the Red-Green Alliance handed over 30,000 DKK to PYD chairman Salih Muslim on his first visit to Denmark. The money was given without conditions (Andersen 2014). The party has also adopted the armed struggle of the YPG and YPJ, which they perceive to be legitimate defence forces of the self-declared autonomous areas of northern Syria as well as crucial fighters against Islamic State. Instead of the Danish contribution to the American-led coalition against Islamic State, which the party voted against, the Red-Green Alliance has proposed to supply weapons to the YPG and YPJ. The party has also voted against the laws that ban travel and intent to travel to war zones. The party is against the laws as they criminalise joining Kurdish forces against Islamic State by failing to discriminate between the secular Kurdish forces and the forces of terrorist Islamic State. The party has also praised the actions of the PKK during the liberation of Yezidis on Mount Sinjar. This has led to renewed efforts to decriminalise the PKK by removing the organisation from the EU terrorist list (Enhedslisten 2014). Finally, the party has hosted a public meeting with Macer Gifford, a British man who fought with YPG and now travels as a spokesperson for YPG in Europe. The Kemal Koç case also led to large-scale recruitment of Kurds by the Red-Green Alliance. Today, there are a number of Kurds engaged within the party, some of whom run for district and national level elections. Over the years, this has ensured heightened attention to the Kurdish cause within the party.

The Kurdish-Danish politician

The politician with a Kurdish background is engaged in the Kurdish cause based on his or her personal background and networks. There are currently three politicians with Kurdish backgrounds in parliament. Only one has been elected, though. The others have replaced politicians on leave for different reasons. However, many Kurds are engaged at district level. I want to single out this group because the politician being a Kurd is part of a Kurdish milieu that may put expectations on him or her, which the politician may not want to disappoint. At the same time, the politician has his or her own political agenda, which may relate to non-ethnic issues and may be the reason he or she went into politics. Thus, the Kurdish politician navigates between at least two agendas: the Kurdish, which they more or less adhere to, and their own political agenda, which needs to be aligned with the comprehensive agenda of the party they belong to. When approached by one of the Kurdish factions, the Kurdish politician has to consider whether he or she will benefit from the encounter. This can restrict the involvement of the politician. It is obvious, though, that the Kurds also represent potential voters who may be more accessible to the Kurdish politician. Some of the non-Kurdish politicians I spoke to also indicated that this is an important side effect of supporting the Kurdish cause.

The transnational Kurdish community

Yet another audience, or actor, that Kurdish groups seek to reach through political activism is the transnational Kurdish community. While Danish decision-makers are the direct target of Kurdish lobbyism, the Kurdish community in Denmark, in the homeland and worldwide is an indirect target, which Kurdish activists attempt to reach by media coverage of the events on various platforms. Photos and videos are posted on social media and news updates are spread through Kurdish media in Denmark. Kurdish media outlets from the homeland are also invited to transmit the events internationally. At the big demonstration on 2 September 2017, at City Hall Square in support of the independence referendum in the Kurdistan Region of Iraq, several Kurdish media outlets from Kurdistan were present, broadcasting from the square. When I asked one of the Kurdish politicians I interviewed whom the rally addressed, he highlighted the link to the Kurds in Kurdistan, stating that '[w]e show that we support the political process in Kurdistan, right? We support the vision of President Barzani and their agenda on independence. The Kurdish people in Kurdistan must know that we support them [. . .] we show them our solidarity' (L, male, 60s). As a reward for the diaspora's commitment to the independence referendum campaign, an address by Masoud Barzani, president of the Kurdistan Region of Iraq, was read aloud at the demonstration. This shows that the engagement and activism of the diaspora are also highly valued by the Kurdish political actors in the homeland, even though the Kurds in Denmark only constitute a group of around 30,000 people.

The Kurdish actors in Denmark primarily seek to influence a Danish audience as they take advantage of being locally rooted in Danish society. Parallel to this, Kurdish groups in Germany seek to influence German decision-makers; the Kurds in Sweden address Swedish politicians, and so on. However, through their political activism, Kurdish actors also seek to maintain and renew the relations with fellow Kurds in Denmark, the Kurdish actors in the homeland and the global trans-border Kurdish community. In doing so, they form and recreate a transnational Kurdish community which acts locally and connects globally.

Kurdish Rivalry

Interaction between Kurdish actors within the diaspora

It is clear from the political lobbyism of the Kurdish diaspora related to the Kurdish struggle in Syria that the various Kurdish associations and parties pursue more or less the same path, as shown above. This entails raising awareness of the Kurdish suffering and struggle among a Danish audience and, more specifically, persuading the Danish politicians to respond to the position of the Kurds. However, it does not take more than a cursory examination of the Kurdish diaspora to realise that it is factionalised along various lines, including cultural, social and political divisions. As described in a previous chapter, two main factions have emerged in Denmark, reflecting the two main factions within the transnational Kurdish community. These are the Öcalan movement and the Kurdistan movement, which are providers of two rather different political solutions to the Kurdish struggle in general:

democratic confederalism and Kurdish independence, respectively. Likewise, when it comes to political lobbyism in support of the Kurdish struggle in Syria, the two factions lobby for two different sets of issues although, when facing a Danish audience, they both claim to speak on behalf of the Kurdish diaspora in Denmark as a whole.

Which strategies do the Kurdish factions pursue to become the most successful political lobbyists, that is, to win the battle against each other in the political arena in Denmark? In other words, how do they fine-tune their political goals in the light of events in the Syrian Kurdish struggle and vis-à-vis each other in order to gain backing? Also, which tactics do they choose in their attempt to outmanoeuvre each other? This section looks into the inner dynamics of the Kurdish diaspora, that is, the interaction between Kurdish actors within the diaspora. I will argue that the two main Kurdish diaspora groups 'engage in a fierce competition for material and symbolic resources' (Gürbüz 2016, p. 24), including access and influence in the political arena as well as recognition of their respective cause.

Political goals

For the Öcalan movement, the Syrian Civil War and the fight against Islamic State have created an unrivalled opportunity for realising the ideology of democratic confederalism. In 2012, the Syrian armed forces withdrew from the Kurdish areas to concentrate troops in the south and centre of the country. In doing so, they left a power vacuum in northern Syria. PYD and YPG filled the gap and took the first step of the Rojava revolution. During the fight against Islamic State, which began in 2014, the American-led international coalition found the Syrian Kurdish forces of YPG the most reliable ally on the Syrian front of the battle. In 2015, this led to the formation of the multi-ethnic forces, SDF, which have received heavy weapons supply and military assistance primarily from the US. All this led to the stabilisation of the Kurdish-led autonomy in northern Syria.

Unsurprisingly, the main goal of political lobbyism of the Öcalan supporters in Denmark and elsewhere in relation to Syria is support for all aspects of this political project. The focus varied from 2014 to 2018 as the challenges of upholding autonomy have changed. The battle of Kobane triggered the call for military support and humanitarian aid. The claims were raised in parliament by the Red-Green Alliance (Eltard-Sørensen 2014). Later, when the military fight of YPG gained momentum, the movement called for reconstruction of the devastated Kurdish cities and political recognition of the ongoing revolution, as per the tagline of World Kobane Day, 1 November 2016, 'Freedom and reconstruction in Kobane'. The movement has continuously argued that the Kurds are friends of the West. They are democratic and secular and pursue gender equality. The Syrian Kurds are therefore the most likely ally in the fight against the Islamic State, who conversely are perceived as fascists, totalitarian and oppressive towards women. When the Afrin crisis arose in January 2018, the main goal was to criticise Turkey and lobby the Foreign Minister into officially criticising Turkey. At this point, the lobbyism in support of the Syrian Kurds merged with the overall agenda of the Öcalan movement, namely the struggle against the oppression of the Kurds by the Turkish Republic.

For the other Kurdish parties, this strategic narrative has been difficult to counter in a Danish political context. Since 2014, Danish politicians have voted for a number of military contributions to the American-led international coalition against Islamic State, whose success relied on the contribution of Kurdish YPG and YPJ forces. Only the Red-Green Alliance has steadily opposed these contributions, but as they are the strongest advocates of the Rojava revolution, they are not the ones to criticise the PYD and the other groupings within the Öcalan movement. Small delegations of Syrian Kurdish politicians from the Kurdistan movement have approached selected politicians, but it seems that poor language skills (many of them having only recently come to Denmark) and a lack of political networks have made it hard for them to have their voices heard. Their main goal is autonomy for the Kurds within a nation state encompassing all parts of Kurdistan. Being realists of sorts, their short-term goal is Kurdish autonomy in Syria within a federal state. However, in the Syrian context, the parties of the Kurdish National Council, KNC, cooperate with the Arab opposition, which opposes any concession to the Kurds regarding the future of Syria. This is perceived as a tricky path for the other actors within the Kurdistan movement in Denmark, who have eschewed lobbying for political solutions with regard to the Syrian Kurds and instead pursued a humanitarian agenda. This was also the case when a demonstration was organised in support of the Kurds in Afrin at the beginning of 2018. The agenda was solely humanitarian. For the Kurdistan movement, the main task in this situation was to beg the big powers, the US and Russia, to intervene to avoid a humanitarian catastrophe. They did not criticise the Turkish attack on YPG positions or lament the fall of Kurdish institutions in the region as the hatred towards the PYD, YPG and the Öcalan movement is absolute. I even once heard a participant hiss praise of the Turkish attack at a demonstration. While supporting the Syrian Kurds has become a troublesome affair for the Kurdistan movement, the support of the Yezidis of Sinjar has proved to be more straightforward. Political lobbyism to raise awareness of the Yezidi genocide and urging the politicians to take action and provide aid for the female victims have thus become the main focus of the Kurdistan movement in their struggle against Islamic State. This is also thanks to the leadership of the Yezidi Cultural Association in Denmark, Komela Kultûrî a Êzîdiyan li Danîmark, who have persistently pushed for attention and meetings with the Foreign Affairs Committee. At least twice since 2014, representatives of the Yezidi Cultural Association in Denmark have succeeded in being invited by the Foreign Affairs Committee to explain the position of the Yezidis.

During the summer of 2017, the independence referendum in the Kurdistan Region of Iraq provided the Kurdistan movement with an opportunity to feel pride in having a political solution of their own to the Kurdish struggles. The Syrian Kurds as well as Kurds from other parts of Kurdistan campaigned on equal terms for the independence of Southern Kurdistan. Up until the referendum day of 25 September, social media was flooded with declarations of support and several events lobbied for support. On 2 September, a demonstration was held at the City Hall Square marking the temporary culmination of the campaign. The organisers, i.e., the Federation of Kurdish Associations in Denmark and the Platform of Kurdish Political Parties, were able to mobilise several hundred people. Later, on 17 September, a concert by the Kurdish singer Şivan Perver attracted around 1,000 guests. The concert was organised by KOMKAR-DK as a tribute to the referendum. Accordingly, a poster with the face of President Masoud Barzani supervising the concert hall adorned one of the walls. However, the failure of the referendum to yield a higher position for the Kurds within the Iraqi state has put the political agenda in support of Kurdish independence on hold in the homeland as well as among diaspora groups.

The referendum campaign also gave rise to criticism and delegitimisation by Öcalan supporters. One young activist representing the Öcalan movement told me that she valued the wish for liberation, but she did not see a nation state under the rule of Barzani as the solution. She pointed to the prerequisites of an independent state, which were currently lacking in Southern Kurdistan: political freedom, a sound economy and recognition from international society. In her opinion, the problem is the KDP, which for her stands for corruption and tribalism (H, female, 20s). In addition, the Öcalan movement had previously condemned the Barzani government for not coming to the rescue of the Yezidis in 2014. Instead, they propagate the fact that the PKK and YPG intervened and saved many Yezidis from the slaughter of Islamic State. The Kurdish opponents of the Rojava revolution whom I interviewed did not hold back their criticism either. Thus, the PYD is perceived as a branch of the PKK and a terrorist organisation, which has created a totalitarian regime in northern Syria that cooperates with Syrian rule in Damascus (X, male, 20s). Just like the two Kurdish factions try to compromise each other verbally in order to present themselves as the true representatives of the Kurdish diaspora, they also try to organise events giving the impression of being the sole representative of the Kurdish diaspora.

Tactics

As shown above, the Kurdish diaspora groups in Denmark have chosen rather traditional ways of political lobbyism. These ways include demonstrations in the public space, encounters with political actors in an attempt to persuade them to support the Kurdish cause, and becoming politicians themselves to influence the political debate from within. However, the repertoires are constantly revised and adjusted. I have identified three distinct ways by which one or the other of the two factions try to outmanoeuvre the other to claim the position of true representative of the Kurdish diaspora. These are mirroring, being first movers and hijacking.

Mirroring

Many times during my fieldwork, I felt that I was witnessing a revival or entering a parallel universe; that I was in the same place but with another group, or even experiencing the performance of more or less the same repertoire twice.

Naturally, the various Kurdish groups prefer the same locations, such as the squares, the Castle and even community centres and reception rooms, but they also seem to take inspiration from each other regarding how to conduct their lobbying. Sometimes, they seem to deliberately imitate each other or adopt the success of the other faction. Other times, similar repertoire stems from the steady adjustment of the repertoire, where the inspiration comes from different angles.

In 2016, the Kurdish Forum arranged a Newroz reception at the Castle, inviting politicians from all parties as well as Kurdish supporters. It was a big event within the Öcalan movement, even though the organisers did not reach the political goal they had set of establishing networks with political actors outside the circles of the usual collaborators as described above. The following year, the Kurdistan supporters decided to host their own reception, seemingly with the aim of imitating the success of the other faction. Thus, in 2017, both Kurdish factions arranged a Newroz reception at the Castle. One group held the reception one day; the other group held their reception another day. This time, both factions restricted the events to invited groups and guests. However, while the Öcalan supporters were able to attract politicians from all the left-wing parties – the Red-Green Alliance, the Socialist People's Party, the Social Democrats and the Alternative – the Kurdistan movement only managed to get hold of one politician: a social democrat. This politician participated in both receptions, however, and was careful to deliver the same message and give equal support to the two factions.

The mirroring also takes place in the streets. In the late summer of 2017, the City Hall Square hosted two big Kurdish events. On 2 September, the Kurdistan movement held a demonstration celebrating the upcoming referendum. Besides the expected political speeches, a number of Kurdish musicians were invited to create a festive atmosphere. The weekend before, 25–6 August, the Kurdish People's Assembly and the Kurdish Women's Association celebrated intercultural exchange at the Kurdish Culture Festival. The Festival ran for two days, presenting more than ten popular Kurdish musicians and bands. Whether intended or not, the Öcalan supporters did not let the Kurdistan supporters take over the streets from the otherwise dominant Kurdish People's Assembly. This involved preventing the Kurdistan movement from presenting itself as the true representatives of the Kurdish diaspora at a time when the referendum was making media headlines. This points to the next tactic to be explained: being first movers.

Being first movers

Another way to dominate the political arena is to be first movers. This includes being the best organised group and securing the most desirable square. As mentioned earlier, the various Kurdish associations consider the City Hall Square the best and most attractive square in Copenhagen when it comes to attracting public attention. In addition, the closeness to City Hall adds political value to the square. In 2015 and 2016, the Federation of Kurdish Associations in Denmark held their Newroz celebrations on the square. In 2015, the year after the emergence of Islamic State, the association was able to attract top politicians from across the political spectrum. Among these were the then Foreign Minister, Martin Lidegaard, from the Danish Social Liberal Party, the previous Foreign Minister, Holger K. Nielsen, from the Socialist People's Party, and Bertel Haarder, who is the longest-serving Danish minister in modern times, from the Liberal Party. However, since Newroz 2017, the Öcalan supporters have been able to take over the square and relegate the other faction to minor squares in the centre of the city. According to employees at the municipal administration of 'urban life', who process the booking applications for public spaces, spaces are granted on the basis of first in, first served. Only on rare occasions will they transfer an already booked group to another place to accommodate a later applicant. This means that strategic planning in advance pays off. The pay-off in this case should primarily be ascribed to the well organised youth association, FOKUS-A, which is responsible for drawing up the annual event plan of the Kurdish People's Assembly.

Hijacking

While mirroring and being first movers are abstract ways of interacting, 'hijacking' requires being present in the same physical space. By hijacking, in connection with political lobbying, I refer to the actions carried out by one group in order to take over the control of an event organised by another group. On 24 January 2018, when the Turkish state had launched its attack on Afrin, the Syrian Kurds within the Kurdistan movement held a demonstration in front of the American and Russian embassies. The group appealed for help from the American and Russian leaders to stop the humanitarian catastrophe. One poster read 'We condemn the attack of the Turkish forces against the Kurdish city Afrin in Syria'. The demonstrators, around fifty people, shouted 'bijî Kurdistan' and 'bijî Afrin', meaning 'long live Kurdistan' and 'long live Afrin'. However, some of the young male attendees then tried to drown the cries by shouting 'bijî berxwedana YPG' (long live the resistance of YPG) even louder. Reacting to this, the organisers then made attempts to overdo it by shouting 'yeke, yeke, yeke, gele Kurd yeke' ('unity, unity, unity, the Kurdish people is united'). Among the Kurdish flags, I also saw a YPG flag, waved above all the other flags. To justify the presence of the rival flag, one of the organisers said, 'it is ok, when there is only one' (J, female, 40s). However, there was more than one. The shouting battle continued for some time, leaving the impression on the accidental passer-by that the demonstration was, at least partly, in support of the YPG.

The same battle was played out at the demonstration at the Christiansborg Palace Square on 8 August 2014, described at the beginning of this chapter. What looked like a unified Kurdish diaspora event in support of the Yezidis on Mount Sinjar can also be seen as an attempt to hijack the event. In defiance of the instructions from the Yezidi Cultural Association, who organised the event, that only the Kurdish flag should be brought to the demonstration, Öcalan supporters waved the flags of PYD, YPG and Rojava, flags with Öcalan pictures and posters with photos of YPG martyrs. This was perceived as an attempt to claim the event. As one of the participants told me, they became even more frustrated when the flags were placed strategically behind politicians just as they were about to be interviewed by Danish media. This turned the demonstration into a politicised event, which the organisers had tried to avoid in order to focus on the humanitarian catastrophe of the Yezidis.

How to dominate

In the competition for prestige and legitimacy, the two Kurdish factions become rivals trying to outmanoeuvre each other by various means (Gürbüz 2016). First, they pursue different political goals. In doing so, they carve out a niche regarding the events in the homeland that reflects their overall ideological position. While the Öcalan movement promotes the political solution of the Rojava revolution and all that it brings, the Kurdistan movement has primarily chosen to be the humanitarian advocates for the suffering Kurds (niche-building). Second, they both present themselves as morally superior, either by depicting the other as terrorists and totalitarians or as corrupt and led by tribalism (strategic subversion). Third, they try to imitate each other's repertoire when it proves successful (resemblance). Being first movers and hijacking events, the Öcalan supporters also seek to take over the political arena by combining all three means at the same time. On these occasions, they enter the scene like a Dostoyevskyan doppelgänger by resembling the other group (similar repertoire) but posing as another and better version of the Kurdish activist (presenting their alternative flags and slogans). By acting as the hegemonic Kurdish player, they present themselves as the true version of Kurdish diaspora (subversion). The domination of the Öcalan movement in the Square and their easier access to the Castle obviously may cause frustration among members of the Kurdistan movement.

Compared with the Kurdish interaction in earlier days, the Kurdish diaspora groups have moved from being enemies to being rivals. In the 1980s and 1990s, a number of murders were committed in Germany and Sweden by PKK supporters, aimed at eliminating political enemies (Baser 2015, p. 136 and p. 155). In Denmark, one murder has been ascribed to the conflict (Serinci 2015, November 4). In the current Danish political arena, the Kurdish diaspora groups interact as rivals targeting the same resources of prestige and legitimacy. However, the Turkish attack on Afrin has revealed a deeper enmity between the two Kurdish movements, since one group claims that the other group is contributing to the suffering of the Kurds in Afrin. Conversely, the other group perceives the first group as obstructive to the democratic revolution and as henchmen of the Turkish regime.

The Success of Kurdish Lobbyism

Ambiguous recognition

Kurdish lobbyism seems to reach only a certain level of success in terms of achieving its goals, that is, access to the political arena and ability to influence the decision-makers as well as the public. This is mainly due to the ambiguous embrace of the Kurdish cause by both Danish authorities and the general public. As I have argued, access to the public space seems unrestricted. Due to freedom of assembly and the strategy on urban life, the Copenhagen municipal authorities embrace Kurdish activism in the public space. The municipality is even rebuilding the city squares to be able to host lively demonstrations of various kinds. In line with this, the applications submitted by Kurdish actors for permits to stage demonstrations in support of the Kurdish cause have always been approved. In contrast, the access to the Castle – the ability to reach the politicians directly – is restricted, as the politicians inside the Castle need to perceive the Kurdish activists as reliable representatives in order invite them. When major events take place in the Middle East, and public attention is captured, restrictions are relaxed, though, and Kurdish activists are invited to meet politicians or to speak to the Foreign Affairs Committee. However, access is only the first step towards successful lobbying. The next step is the ability to pressure the decision-makers to take action in support of the Kurdish cause. While the public have shuttled between great dedication and ignorance, politicians have offered limited support regardless of whether it is support for the Rojava revolution, Yezidi survivors or the independence referendum in Iraqi Kurdistan. The Kurdish cause has wide appeal, but at the same time, few politicians are willing to act on it and propose bills that offer financial, military or political support for the Kurds. The situation has become even more complicated after Turkish-backed rebels captured the Kurdish region of Afrin. While every politician denounced Islamic State, which the Kurdish forces have fought against since Kobane, the Danish government did not explicitly criticise Turkey at the time of the attack on Afrin, leaving the Syrian Kurds without even moral support in a very critical situation. This ambiguous recognition of the Kurdish cause has had a huge impact on the (mixed) success of the Kurdish lobbyism in support of the Kurds in Syria.

Determinants of success

However, the rivalry between the two main Kurdish movements in Denmark and the domination of the Öcalan movement suggest that some determinants of success are identifiable. First, having allies among Danish decision-makers is of utmost importance. Political allies can ease the access to other political actors within the Castle, such as the Foreign Affairs Committee. Within the Castle, they can advocate for the Kurdish cause in parliament when passing bills and in front of the government at times of crisis. By attending Kurdish political events, political allies will also legitimise the Kurdish cause for supporters among Danes as well as Kurds. Second, having a strong message that appeals to young activists, which makes mass recruitment for demonstrations possible, is also a determining factor. Numbers are crucial to putting pressure on the politicians, as the number and visibility of the demonstrators seem to be perceived as equal to the strength of the group. Numbers are also crucial to be able to hijack an event organised by a rival group. Third, being well organised and persistent, i.e., having loyal and dedicated followers who are willing to be first movers and who will repeatedly organise or attend the political events, will also make the organisation succeed compared with other less organised groups. This also points to the fourth determining factor: transnational linking. The transnational network will provide the group with campaigns and repertoires that only need to be realised in a Danish setting, leaving strategic considerations to the stronger mother organisations.

Becoming an activist, becoming a Kurd

What is the impact of Kurdish political lobbyism on being a Kurd in Denmark? Becoming a Kurd is an identification process that can be analysed at various levels (Jenkins 1994). In the following, I want to examine how Kurdish identity is formed at the individual level and at the in-group level. The recognition by non-Kurdish actors is touched upon above.

At the individual level, identification as a Kurd is related to the desire for political action; being a Kurd means reacting to the call from the Kurdish people in need by going to the Square or to the Castle. When one of the Kurdish activists reflected on the question of why she demonstrates when the outcome is poor, she answered that she would otherwise feel powerless (H, female, 20s). By acting and becoming an activist, she attains a voice and becomes someone. By acting in support of the Kurdish cause, she becomes a Kurd. Another of my interviewees also emphasised that being a Kurd implies supporting the suffering Kurds in the homeland. He stressed that the will to take action 'is in our blood' (R, male, 40s), which logically implies that if an individual desists from acting, he or she will not be considered a true Kurd.

At the in-group level, the individual's fight to make the Kurdish voice heard is confirmed and encouraged by other group members and by the collective framing of how the individual should act to become a true Kurd. The individuals' negotiation of goals and means is thus what brings a Kurdish 'we' into being (Melucci 1989, p. 26). The Kurdish collective identity relies on a widespread presumption that a Kurd is one who opposes injustice and fights repression by making his or her voice heard. Within the Öcalan movement, Öcalan is presented as the role model for the Kurdish activist proclaiming that 'Abdullah Öcalan is fighting in jail. You must also fight'. In the same way, the myth about Kawa the Blacksmith is recounted at Newroz to remind the Kurds that they must fight for their freedom as Kawa fought against tyranny in ancient times. For members of the Öcalan movement, fighting encompasses both military and political fight. However, according to the division of labour, diaspora members undertake political lobbying, while the Kurds in the homeland pursue military goals; the call to fight for the diasporic members is thus considered a call to political activism. The political struggle is also a core element of the Kurdistan movement, and the rivalry between the two movements is primarily related to who is representing the Kurdish diaspora in the political arena vis-à-vis the public and vis-à-vis the political decision-makers.

The political activism of the Kurds in Denmark is also acknowledged by the transnational Kurdish community. Leading members of Kurdish political parties and organisations visit Denmark from time to time to participate in public meetings and panel debates organised by Kurdish diaspora groups. Their presence infuses Kurdish diaspora members with the spirit to fight and encourages them to continue their struggle. At every Kurdish event, Kurdish activists post photos and films on social media to document what is going on in the diaspora and thereby to secure a position as political fighters within the transnational Kurdish community.

A constituent characteristic of the Kurdish diaspora is memories of the homeland. As I have pointed out in the chapter on the theoretical framework, these memories are prosthetic memories (Landsberg 2004), meaning they are collective memories which may or may not represent genuine experience from the homeland. When conflict unfolds in the homeland, as we saw during the battle of Kobane, the transnational ties are strengthened by direct interaction between diaspora and homeland political actors. Salih Muslim has visited Denmark a number of times since 2014, as have other Kurdish political actors from Syria, to appeal for support for the political and military struggle. Likewise, Kurds from Denmark have travelled to

Rojava to participate in political developments there. These encounters are of great importance as they fuel the Kurdish diaspora identity by renewing the memory of home. For the Kurds who do not originate from Syria, the battle of Kobane and the encounters with representatives of the Syrian Kurds has spurred what I call an alter-territorial identification with the Kurdish homeland. This alter-territorial identification with the Syrian part of Kurdistan is based partly on de-territorial solidarity with the transnational Kurdish community and partly on re-orientation towards the homeland as a concrete place, however, a different part of Kurdistan from the area from which they originate. In similar ways, Kurds who do not originate from the Iraqi part of Kurdistan, identify alter-territorially with the Kurdistan Region of Iraq. Strong political visions of the Rojava revolution and of an independent Kurdistan in northern Iraq are shared among diasporic Kurds. This suggests that in most cases the alter-territorial identifications with Rojava and the Kurdistan Region of Iraq are based on political mobilisation. For the Öcalan movement, the battle of Kobane has also been an opportunity to identify as something new. The Kurdish identity has transformed the perception of the role of Kurdish people from that of fighters to conquerors of tyranny. Even though opponents of the Öcalan movement refuse to accept the framing of the victory at Kobane as a victory of the democratic revolution, the battle of Kobane inspired pride in almost all Kurds, regardless of political convictions.

7

THE COURTROOM: LEGAL STRUGGLE
FOR MILITARY SUPPORT

Introduction

No political prisoners in Denmark

On 8 June 2016, ten Kurdish men went on trial at the High Court of Eastern Denmark charged with supporting terrorism. They were accused of collecting money and handing it over to the PKK by donating money to ROJ TV. The ten men were found not guilty by the City Court of Copenhagen, but the prosecutor decided to appeal the case to the High Court. On 8 June, the litigation was coming to an end and the verdict was about to be announced. In front of the court, a demonstration had gathered to condemn the litigation under the slogan 'no political prisoners in Denmark'. The slogan pointed to the alleged relationship between the charges against the ten Kurds (and prior to that, the charges against ROJ TV) and the appointment of former Danish Prime Minister Anders Fogh Rasmussen as Secretary General of NATO. Turkey objected to the appointment of Anders Fogh Rasmussen because Denmark hosted the Kurdish broadcasting media ROJ TV, which Turkey considered a mouthpiece of the PKK. In order to sway Turkey, Danish representatives seemingly pledged 'to intensify efforts against ROJ TV' (Embassy Copenhagen 2006, May 26). Following Anders Fogh Rasmussen's appointment, ROJ TV was charged with terrorism, as were the ten Kurdish men. The demonstration was arranged partly by FEY-KURD and was announced on social media. Around fifty people showed up to support the Kurds and listen to the speeches by members of Parliament from the Red-Green Alliance, Kurdish district politicians, Danish supporters of Kurdish Forum and some of the defence lawyers. In court, the defence lawyers had tried to prove that the PKK was not a terror organisation, and that the accused individuals were unaware they were acting illegally. They failed to do so for two of the accused, who received suspended sentences due to the passing of time since the crime was committed.

The Kurdish supporters of Öcalan were dragged into the courtroom and became courtroom activists by necessity rather than choice. Despite their reluctance to reveal their agendas and strategies in court, they chose to take advantage of the situation and turned it into a political platform by addressing the injustice committed against the Kurds in Denmark as well as in Turkey.

Kurdish activism in the judicial arena

The aim of this chapter is to analyse Kurdish courtroom activism in relation to the ongoing conflicts in Syria and Iraq. The courtroom is an important arena to study for a number of reasons. It is important in the study of Kurdish diaspora activism as the courtroom is a place where the state seeks to subjugate the Kurds to the will and interests of the state. While the Kurds have the freedom to decide what cultural activities to engage in as well as the capacity to influence the political agenda to some degree (investigated in the previous chapters), they are reluctantly dragged into the legal arena where the state determines the rules, established through decades of political negotiations.

The courtroom arena is also important to study as the courtroom is where the boundaries of legal and illegal practices are determined. The verdict will establish the future framework for the assessment of legal opportunities and constraints and will thus have *direct* consequences for further activities and choice of tactics. The verdict will also have *indirect* consequences (Boutcher 2011, p. 178) as the courtroom provides the Kurds with a rostrum from which they can promote their cause to a wider public audience. The legal setting will ensure that the message that justice has prevailed – or injustice has occurred – is conveyed clearly and easily. Litigation can thus potentially become a mobilising event.

The chapter will present a study of the passport case against Joanna Palani, which also led to a criminal case against her. A number of fighters from Denmark have had their passports confiscated as a result of the revision of the Passport Act in March 2015. The revisions grant the police the authority to confiscate a passport and issue a travel ban if they suspect the person will travel abroad and participate in activities that may pose a threat to national security. However, only one of the people who has had their passport confiscated is Kurdish and thus relevant to this study of Kurdish activism in support of the Kurdish cause in Syria. Her name is Joanna Palani. She is a Danish citizen, born in Iraq to Kurdish parents from Iran, and was 22 years old in 2015, when her passport was confiscated. Besides being the only case of a Kurdish individual being accused of joining Kurdish forces, her case is important for a number of reasons. First, her case appears to be a test case as she is the first supporter of the YPG/J to have her passport confiscation tested in court. Second, she is a representative of the Kurdish female fighters, who have been praised by a variety of actors for their bravery and dedication. Third, she is a public figure, who was interviewed by Danish media several times before leaving Denmark to fight Islamic State and has thus contributed to the stories of Kurdish military activism. Her case will be analysed as a single case study but will also uncover the challenges of the Kurdish transnational activism in support of the Kurdish homeland in general. The Kurdish actors face a number of other actors with unique agendas that they have to cope with. The strategies of these actors will be included in the analysis.

In the following, I will provide a conceptual framework for analysing courtroom activism in line with the social movement theory perspective outlined in the theoretical chapter. Then, I will analyse the case by looking at both the direct and indirect consequences of the verdict.

The literature on courts and social movements has mainly tried to answer two essential questions, namely, what is the outcome of taking a case to court, and why do social movements choose litigation as a strategy? While the first question was raised by early research in the field, the second question dominates more recent research. In the following sketch of the research on social movement and legal strategies, I draw on categorisations by Steven A. Boutcher (2013), Siri Gloppen (2013) and Chris Hilson (2013).

The early research on social movements and litigation was conducted in the law and society tradition by scholars who studied various aspects of law across multiple social contexts. They studied the social and political goals of social movements, whether related to civil rights, women's rights or legalisation of homosexuality, and thus their ability to bring about social change (Boutcher 2013). The main question was whether social movements succeed in bringing about social change by choosing litigation as a strategy. In general, early scholarship on social movements and law was sceptical about the role of litigation in pushing the boundaries of legal behaviour. Thus, the reference article on the topic asked 'Why the "haves" come out ahead' (Galanter 1974). Other researchers suggested that court-centred activism legitimises the system (Scheingold 2004), and that court victories are 'hollow hopes' bringing no real change (Rosenberg 1991).

More recent research on courts and social movement draws explicitly on social movement theory, focusing on mobilisation processes rather than the outcome of litigation. Thus, the main question has become 'How, when and why do social movements decide to use the court as a strategy for pursuing their goals?' (Gloppen 2013). This points to core explanations by social movement theory, such as political opportunity structures and resource mobilisation. When litigation became recognised as a distinct strategy along with political strategies, the concept of legal opportunity structure was introduced to explain why social movements choose litigation (Hilson 2002). Other studies have argued that there is no simple correlation between legal opportunities and choosing litigation. Litigation may in fact be perceived as the best strategy if political mobilisation has failed, even if litigation seems unfavourable in itself (Gloppen 2013). Some studies focus on the indirect consequences, meaning that litigation becomes an opportunity for political and social mobilisation (McCann 1994), as it may attract attention from interest groups and policy makers as well as the general public. Even defeat in court may be translated into mobilisation (Boutcher 2011), with some movements 'Winning Through Losing' (NeJaime 2011).

Most of the literature on social movements and litigation focuses on litigation as an active strategy, but some research distinguishes between *proactive* and *reactive* litigation strategies (Harlow and Rawlings 1992; Vanhala 2009). While the proactive strategy describes situations where a group seeks to *take* their cause to court, the reactive strategy includes situations where a group will undertake acts of civil obedience in order to *be taken* to court. By choosing a reactive strategy, the group hope that the court will bring justice by overriding unjust legislation (Vanhala 2009, p. 741), or they may seek prosecution in court to mobilise politically by exposing an unjust system (Doherty and Hayes 2012, pp. 7–8). While the former addresses the direct consequences of courtroom action, the latter relates to the indirect consequences.

I aim to go beyond imprecise questions of whether social movements will succeed in court, and which strategies the legal opportunity structures result in. Drawing on strategic interactionism, the first part of the analysis will focus on the interaction in the courtroom arena between the two main players, Joanna Palani and her defence on the one hand, and the prosecution authorities on the other. It will also look at how they negotiate the legal boundaries for military activism in support of the Kurds in Syria. Focusing on courtroom interactions, I will also investigate how the prosecuted adapt tactically to the choices available in this specific and very formal setting (Doherty and Hayes 2015, p. 29). Thus, I will investigate the goals and arguments of the two players and analyse the direct outcome of the negotiation. However, courtroom interactions do not take place in a vacuum but are related both to activities in the battlefield in Syria and political negotiations in parliament. While Joanna Palani's courtroom activism is a continuation of her actions in the military arena, the legal basis of her case is the product of negotiations in the political arena. The reasoning behind her military activism and the legal amendments will also be included in the analysis. The second part of the analysis will focus on the indirect outcome of the litigation, namely Joanna Palani's attempts to mobilise support, since the verdict was not in her favour. I have identified three main players whose interventions, albeit ambiguous, form the outcome of the mobilisation: the politicians (once again), the Kurdish diaspora and the public.

This analysis will also contribute to the analytical process of 'Breaking Down [of] the State' called for by Jan W. Duyvendak and James M. Jasper, as in the title of their second edited volume (Duyvendak and Jasper 2015). Accordingly, the state will be perceived as a web of sub-players who interact and negotiate with other actors using different strategies in different arenas (Jasper 2015, p. 11).

Military Activism

Fighters from Denmark joining Kurdish forces: An overview

Since the police was given the authority to seize passports and impose a travel ban, at least six Danish citizens have had their passports confiscated on suspicion that they would travel to Syria or Iraq to join the Kurdish fight against Islamic State. Three of them have taken the police decision to court: Joanna Palani, of Iranian-Kurdish background, and Martin of Danish background as well as Anne Dalum of Danish background. Joanna Palani fought in both Syria and Iraqi Kurdistan, while Martin, or 'Martin from Esbjerg', as the media named him, fought with Peshmerga in Iraqi Kurdistan. Anne Dalum planned to join the Internationalist Commune of Rojava, but had her passport confiscated before leaving. Tommy Mørck, one of the remaining three, who all have Danish backgrounds, was also charged with a criminal case. In February 2018, the prosecution authorities filed charges against him for fighting with YPG in Syria. The remaining two, who are young men with some military training from the Danish armed forces, had their passports confiscated as they allegedly were about to leave the country to join YPG against Islamic State (Jensen and Sørensen 2015; Saxtorph-Poulsen and Underbjerg 2017).

Like Tommy Mørck, another young man, Aske Barfod Sivesgaard, faced a criminal lawsuit for fighting alongside YPG. Thus, in 2019, he was charged with travelling to the war zone in Syria. The very first man with a Danish background to leave Denmark to fight with YPG was Jørgen Nicolai. As he left in 2014 before the passport law was amended, he evaded legal prosecution (Eskesen 2015).

Joanna Palani is the only Kurd fighting for the Kurdish cause who has had her passport confiscated. A number of other Kurds interviewed by Danish media joined the Kurdish fight against Islamic State (Serinci 2015, pp. 129–30; Vittus 2016) without having their passports confiscated. Almost all of them joined the Peshmerga Forces in Iraqi Kurdistan. Some were even experienced fighters from the Kurdish struggle, having fought with the Peshmergas before leaving Kurdistan in the 1980s and 1990s. Only one other Danish citizen with Kurdish background has openly talked to Danish media about his fight with the YPG in Syria. That is Ari, who was interviewed while fighting with YPG and SDF in Raqqa to overthrow Islamic State (Damsgård 2017). It is likely that there are a number of Kurdish foreign fighters unknown to the public, as planning and carrying out military activism in Syria and Iraq could have legal consequences after the new laws were introduced. In 2016, *Jyllands-Posten*, a Danish newspaper, estimated that 20 to 25 Kurds have left Denmark to fight in Iraq or Syria with Peshmerga Forces or YPG or the PKK (Serinci 2016). This number may be higher as the fight against Islamic State has continued since then, including the battles for Mosul and Raqqa. Both cities were recaptured from Islamic State in 2017, Mosul in July and Raqqa in October. In addition, the fight against Turkish and Turkish-backed forces in Afrin and northeastern Syria has taken place since 2018. However, the Peshmerga forces of the Kurdistan Region have renounced foreign fighters, as inexperienced fighters are difficult to incorporate into the professional ranks. The recruitment of volunteers for YPG and YPJ has also been abandoned to avoid provoking European partners, since many European countries have criminalised volunteering for Kurdish military actors as well as Islamic State and others.

It should be mentioned that a relatively high number of Kurds from Denmark have joined Islamic State and other Islamist and Salafist groups. In January 2018, the Center for Terror Analysis (CTA), which is a research unit within the Danish Security and Intelligence Service (PET), estimated that since 2012, at least 150 fighters have left Denmark to join different Islamist groups in Syria and Iraq (The Center for Terror Analysis 2018, p. 5). Most of them are men, but an increasing number of women have followed suit. Among the 150 foreign fighters from Denmark, 20 to 26 are Kurds who have joined Islamic State (Serinci and Villemoes 2017). Thus, the Kurds constitute the biggest group among the Islamist fighters according to ethnic background – around 15 per cent. The majority of them originate from the Konya province in central Turkey, which has also coincidentally produced a disproportionate number of Kurds among Turkey's jihadi foreign fighters (Necef 2018, p. 7). Among the Kurds from Iraq who have joined Islamic State, eighty are from Halabja alone (Eliassi 2018). Women are also represented among the Kurds who travelled from Denmark to join Islamic State. In 2016, the story about two Kurdish sisters from Turkey, who left Denmark together to join Islamic State, reached the media as the father asked for help in finding them (Moestrup and Vesterlund 2017). In early 2020, he allegedly succeeded in bringing them out of Syria (Vesterlund 2020). Like other Islamic State supporters, some of the Kurdish fighters have been killed or have disappeared, and some have returned to Denmark. Some of them have been taken to court. In 2017, Hamza Cakan, also a Kurd from Turkey formerly known as Enes Ciftci, was sentenced by the Supreme Court to six years in prison, deportation and revocation of his Danish citizenship (Ritzau 2017). Revocation of citizenship is possible if the convicted has dual citizenship. In this case, he was Danish and Turkish. To date this has been the harshest sentence in Denmark imposed on a foreign fighter supporting Islamic State. He was convicted of joining Islamic State twice and of attempts to support the organisation financially. He was also convicted of condoning the terror attack by Omar el-Hussein, who killed two people in Copenhagen in February 2015 (The Supreme Court 2017). One person was shot at Krudttønden, which hosted a debate event on 'Art, Blasphemy and Freedom of Speech', and the other, a security guard, was shot in front of the Great Synagogue in Copenhagen.

This shows that the identity of migrants with a Kurdish background, especially from Turkey, is very diverse. Some feel strongly connected to their ethnic background, while others identify more closely with their religious identity, whether Muslim, Alevi or Yezidi. However, identifying with military actions committed by Islamic State would be considered an act of extremism. To understand this, individual factors need to be considered, such as an individual's experience with violence as well as how appealing anti-Western countercultures seem to the person (Crone 2016). The same factors may apply to fighters joining Kurdish forces. I will recapitulate on their motivation later.

It is interesting that the estimated number of Kurdish fighters for Islamic State corresponds almost exactly to the estimated number of Kurdish fighters against Islamic State. Likewise, the explanations of the fighters for the Kurdish cause resonate with those of the fighters for Islamic State: our brothers are threatened; someone needs to sacrifice themselves to save others; I am part of the creation of a new society (Sheikh 2015).

What do they fight for?

So how do the Kurds from Denmark interpret and assess the situation in the Kurdish areas to legitimise their military activism? In other words, what do they fight for?

First of all, the decision to take up arms is a reaction to the atrocities committed against 'my people'. Military activism is thus in line with other forms of Kurdish diasporic activism motivated by the suffering of the Kurdish people, either because of family connections or identification with the Kurdish collective or both. What differentiates military activism from other forms of Kurdish activism is the type of action chosen. For some Kurds, it is imperative to take up armed resistance against the cruel and violent Islamic State as it is perceived an existential threat to the Kurdish communities.

The conquest by Islamic State of large areas of Iraq, including the major city of Mosul, during the summer of 2014 mobilised both young and elderly Kurdish men from abroad to take up arms, join the Peshmergas and defend their people just as their fathers or uncles had done before them. One of them, Shaho Pirani, a father of two, has repeatedly been interviewed by Danish media and also participated in a documentary about Kurdish military resistance in Iran (Kanal 5, 4 Nov 2015). In 2014, then 30 years old, he told the Kurdish media network *Rudaw* 'If ISIS wins, we lose everything. As soon as the Kurds need my support, I'll be there for my people'. His declaration was supported by another young Danish Kurd, who stated that 'My ancestors have given their blood for us, so we could have Kurdish autonomy. I will not just watch ISIS come and take it all' (Serinci 2014).

For the Kurds fighting for the Peshmergas, military activism is also an act of propagating Kurdish autonomy in the Kurdistan Region of Iraq. Alan Gredar, 47 years old and living in Copenhagen with his wife and three children, stresses the importance of 'signal[ing] to both IS and the Western world that we are ready to protect what we have created in the Kurdish part of Iraq' (Vittus 2016).

For the Danish Kurds joining the YPG and YPJ at the Syrian front of the battle against Islamic State, the battle of Kobane during the winter of 2014–15 was the defining movement. Even though the battle of Kobane became a widely supported event among various Kurdish groups, it mobilised fighters mostly for the YPG and YPJ. Like the Peshmergas, the YPG and YPJ fighters pursue an agenda of fighting both against the inhumane Islamic forces and for a Kurdish alternative. Ari Hussein, a 23-year-old Danish Kurd with family in Qamishlo, was interviewed while fighting at the front in Raqqa. He highlighted the necessity of fighting against Islamic State, arguing that he 'went to Syria to liberate people from IS, which is a crazy death cult killing and suppressing civilians. Think about what happened to the women who have been used as sex slaves'. He further believes that 'Death and destruction do not lead to anything good. But it has come so far that we have to do it. It's pure desperation' (Damsgård 2017). The necessity of countering the military actions of Islamic State was also emphasised by Joanna Palani in an early interview after her first trip to the front. She stated that '[i]t feels good to save lives. I just wish that it was not necessary to do it this way' (Bendtsen and Sørensen 2015).

Joanna Palani was first interviewed in the autumn of 2014 and has since talked to different Danish as well as international media about the need to fight Islamic State and why she felt obliged to join the fight. For her, as for the other Kurdish fighters, political activism was not enough. She had to act militarily to protect the civilian Kurds in Kobane. In addition to wanting to support the Kurdish fight against Islamic State, she sees herself in a larger war in the Middle East promoting Western values, including women's rights and democracy (Skjoldager 2014). In this way, she inscribes herself in the narrative of the democratic revolution in Rojava, the Kurdish region in Syria, which she has more and more explicitly dedicated herself to. At a film and debate event in February of 2018, she was invited to talk about female fighters based on her experiences of fighting with Kurdish forces against Islamic State. Wearing a YPJ uniform, she elaborated on the ideas of jineology, the Kurdish version of women's liberation developed by Abdullah Öcalan and one of the pillars of the revolution. Referring to the concept of womanism by Alice Walker, a black American writer and women's activist, she underscored that jineology starts with Kurdish women's liberation and that it will spread from there. In line with this, Joanna Palani argued that jineology is different from feminism as jineology is intertwined with a broader social and political revolution. Denouncing Western ideals of female beauty, such as wearing makeup and having cosmetic surgery, she has now dedicated herself to the Kurdish women's rebellion prescribed by Abdullah Öcalan. 'That is my radicalisation', she said. By doing so, she points to not only the Kurdish fighters as the West's secular and democratic ally in the fight against a totalitarian Islamic State but also the uniqueness of the Rojava revolution.

The non-Kurdish international fighters use the same three basic explanations as the Kurdish fighters when wanting to join the Kurdish military fight against Islamic State: personal relations, moral condemnation of the atrocities committed by Islamic State, and ideological support for Kurdish autonomy in either Iraq or Syria. This applies to Danish fighters as well as other Western volunteers.

A number of ethnic Danes have joined Kurdish forces. The first Dane volunteering for the Kurdish fight against Islamic State was Jørgen Nicolai, who, besides being interviewed by Danish media, also wrote a book about his experiences. The title of the book is *Heval*, which means comrade in Kurdish (Nicolai 2015). He explains that he was primarily motivated by anger, having witnessed the atrocities committed against civilians, but also by moral considerations. He felt guilty about doing nothing (Nicolai 2015, p. 31). Having worked as a development worker in Aleppo at the beginning of the 2000s, he had friends whose lives were directly affected by Islamic State. He tried to join the Peshmerga in Iraq, but ended up with YPG. Martin from Esbjerg, as he was called in the media, was another Dane who joined the Kurds fighting IS. He was 30 years old when he left Denmark in 2015 to fight with the Peshmerga in Iraqi Kurdistan. He, too, became enraged when watching reports of rape, killing and tyranny against children, women and men and decided to take action as he was still 'young and strong' (Lindhardt et al. 2016). Yet another Dane, who represents the growing group of international revolutionaries joining YPG and YPJ for ideological reasons, is Tommy Mørck, who has spoken very openly about his experiences of fighting with the Syrian Kurds in the spring of 2017. He left Denmark in order to participate in the revolution either as a civilian or as a fighter. He was not necessarily seeking the battlefield but would be willing to fight if asked to. What fascinated him the most about the Kurds in Rojava was their ability to create a new society based on radical democracy while fighting was going on (Staghøj 2017).

All of the fighters from Denmark, Kurds as well as Danes, have returned to Denmark after weeks or months of fighting. Although they claim to be willing to sacrifice their life for the cause, apparently none of the fighters from Denmark have so far paid the ultimate price of losing his or her life in combat.

The volunteers face legal repercussions, though, as Danish politicians have tightened the rules and regulations on travelling abroad to fight alongside other military forces or militias. Many of them give this some thought before leaving Denmark, but the feeling of urgency dissolves their concerns. This applies primarily to the fighters joining YPG/J as the case against 'Martin from Esbjerg' proved that fighting for the Peshmerga is not sufficient reason to have the passport confiscated (see below). However, even before the laws were implemented, the fighters joining YPG and YPJ were aware of the terrorist label on the PKK, and that this may affect the evaluation of their activities as YPG and YPJ fighters in a Danish legal setting. In 2014, Joanna Palani stressed that '[i]f I choose to travel to fight and later am charged with terrorism [. . .] I have to accept this' (Skjoldager 2014). Apart from being willing to speak to the media, she follows the tradition of other young Kurds living in Europe, mainly from Germany and France, who since the 1980s have joined the ranks of the PKK in Turkey. It is of course difficult to assess precisely how many Kurds from Europe have joined the PKK. The German police have estimated that the vast majority of the 1,800–2,000 Kurdish children and teenagers who have died since the 1990s while fighting for the PKK against the Turkish state came from Germany (Eccarius-Kelly 2011, pp. 178–9). Likewise, it is evident that clandestine activities related to military support for YPG in Syria occur, just as the support for the PKK has existed through the years. This also suggests that Kurdish activists seen at a number of PYD events in Copenhagen wearing military uniform are experienced YPG fighters.

The majority of Kurdish fighters and international volunteers do not readily accept the legal charges they are faced with after returning to Denmark. According to Joanna Palani and others who have had their passports confiscated due to their connections with Kurdish militias, it should not be illegal to fight alongside the forces that cooperate with the Danish defence and the international coalition against Islamic State. By questioning this allegedly unjust system and legally challenging the administrative confiscation of their passport, the fighters become courtroom activists. They could have accepted the police decision, as they said they would. Instead, they have chosen a form of proactive strategy to override the indiscriminate application of the law, which treats fighters against Islamic State in the same way as fighters for Islamic State and other jihadi groups. Since Joanna Palani's legal defence failed to prove that her travel activities were legal, Palani and her defence lawyers tried to mobilise the public as well as the Kurdish diaspora milieu, which has not yet, however, adopted her case. Joanna Palani and her defence are thus aiming for direct as well as indirect consequences. In the following, I will go through her cases and the laws they are based on. Later, I will look at her attempts to broaden courtroom activism by investigating the public support for her situation and the lack of support from the Kurdish diaspora.

Courtroom Activism

The cases against Joanna Palani

The first time I saw Joanna Palani was in January 2016 at a public meeting in Copenhagen with Salih Muslim, then co-chair of PYD. She attended the meeting as one of around 300 guests, who showed up to listen to the speeches of Salih Muslim and Nikolaj Villumsen from the Red-Green Alliance. Salih Muslim was invited by PYD Denmark and FEY-KURD to discuss the latest developments in Rojava. The last time I saw her was at the debate event on female fighters in February 2018. In the meantime, she had lost three cases at the City Court of Copenhagen, two related to the administrative confiscation of her passport and one to her alleged violation of the travel ban.

The first of the three cases relates to her passport confiscation and travel ban. On 29 September 2015, the police decided to confiscate Joanna Palani's passport and impose a one-year travel ban on her. Based on her interviews with Danish media, the police claimed that she intended to leave Denmark again in order to travel to conflict zones in Syria. They also argued that if she was to leave again, she would receive further military training and thus become a security threat to Denmark and other states as well as to public order (The City Court of Copenhagen 2016). Taking the police decision to court, Joanna and her defence tried to reverse the decision to confiscate her passport and ban her from leaving the country. The main argument of the defence was that Joanna was not part of YPG/YPJ, but at the time, she was involved with the Peshmerga in Iraq. Fighting for an allied force, she was not subject to the regulations of the Passport Act. The defence also criticised the police for basing their decision on inaccurate information about the Kurdish forces in Iraq and Syria, and for failing to interview her to obtain the correct information (The City Court of Copenhagen 2016). On 4 February 2016, the court decided in favour of the police, stressing that further military training would contribute to her ability to 'commit serious criminal offences'. In addition, the fact that she had spent time with the YPG/YPJ made it unlikely that she was now enrolled with the Peshmerga as 'it is not possible to fight with both YPG/J and the Peshmerga as you like' (The City Court of Copenhagen 2016). She does not, therefore, as claimed, have a 'creditable purpose' in relation to the coalition that will justify her travelling to the conflict zones (The City Court of Copenhagen 2016). The verdict was not appealed, and in September 2016, the decision to confiscate her passport and impose a travel ban on her was prolonged for another year as the police discovered, during the summer of 2016, that she yet 'again appear[s] in conflict areas participating in combat' (The City Court of Copenhagen 2017a). After being taken into custody for two weeks in December 2016, she once more decided to try the police decision in court. She appointed a new defence lawyer, Erbil Kaya, who won the court case for Martin at the District Court in Esbjerg.

Martin from Esbjerg also had his passport confiscated and a six-month travel ban imposed on him from August 2016. Martin travelled to Iraqi Kurdistan and fought with the Peshmerga during the summer of 2015. The travel ban was imposed as he was overheard talking about travelling to Syria. Martin successfully argued that he did not intend to leave Denmark to fight as he had settled down with his girlfriend, bought a new car and rented an apartment. He also stressed that he had only fought for the Peshmerga forces, which was not illegal as the Peshmerga is perceived as a regular army by the Ministry of Justice (Ministry of Justice 2016, July 1). The verdict of 5 December 2016 was passed in his favour, highlighting that Martin had a creditable purpose as he only fought for the Peshmerga, a Western and thus Danish ally in the battle against Islamic State (The District Court of Esbjerg 2016). Thus, the passport law did not apply to the case. On 22 June 2017, the acquittal was settled by the appeal court. The court added that no fighter joining the Kurdish forces has committed acts of terrorism or other serious crimes after returning to Europe (The High Court of Western Denmark 2017).

The second time Joanna Palani tried the police decision in court, defending her right to reclaim her passport, she once again argued that the Passport Act did not apply in her case, adding that she had settled in Denmark and no longer intended to leave the country to fight (The City Court of Copenhagen 2017a). The police, however, succeeded in portraying Joanna Palani as a confused person partly because she had fought with both Peshmerga in Iraq and YPJ in Syria, which they claimed to be rather unusual and thus suspicious (p. 19), and partly because of 'her fragile mental condition' (p. 19). Thus, on 26 October 2017, the City Court once again confirmed that the police decision to confiscate her passport and ban her from travelling abroad was justified, stressing that she still intended to travel to the conflict zones, had no creditable purpose for being there, and by staying there she would further develop her ability to 'commit serious criminal offences' in Denmark (The City Court of Copenhagen 2017a). Joanna Palani appealed the decision, but on 16 August 2018, the High Court of Eastern Denmark confirmed the verdict of the City Court. Once again, the verdict was based on her personal and mental conditions. This time with stronger weight as a schizophrenia diagnosis and the pressure placed on her by the PKK were added to the description of her (The High Court of Eastern Denmark 2018). Interestingly, the emphasis on her personal affairs opened up for decriminalising fighting with YPG/J per se, as her affiliation with YPJ was disregarded in the court ruling.

Joanna Palani was also charged with being in breach of the travel ban (the Passport Law, § 5 (1) cf. § 2 b (1)) by leaving Denmark from June to October in 2016. The prosecution claimed that she had participated in combat in Syria, which she had reached through Qatar and Iraq. Joanna insisted that she just needed to get away and that she had stayed in Qatar for some weeks during the summer. She also pointed out that she had used her own passport, which the police had never confiscated. The verdict, pronounced on 22 November 2017, confirmed the charges and sentenced her to nine months in prison (The City Court of Copenhagen 2017b). The fact that she had returned to the conflict areas, which had caused her travel ban in the first place, was an aggravating condition. Joanna Palani did not appeal this verdict.

Joanna Palani became a courtroom activist when she allowed the police to take the passport confiscation to court. She could have obeyed the police decision as a number of other volunteers have done, but she did not. The second time she took the police decision to court, it was as an immediate reaction to the police investigation of her alleged breach of the travel ban in December 2016. By going to court to overturn the police decision, she chose a proactive strategy. Thus, her agenda differs from that of the ten Kurdish men, who were subjected to court without any desire to be courtroom activists. In this way, the litigations are a continuation of her military fight against injustice in Syria and Iraq.

The regulation on travel to conflict zones

The increasing number of foreign fighters joining Islamist and jihadi groups in Syria raised concerns in Western countries, especially after the announcement of the Islamic Caliphate in the summer of 2014. On 24 September 2014, the UN Security Council agreed on resolution 2178, deciding that with regard to foreign terrorist fighters, member states shall

> prevent and suppress the recruiting, organizing, transporting or equipping of individuals who travel to a State other than their States of residence or nationality for the purpose of the perpetration, planning, or preparation of, or participation in, terrorist acts or the providing or receiving of terrorist training, and the financing of their travel and of their activities. (UNSCR 2178, Art. 5)

The Danish government followed suit by proposing measures to prevent potential foreign fighters travelling abroad. The government also suggested criminalising participation in armed combat abroad. As a result, the Danish parliament adopted amendments to the Passport Act, implemented 1 March 2015, and amendments to the Criminal Code, implemented 1 July 2016.

The Passport Act

The amendments to the Passport Act mean that the police are entrusted with the authority to confiscate or refuse to issue a passport to a Danish citizen. They also have the authority to impose a travel ban on the individual for up to one year at a time (The Passport Act, § 2 and 2 b). This applies when there is reason to assume that 'the individual intends to participate in activities abroad where this may involve or increase the threat toward national state security, security of other states or pose a serious threat toward public order' (The Passport Act, § 2 (1) no. 4). The individual to whom the articles apply can have the police decision tested in court (§ 2 (4) and 2 b (3)). If the travel ban is violated, the individual will be fined or sentenced to imprisonment (§ 5). Similar amendments aimed at non-Danish citizens residing in Denmark were also approved. Consequently, a residency permit holder can have his or her residency permit withdrawn on the same grounds as those mentioned above (The Aliens Act, § 21 b (1)) (Vestergaard 2016, p. 542).

By the end of 2018, at least five individuals, who have fought with or intended to fight with Kurdish forces, have had their passports withdrawn and been prevented from travelling abroad. Two of them have had the police decision tried in court. One, Martin from Esbjerg, had the decision annulled by the court, but Joanna did not. In addition to these five individuals, Anne Dalum, who planned to join the Internationalist Commune of Rojava, had the police decision to withdraw her passport annulled in court as her defence succeeded in convincing the court that she was going to participate in a rebuilding programme and not in military fighting (Ritzau 2019).

The Criminal Code

Prior to the formation of Islamic State, Denmark had tougher legislation on terrorism than the other Scandinavian countries. Following the terror attacks of 11 September 2001, the Danish parliament adopted an expansion of the terrorism paragraph (§ 114), criminalising many activities which had not been regulated before. Thus, participation in and financing a terror organisation as well as recruiting and training others to commit terror attacks were criminalised.

In 2016, the Danish parliament adopted yet another expansion of the terrorism paragraph with the aim of criminalising terror-related travel, as in UNSC Resolution 2178. Thus, § 114 j was implemented to ban travel to specific conflict zones identified by the Danish Minister of Justice after negotiation with the Minister of Foreign Affairs and the Minister of Defence. These 'no-go zones' were confined to specific areas in northern Iraq and northern Syria, namely the district of Mosul and four districts around the river Euphrates in Syria. These were the areas where the heaviest Islamic State fighting took place around the time of the announcement (Ministry of Justice 2016, September 28). The law was implemented too late to have a real effect on the sentencing of foreign fighters who had joined Islamic State, al-Nusra Front and other militant Islamist groups. In their terror threat assessment report of 28 April 2016, the Center for Terror Analysis under the Police Intelligence Service estimated that 'a minimum of 135 individuals have left Denmark for Syria/Iraq since the summer of 2012' (The Center for Terror

Analysis 2016). In 2018, CTA estimated the number to be 150 (The Center for Terror Analysis 2018). Until now, only two people have been charged according to § 114 j. The most prominent defendant was the former Danish YPG fighter Tommy Mørck, who was charged with violating the travel ban while fighting with the YPG. On 4 June 2018, he was sentenced to six months in prison at the district Court of Aarhus. On 12 November, the verdict was upheld by the High Court of Western Denmark, and on 27 August 2019, the Supreme Court of Denmark also ruled in favour of the Prosecution Service after accepting the case as a test case (Elkjær 2019). Two weeks later, at the City Court of Copenhagen, Aske Barfod Sivesgaard was sentenced to six months in prison for his travel to Syria in 2017–18 (Nielsen 2019). In order to adapt to the developments in the battlefield in 2019, the government revised the area map displaying the no-go zones. The districts around Raqqa, among others, are no longer included (Ministry of Justice 2019).

The amendment to the Passport Act and the Criminal Code reflect the legislators' intention to prevent individuals from participating in terror-related travel and punish those who do. The main argument of the legislators is that individuals who travel abroad to fight with militant Islamist groups have military training and will be exposed to brutal acts of war that can increase their ability and intent to commit terrorism in Denmark or recruit others to do so (L 99 2014, pp. 5–6; L 187 2016, p. 6). However, as it is worded, the legislation applies to every individual who intends to travel abroad to fight without a creditable purpose or who travels to the no-go zones without permission. When the amendments to the Passport Act were debated in the Legal Affairs Committee, this was one of the concerns expressed by the members (L 99 – Questions 2015). The Red-Green Alliance member Pernille Skipper questioned the law's applicability to fighters joining Kurdish forces, and the Danish People's Party member Karina Lorentzen also wanted to ensure that fighters joining the Israel Defence Forces were not subject to the law. Another concern raised by Pernille Skipper regarded the evidence required by the police before withdrawing a passport. According to the new law, the police only need to have 'reason to assume' that the individual intends to participate in activities abroad that may increase the national security threat (Passport Act, § 2 (1) no. 4). The Red-Green Alliance voted against the Passport Act due to these two concerns, as did one non-party member,

Uffe Elbæk, who later founded the party The Alternative (L 99 – Voting 2015). The Passport Act was adopted with broad support in parliament, however. When the amendments to the Criminal Code were debated in parliament, the main concern of the parties voting against the law (the Red-Green Alliance, The Alternative, the Danish Social Liberal Party and the Socialist People's Party) was the restrictions on freedom of movement, which would authorise the Ministry of Justice to assess who have a recognisable purpose for travelling and who do not. In addition, the Red-Green Alliance once again criticised the lack of discrimination between the individuals fighting for and against Islamic State (L 187 – Debate 2016).

Compared with the other Scandinavian countries, Denmark has adopted a tough approach to militant Islamist foreign fighters (Andersson, Høgestøl and Lie 2018, pp. 15–16). Denmark is the only Scandinavian country that has adopted laws on passport withdrawal and no-go zones. Norway has adopted a general criminalisation of participation in military activities in armed conflicts abroad (the Criminal Code, § 145) and criminalised participation in a terror organisation (the Criminal Code, § 135 a). Sweden, on the other hand, only criminalises individuals who travel abroad with the intent of committing serious crimes. Intent is very difficult to prove, and so far, Sweden has only convicted two foreign fighters (Andersson et al. 2018, p. 17) out of 300 people who are estimated to have travelled from Sweden to Syria and Iraq to join terrorist groups (Gustafsson and Ranstorp 2017, p. 5).

In 2019, after the defeat of Islamic State in Baghouz, the Danish legislators toughened the regulation on foreign fighters even further. As a result, citizens with dual citizenship can have their Danish citizenship administratively revoked by the Minister of Immigration and Integration if they pose a threat to 'vital Danish interests' (Ministry of Immigration and Integration 2020).

The courtroom as a mobilisation rostrum

This section looks into how Joanna has tried to mobilise in the wake of the unsuccessful litigations, which were intended to regain her passport and repeal the travel ban imposed on her administratively. As she has not succeeded in convincing the prosecution of her just cause to fight in Syria and Iraq, she has been particularly eager to convince the Danish public. In other words, as she has failed to prove her case, that is, to turn military activism

in support of YPG into a legal act, the political consequences of the litigation seem even more important. This is why she decided to participate in
a documentary, 'Criminal or Freedom Fighter', which was broadcast on
national television (DR) in the evening of 26 October 2017, the day when
the verdict of her second passport case was read. In the film, she explains
that her courtroom activism is a continuation of her military activism,
pointing out that, 'I am now in a position where I have fought for freedom in the Middle East and now I am fighting for justice here' (Klitgaard
2017). Thus, Joanna equates fighting for freedom, democracy and women's
rights in Syria with fighting for Denmark. She also equates fighting in the
Danish courtroom for her right to travel with fighting for the recognition
of the YPG. She therefore feels betrayed by the Danish government as she
has fought shoulder to shoulder with the coalition, and then she got 'a stab
in the back by the Danish government', which is on the same side in the
war against Islamic State. She still has hope for the Danish people, as it is
crucially important to her that 'people understand why we have fought and
what we are fighting for'. It should be noted that she does not mention
the Kurdish diaspora when talking about the Danish people. The diaspora
groups supporting PYD, YPG and YPJ have been very eager to support the
women's revolution in Rojava and celebrate the female YPJ fighters. They
would be expected to be on the same side as her. However, there has been
complete silence from the Kurdish groups about her litigation. This will be
discussed later in this chapter.

In the following, I will examine the position of the Danish government
and the Kurdish diaspora toward the Kurdish fight in Syria and subsequently
their position toward Joanna Palani. First, I will examine the strategy of the
Danish government, or rather, I will examine the strategy of the Danish parliament, as there has been broad political consensus in Denmark concerning
countermeasures against Islamic State in Iraq and Syria and countermeasures
against the terror threat in Denmark. Second, I will examine the position of
the Kurdish diaspora toward the female Kurdish fighters in Syria and toward
Kurdish volunteers from Europe joining the Kurdish fight in Syria. I will
then discuss where this cross-pressure leaves Joanna Palani and include a discussion of her call to the Danish public. Finally, I will identify the challenges
of Kurdish courtroom activism in a Danish setting.

Responses to Courtroom Activism

The official Danish response to the Kurdish struggle in Syria

In 2014, following the expansion of Islamic State in Iraq and the attack on the Yezidis in Sinjar, the Danish Parliament decided to join the American-led coalition against Islamic State. On 8 August, the United States launched the first military attack on Islamic State, responding to the international call for support made by the Iraqi state through the UN Security Council. A few weeks later, the Danish parliament decided to follow suit by voting in favour of a military contribution to the coalition against Islamic State. From 2014 until today, the parliament has adopted a number of contributions, including a transport aircraft (B 122 2014); fighter aircraft (F-16) deployed for up to twelve months, and staff officers and military instructors for the Iraqi and Kurdish security forces (B 123 2014); a mobile radar (B 8 2015, renewed until January 2020); redeployment of fighter aircraft (F-16) and special operation forces (B 108 2016); and a frigate (B 56 2017). In addition, Denmark has offered to lead the NATO training mission in Iraq from the end of 2020 (Reuters 2019). While the first contribution of fighter aircraft (B 123), adopted in 2014, was restricted to operations in Iraq, the contribution of fighters and special operation forces (B 108), adopted in 2016, was allowed to enter Syria as well. The first decision was broadly accepted in parliament and passed. Only the Red-Green Alliance voted against it. When the decision to allow participation in the coalition's interventions in Syria was approved, the oppositional stance of the Red-Green Alliance was supported by the Socialist People's Party and the newly formed party The Alternative.

The aim of the Danish contributions to the international coalition was to 'support Iraq's military campaign against the terrorist organisation Islamic State' and to 'assist the Iraqi authorities in protecting the civilian population against severe assault'. The contribution was based on the invitation of the Iraqi state and intended to avert the humanitarian crisis caused by Islamic State. At the press meeting in September 2014, where the Danish contribution of fighter aircraft (F-16) was announced, the Danish Prime Minister Helle Thorning-Schmidt publicly emphasised the anti-terror agenda in order to legitimise yet another military contribution to an international conflict. She stated that 'The terrorist organisation IS is an atrocious organisation that

Denmark must participate in annihilating. IS poses a threat to Denmark and to our allies. If we do nothing, things will only get worse. So ignoring the situation and turning a blind eye is not an option' (Kongstad and Kaae 2014).

Thus, the humanitarian agenda for the situation in Iraq was justified by the argument that the international coalition was providing international security by defeating Islamic State. The Danish contribution to the American-led coalition represents the culmination of Danish military activism since the Cold War. This military activism is proof of Denmark's will and desire to participate in international military intervention without national caveats. By participating in 'Operation Inherent Resolve', as the military intervention of the American-led coalition against Islamic State was called, Denmark subscribed to the American strategy against Islamic State. The strategy toward Islamic State was presented in an address to the nation by President Barak Obama, who stated that 'Our objective is clear: We will degrade, and ultimately destroy, ISIL through a comprehensive and sustained counter-terrorism strategy'. The strategy included four key elements: (1) a systematic campaign of airstrikes; (2) support for Iraqi and Kurdish forces fighting on the ground in Iraq; (3) counter-terrorism activities to prevent terror attacks; and (4) humanitarian assistance to internally displaced persons (Obama 2014).

However, the American strategy against Islamic State was not restricted to Iraqi territory as the organisation had also settled around Raqqa, taking advantage of the turmoil of the Syrian Civil War. In order to fulfil the objective of destroying Islamic State, a tactical alliance with the Syrian Kurdish forces, YPG and YPJ, emerged during the battle of Kobane in late 2014. As the YPG/J proved to be a strong and dedicated ally in the fight against Islamic State at the Syrian front of the battle, the partnership has become even stronger since then. The Kurdish forces are provided with heavy weaponry, including 'heavy machine guns, mortars, anti-tank weapons, armoured cars and engineering equipment' (Gordon and Schmitt 2017). Additionally, up to 2,000 soldiers and special operation forces were deployed to the Kurdish held areas of Syria during the battle of Raqqa. From November 2015, the cooperation with YPG/J continued within the multi-ethnic alliance of the Syrian Democratic Forces (SDF), which was formed with the backing of the United States to deflect the Turkish condemnation of the American-

Kurdish partnership. As part of the American-led international coalition against Islamic State, Denmark joined this tactical alliance, placing the Danish forces and YPG/J on the same side of the battle against Islamic State. In 2016, when the Danish parliament decided to extend the mandate to the Syrian territory, Danish fighter aircraft and special operation forces became even closer allies of the YPG/J engaged in the same attacks on Islamic State.

The same determination to react to terrorist threats also characterises Danish domestic policy. As explained above, since 9/11, Denmark has implemented several measures to counter the threat from militant Islamism, the amendments to the Passport Act and Criminal Code being the most recent. However, as the Joanna Palani case has shown, there seems to be a discrepancy between foreign policy and domestic policy on counter-terrorism. While Danish Members of Parliament express themselves clearly when it comes to whom to target in the Iraqi and Syrian context, namely the fighters of Islamic State, they do not make the same clear definition in the amendments to the Passport Act and the Criminal Code. In the battlefields of Syria and Iraq, Danish forces fight with Kurdish forces against Islamic State, while the Danish courtroom does not distinguish between Kurdish and Islamic State fighters.

Joanna Palani and other activists have criticised this inconsistency between Danish foreign policy and domestic policy with regard to how Kurdish fighters are treated: as valued allies and ignoble criminals. Consequently, she has declared the legislation grossly unfair, which is hardly surprising. However, other actors, like the director of the Danish judicial think tank Justitia, Jacob Mchangama, has also criticised the Passport Act for being inconsistent with the Danish participation in the international military operation against Islamic State. In an analysis of the bill, he and a co-author criticise the law based on principles of legal certainty (Mchangama and Prener 2014). The authors point to the vague formulation of the field of application as the law does not specify what is and is not 'a recognisable purpose' when entering a conflict area. They also point to the vague formulation of 'reasons to assume', referring to the basis which is required for the police to take action. To limit the consequences of the restriction on individual freedom, the authors suggest introducing a sunset clause that terminates the amendments to the law in 2020. While the criticism of the vague and indefinite formulations of the law was ignored, the sunset clause was implemented when the law was passed in Parliament in 2015 (Mchangama 2015, November 24). However, in 2020, when the Parliament renegotiated the amendments of the law, the majority decided to make the amendments permanent, ignoring the sunset clause (L 92, 2020). Jacob Mchangama has also commented specifically on the Joanna Palani case on several occasions. In 2015 in the blog 'Terrorist or freedom fighter: should they be treated alike?', he discusses whether the law applies to Joanna Palani or not. He concludes that the law indiscriminately applies to her as well as to fighters who want to join Islamic State and suggests that the law be made more specific. He argues that it could be added that the police should have 'specific reasons to assume that an individual intends to participate in activities which can cause or increase the threat of terror' before they confiscate a passport (Mchangama 2015, June 8). He repeated his criticism of the Passport Law just before the trial of Joanna Palani in 2017 in the documentary 'Criminal or Freedom Fighter'.

The legislators do not intend to change the law even though it might have consequences for fighters who support the Kurdish cause. While they emphasised the terror threat posed by returned militant Islamists when adopting the law, they have now shifted their argument to the psychological effects of joining combat and the manageability of the law when defending. In the documentary 'Criminal or Freedom Fighter' about the military activism of Joanna Palani and Tommy Mørck, two Members of Parliament, Preben Bang Henriksen from the Liberal Party and Peter Kofod Poulsen from the Danish People's Party, defended the law, pointing to the psychological consequences of being exposed to explosions and learning to handle weapons (Klitgaard 2017). Preben Bang Henriksen stressed that 'no matter which side you have been fighting on, you may have experienced brutalisation'. Peter Kofod Poulsen added that war is not 'a case for independent actors'. He further stressed that the law is manageable because it does not list legal and illegal groups. The legislators seem to want to be 'better safe than sorry', as Jacob Mchangama points out. The question should therefore not be whether Joanna Palani is a criminal or a freedom fighter, but how she can possibly be both? The inconsistency of the legislators' approach to Kurdish military activism dissolves into ambiguity when the political rationale behind the Danish military activism which has emerged after the Cold War is examined more closely.

Political scientists who study Danish contributions to international military interventions argue that the main political rationale behind the politicians' decision to send Danish troops to war is prestige-seeking (Jakobsen 2016; Jakobsen, Ringsmose and Saxi 2018; Pedersen 2018). They claim that interest-based arguments, like reputation, are downplayed in favour of humanitarian and legal arguments in order to legitimise military contributions to the population (Jakobsen et al. 2018, p. 264), even though the Danish population seem more accepting of military deployment than other European countries (Jakobsen 2016, p. 194). A survey found that 59 per cent of the Danes agreed that Denmark should continually engage militarily in international conflicts. Nevertheless, the prestige-seeking discourse has become more and more explicit, primarily among liberal politicians to repair what they believe to be a strained relationship between Denmark and the Unites States due to the Danish opposition to NATO's decision to place nuclear missiles in Western Europe in the 1980s (Jakobsen et al. 2018, p. 265). Gradually, Danish military activism has evolved into a strategic culture (Wæver 2016) characterised by a willingness, which has been broadly adopted in Parliament, to deliver when the big powers, especially the United States, call. However, when the desire to be 'out in the front' to earn 'pride, praise, and position' (Jakobsen 2016, p. 192) is predominant, 'the 'big' decisions concerning where, when, and how to fight' are left to others, and the Danish decision-makers seem happy about this (Jakobsen 2016, p. 207). The Danish decision makers left the decision to ally with the Syrian Kurds to their American counterparts, without considering that they would have to handle Kurdish military activists from Denmark returning from the battlefield. Thus, I will argue that the Danish decision-makers exhibit ambiguity when faced with the Kurdish military activism. They recognise the Kurdish fighters of YPG and YPJ as valued allies as long as they stay in the Kurdish areas, but treat them as terrorists when they appear in Denmark. As I have argued, the ambiguity is based on different political rationales of foreign and domestic interests rather than inconsistency between foreign and domestic policies.

The Kurdish diaspora, female fighters and Kurdish volunteers

Since the PKK took up arms against the Turkish Republic in 1984, military resistance has been a core element of the Öcalan movement. The years following Öcalan's capture in 1999 and the peace talks in 2013–15 are the only exceptions. In Iraq, both the KDP and PUK have Peshmerga forces, but in Turkey, the guerrilla war of the PKK distinguishes them from the other political parties, such as the PSK, HAK-PAR and PAK.

From the early stages of the guerrilla war, female militants played a significant role as symbols of the self-sacrificing fighters devoting themselves to the Kurdish cause (Duzel 2018). They legitimised their identity as fighters through self-inflicted death and suicide bombing missions, thereby solidifying their position in the organisation (Duzel 2018, p. 2). When the civil war broke out in Syria, and especially during the defeat of Islamic State in the battle of Kobane, the female fighters of YPJ were celebrated as the heroic counterparts of the villains of Islamic state. The female martyrs continue to attract specific gendered attention as 'dead goddesses' (Duzel 2018, p. 13), but the living soldiers also attract gendered attention within the movement. Thus, Kurdish female fighters are hailed when photos and films of female fighters are shared transnationally on social media, and when they show up in person at public events in the diaspora. The Kurdish diaspora also takes part in the hype.

In April 2016, FEY-KURD invited representatives from Rojava to Denmark to meet the diaspora. Two hundred and fifty Kurds and a few Danes showed up to meet the Kurds from Syria. The speakers were Sinem Mohammed, by then co-chair of TEV-DEM, and other political representatives, as well as Nesrin Abdullah, commander and spokesperson of YPJ, who earned her reputation as the public face of the military resistance of Kobane. Nesrin Abdullah took the floor when the politicians had delivered their speeches, recapitulating the message, 'we are fighting against evil', 'we are fighting against the same enemy' and 'we are strong'. It turned out that the female commander was the main attraction of the meeting, which culminated in excited selfie sessions involving young women and men taking photos of themselves with the heroine of YPJ.

As a female fighter and fighter for democracy and women's rights against Islamic State, Joanna Palani should be able to mobilise support among the Kurdish diaspora in Denmark as a heroine of their own. But she has not. How come?

When asked about the mobilisation of Kurds in Europe for YPG and YPJ, the official answer of the PYD is that they should stay in Europe and engage in political lobbyism there. The organisation is not in need of fighters as they have succeeded in recruiting local fighters. What the organisation needs are politically active Kurds in Europe to influence politicians and Europeans in general to support their revolution and the fight against Islamic State and Turkey, especially after the attack on Afrin in January 2018. I have interviewed the former co-chair of the PYD and now foreign affairs representative, Salih Muslim, twice in order to challenge the official stance on the role of the diaspora. On both occasions, in March 2017 and August 2017, he stressed the importance of financial support and of raising awareness among Europeans of the Kurdish struggle in northern Syria to put pressure on the politicians. He was not explicit in terms of how to take action, though. When asked about European Kurds, who do join YPG and YPJ, Salih Muslim replied that 'they decide for themselves' (August 2017) and thereby neglected the responsibility of the PYD with regard to their decisions to join the fight. This was also stressed in one of his tweets in the wake of the war in Afrin, 'To all Kurdish activists and friends: our struggle is democratic and for democracy, we should respect democratic rules in countries hosting our people' (@SalehMaslem 2018, March 12). Kurdish power holders in Rojava seem to calculate that in order for the autonomy to persist, international allies need to be the top priority. Rojava, being a landlocked area surrounded by regional powers who do not support Kurdish autonomy in northern Syria, is in most need of international supporters who will guarantee their survival in the military conflict with Turkey and in political negotiations on the future of Syria. Recruiting Kurdish youths in Europe for the military fight in Syria is therefore out of the question due to the regulations on foreign fighters and the EU designation of the PKK as a terrorist organisation. At the same time, Kurds in military uniform wearing YPG badges at cultural and political events in Denmark indicate that the clandestine tradition of young PKK recruits is adopted by young Kurds joining YPG and YPJ with the blessing of the political parties within the Öcalan movement.

This ambiguous support for military activism was also displayed at the funeral of Ari Hussein. As mentioned earlier, Ari was interviewed by DR when fighting with the YPG in Raqqa. In March 2018, he was back in Denmark. According to the tabloid Ekstra Bladet, he was a member of Loyal to Familia (LTF), which is perceived as a criminal gang intermittently engaged in violent fights and infighting in the larger cities in Denmark (Bjerregaard and Kornø 2018). Allegedly, he decided to leave the brotherhood upon his return to Denmark but was shot dead as a result of this decision (Toksvig, Yasar and Bjerregaard 2018). The family wanted to stress his loyalty to the Kurdish struggle, however. At the funeral, the coffin was carried by soldiers wearing YPG uniform, and it was embellished with yellow, red and green ribbons, matching the colours of the Rojava flag. Some of the mourners held photos of the deceased posing as a YPG soldier, and the men carrying the coffin shouted 'şehîd YPG' in Kurdish (martyr of YPG). He was basically celebrated by the family as a martyr for the YPG. One week after the funeral, a memorial ceremony was held by the family in Germany. Once again, he was presented as a martyr. However, the events were promoted only among Syrian Kurds and not utilised as mobilising events within the broader Kurdish community, nor among the public.

The ambiguous interplay

The Danish state and the Kurdish diaspora are both acting ambiguously. The Danish state is not following a consistent policy toward the Kurdish cause, and this has led to conflicting policies when it comes to recognition of fighters for the Kurdish cause in Syria. Danish foreign policy has led to cooperation with Kurdish forces in Syria, and yet volunteer fighters who joined the Kurdish forces in Syria risk lawsuits when they return Denmark. The Kurdish diaspora as part of the Kurdish transnational community seeks to navigate in this field, drawing on their experiences with ambiguous leaders in the Middle East and the ban on the PKK in European countries. Consequently, the Kurdish diaspora themselves have adopted an ambiguous strategy in the European setting toward fighters for YPG and YPJ.

The ambiguity of the Danish state can be ascribed to the different rationales behind the Danish foreign and domestic policies. The Danish legislators support the Kurdish struggle as Denmark pursues a foreign policy which adheres to the international military interventions of the United States. As part of the American-led international coalition against Islamic State, Denmark supports the Syrian Kurds. However, domestically, Danish legislators deny Danish citizens the right to travel to Syria to fight with the Kurds by implementing regulations on travel and intent to travel to conflict zones.

The Kurdish diaspora milieu of Öcalan supporters exhibits a similar ambiguity when interacting with Danish authorities. While it celebrates YPJ fighters visiting Denmark and praises foreign YPG fighters for their dedicated political convictions, it disregards fighters of its own milieu when they try to unmask the ambiguous interplay and ask for a consistent approach from the politicians and the Kurdish diaspora.

So why is Ari embraced by parts of the Kurdish community while Joanna is not? First, Ari did not question the ambiguous support for the Kurdish struggle. When interviewed, he was more realistic than any of the other Kurdish fighters about the consequences of the indiscriminate Danish legislation intending to prevent fighters from being militarily trained in Syria in order to prevent terror attacks in Denmark. He told the journalist, 'of course, if there is a law in Denmark, I expect it to be followed, however crazy it may be. It is the rule of law. I have to accept it' (Damsgaard 2017). These words were uttered by a man who had been jailed in Denmark once before. At that time, his imprisonment was due to illegal weapon possession. Allegedly, he received the punishment on behalf of others (Bjerregaard and Kornø 2018). In line with the interview, his family succeeded in presenting him as a YPG soldier and martyr, thus inscribing him in the collective ideological struggle of the movement.

Joanna, on the other hand, has given interviews several times and participated in two documentaries about her military activism (Ladefoged and Sørensen 2015; Klitgaard 2017), so she has not participated in the ambiguous interplay of open political support and clandestine military activism. Moreover, she has openly joined both the Peshmerga in Iraq and YPJ in Syria, which was perceived as unlikely and thus weakened her testimony and subsequently her case. As Nerina Weiss proves in her study of Norwegian foreign fighters who joined the different Kurdish militias' fight against Islamic State (Weiss 2018), the route to military activism is not the same for different volunteers and is seldom well planned. She explains, 'Things happen in war, and you navigate in the terrain to the best of your ability. The legitimisation of the choices is made along the way and influenced by the different contexts that the volunteers happen to be within' (Weiss 2018, p. 427). Several of the Norwegian volunteers have joined more than one of the rivalling Kurdish groups. Kurdish activists are quite critical of this as it is not clear to them whom the volunteers actually support. When asked if the military activism of Joanna Palani and other fighters is appreciated within the Kurdish activist milieu, one of my informants responded that the main concern within the movement is 'how much [of the activism] is personal agenda and how much is for the cause' (V, female, 30s). If a person appears to be more loyal to self-promotion in the media than to the cause, the movement will be reluctant to support him or her. This explains why neither the court nor the diaspora and their political allies have faith in Joanna Palani, which makes her call for public support seem both desperate and understandable.

Last Call

Call for solidarity

Joanna Palani followed two tracks to mobilise the public. First of all, she reached out to friends of the Kurdish cause. Through her defence lawyer, Joanna Palani appealed for support from the Kurdistan Solidarity Group within the Red-Green Alliance. In response to the request, the Solidarity Group set up a working group that would assemble a support committee for the trials by inviting people from different milieus supportive of the Kurdish cause. The members of the support committee would be present at the courtroom hearings at the appeal court to provide moral support for Joanna Palani. The support committee was not intended to influence the court decision, that is, aim at the direct consequences of the litigations. Nor was it intended to put pressure on the lawmakers to amend the law, that is, aim at the indirect consequences of the litigations, as this was perceived as a task for the members of Parliament. The sole aim was to support the person morally. By doing so, the Kurdistan Solidarity Group avoided adopting the Joanna Palani case. Thus, there was no response in August 2018 when the High Court of Eastern Denmark confirmed the withdrawal of Joanna Palani's passport. Like the diaspora groups, they declined to support her unconditionally, even though they have on other occasions celebrated the volunteers for Rojava and appreciated their will to take action.

The international fighters supporting YPG and YPJ are repeatedly compared to the volunteers who went to Spain from 1936 to fight against the fascists in the Spanish Civil War. Among 35.000 international fighters, around

450 came from Denmark to fight in Spain on the side of the Republic (Christiansen 2017). I also once heard Kobane compared to Stalingrad by a Danish socialist, as Kobane proved to be the turning point of the war against the fascists of Islamic State much as Stalingrad was the turning point of the allies' war against Nazi Germany during World War II. When invited to public events, the volunteers of YPG and YPJ play the role of spokespersons of the Rojava revolution and pose as individuals with first-hand experience from the war against Islamic State. Macer Gifford, a former YPG fighter and an articulate British man, was invited by the Red-Green Alliance to talk about the advance of YPG at the Rojava Days from 30 October to 1 November 2018. The event was organised by the Danish Rojava Committee, who wanted to celebrate and discuss the developments in Rojava. The socialist activist community has also welcomed Tommy Mørck, a former YPG fighter from Denmark, who has dedicated himself to the democratic and organic revolution of Rojava. On several occasions, he has been invited to talk about his experiences and visions for northern Syria. When Tommy Mørck was taken to court for travelling to the forbidden zones of Syria, a group of supporters gathered in front of the court house in Aarhus, some of whom were members of the local Red-Green Alliance's association while others were young internationalist and socialist activists. Even some high-ranking members of PYD stopped by briefly to confirm their endorsement of him, 'our friend', as I often heard him referred to by Kurdish activists. While Tommy Mørck was embraced as an ideological fighter, most recently after the Supreme Court verdict (Hertoft 2019), Joanna Palani is only reluctantly supported by the political allies of the Kurdish diaspora. In this respect, the Red-Green Alliance and the groups of young internationalists and socialists seem to align themselves with the Kurdish diaspora.

Call for public support

The other track followed by Joanna Palani is to reach the public through media appearances and public settings that allow her to express the aim of her struggle. First, she has participated in TV documentaries. The latest, titled 'Criminal or Freedom Fighter' (in Danish: Forbryder eller frihedskæmper) broadcast on national TV on 26 October 2017 (Klitgaard et al. 2017), discusses the justice of the Danish legislation which indiscriminately criminalises fighting for the Kurdish cause and fighting for Islamic State and other militant Islamists. Her participation in the panel debate on female fighters, mentioned above, was also a way to reach a broader audience. Finally, she published an autobiography about her life and struggles in cooperation with reporter Lara Whyte (Palani 2019). However, she has also complained about how the media has capitalised on her story and misrepresented her. From October 2014 to December 2018, Joanna Palani was mentioned in more than 200 articles and notices in Danish national and local newspapers and magazines (see Infomedia[1]) in addition to appearances on social media, radio and television. In some of the appearances, she is allowed to express the aim of her struggle, but in most of the appearances, she is presented as a symbol of the brave and beautiful female combatant. She has posed as one of '100 Danish women who inspire us' in the Danish women's magazine Femina (Bendixen et al. 2015). She is presented as 'the heroine Joanna' who should be hailed and thanked for her courageous fight against Islamic State (Lilleør 2016). The presentation of Joanna Palani is part of the international fascination with the female fighters of YPJ, which increased in the wake of the siege of Kobane.

Numerous international media outlets, such as the BBC, NBC and CNN, published long pieces on the female fighters. Likewise, a feature in the international women's magazine *Marie Claire* in September 2014 included a photo series of female Kurdish combatants in uniform with heavy weapons (Toivanen and Baser 2016, p. 295). Based on a study on the representation of Kurdish female fighters in British and French media in 2014–15, Toivanen and Baser argue that female Kurdish combatants are depicted as a counter-image to the male Islamic State combatants. This bipartite structure emphasises the exceptionalism of the female fighters as femininity is given prominence, while the masculinity of the male fighters is degraded (see also Kardaş and Yesiltaş 2017, p. 272). This glorification of the female fighters as 'heroic', mainly in the British media, and as fighters for 'liberty, equality and unity', mainly in French media, has made the stories of Kurdish fighters palatable in a Western context. The fascination with the female fighters has also created mythical figures

[1] Infomedia is a Danish online media archive collecting and monitoring Danish media including newspapers, journals, magazines and news agencies.

like 'Rehanna', who killed 100 Islamic State fighters during the siege of Kobane. The story was later proved false as the person behind the story did not exist, yet the iconic photo has been reproduced and reprinted on T-shirts as a Kurdish version of the Che Guevara silhouette. The Rojava Committees in Sweden and Denmark have used her photo as their trademark to depict the Rojava revolution including resistance and female liberation. When the mythical narratives dominate the representation of the female Kurdish fighter, a real-life woman will have difficulties representing herself.

Prospects for Kurdish Courtroom Activism

Lack of incentives

When ROJ TV and subsequently the ten Kurds were on trial for allegedly supporting terrorism, it was an undesirable situation for the Kurdish diaspora milieu. Kurdish activists were subjected to the rules and regulations of the state authorities and dragged into the judicial arena without consent, despite being neither proactive nor reactive courtroom activists. As one of my informants told me, 'Actually, we are not happy about the court cases. We are not. It is not what we wish' (U, male, 40s). Besides the personal costs to the incriminated individuals and the interests of the Öcalan movement, their strategies and activities in support of the homeland Kurds were publicly discussed. The Kurds fought back, and they almost succeeded in reaching a positive outcome in terms of the direct as well as the indirect outcome of the litigations. They only partly succeeded in influencing the direct outcome of the litigation – the question of guilt – as two of the Kurds were sentenced for supporting terrorism by transferring money to ROJ TV. However, they succeeded in influencing the indirect outcome of the litigations by raising a political debate. This was the peak of the litigations as the Kurdish activists succeeded in proclaiming that the cases were politically motivated. Thus, they referred to the compliance of the Danish government with the Turkish demand for prosecution of what they considered to be Kurdish terrorists at a time when Danish Prime Minister Anders Fogh Rasmussen was in desperate need of Turkish support for his bid to become Secretary General of NATO.

In 2015, when the Passport Act was passed, public opinion was even more supportive of the Kurdish struggle as the Kurdish forces YPG and YPJ proved to be the most efficient counterforces to Islamic State on the Syrian front of the battle. However, the majority of the decision-makers were not willing to insert a distinction in the legislation between support for Islamic State and the Kurdish forces. Instead, they defended the law, arguing that every fighter who joins a non-state army and experiences violence will be corrupted. They also argued that the law was only manageable without the distinction between different groups. Even though this was criticised by the Kurdish community, the Kurds seem to follow an ambiguous agenda themselves. They criticised the decision-makers' approach to the Kurds for being contradictory, but at the same time they did not support the single individual caught between the political support for the Kurdish struggle in Syria and the law criminalising participation in the same struggle. Instead, they promoted the myth of the heroic and purely ideologically motivated female fighters, while at the same time feeling intimidated by the real person, who was less submissive and seemingly driven by mixed motives. Likewise, the media has portrayed Joanna Palani as a symbol of resistance toward Islamic State, femininity in war and gender equality in the Middle East, disregarding the complicated picture of the real-life woman.

It seems unlikely that the Kurdish diaspora groups in Denmark will engage courtroom activism as an active strategy anytime soon, neither proactively by prosecuting the state in order to claim their rights nor reactively by civilian disobedience in order to use the litigation as a political arena. When the lawmakers across the different political parties agree, the risk of losing control and having all activities and relations investigated is too high. When Joanna Palani chose to become a courtroom activist, she did it on her own. She chose a somewhat proactive strategy when she decided to try the administrative withdrawal of her passport in court. The strategy was proactive in that it was based on her active decision, I will argue, but only partially, as the decision was a response to the administrative decision taken by the police. She expected to be publicly accepted as one who fought against the evil forces of Islamic State and for freedom, democracy and women's rights. She also expected to be welcomed as a freedom fighter within a Kurdish community that praises the struggle for Kurdish rights and female resistance. Joanna Palani also expected the public and the Kurdish community to support her in court when she attempted to turn the litigations into a mobilising event addressing the indirect consequences of the litigations. This resonates with the story of some foreign fighters recounted by Maja Greenwood at her PhD defence on 24 September 2018. According to her, the foreign fighters left Denmark and a violent background to fight for their brothers in the Muslim homeland. When they returned to Denmark, they hoped they would be accepted and reincorporated in the Muslim community as renewed and purified Muslims. However, this did not happen (Greenwood 2018, p. 225).

Germany, in contrast, has witnessed a number of cases of Kurdish courtroom activism all related to the ban on PKK activities issued in 1993. The most prominent example is the case of Aysel Aydin, which was elevated to the European Court of Human Rights. In 2001 following the announcement of the abandonment of armed resistance against the Turkish state, the PKK launched a campaign among its supporters in Europe. Thus, in 2001, Aysel Aydin and other PKK supporters in Germany signed a declaration, which read, 'I also am a follower of the PKK'. The declarations were handed over to various state authorities. When Aydin's action was taken to court in Germany, she was sentenced to 150 daily fines of eight euros. In 2011, when the litigation came to an end at the European Court of Human Rights, the court ruled in favour of Germany, declaring that the sentence was not a violation of her freedom of expression. Additionally, the court noted that the fine did not appear to be disproportionate to the nature of the offence (The European Court of Human Rights 2011). Aysel Aydin carried out reactive activism as her action aimed to provoke an annulment of the ban on PKK activities either directly, by making the court override the law, or indirectly, by mobilising public support.

In 2018, Germany witnessed a case that was an example of proactive courtroom activism. This time, a Syrian Kurd responded to a newly adopted police instruction that prohibited bringing flags related to the PKK onto the streets. He took the prohibition on YPG and YPJ symbols to court in Berlin at the beginning of 2018 when demonstrations in support of the Kurds in Afrin peaked. The court decided in favour of the Kurdish activist, setting a precedent by banning symbols exclusively related to the PKK and not to their Syrian counterpart (Shino 2018).

Legacy of the courtroom activist

How does Kurdish courtroom activism relate to identifying as a Kurd in a Danish setting? I will focus on the interactions at the in-group and out-group level and discuss whether the acts of Joanna Palani – being a military fighter and courtroom activist – contribute to the transformation of Kurdish identity.

As argued above, being a courtroom activist is not an integral part of being a Kurd or a Kurdish activist in Denmark. When Joanna Palani took the police decision to court and went to the media to gain support, her activism seemingly transgressed the boundaries of Kurdish action. According to the Kurdish diaspora, or more precisely the Öcalan milieu of the Kurdish diaspora, being a Kurd is a political identity which implies being engaged in the political liberation of the suppressed Kurds. This also involves praising military resistance, primarily against the Turkish state, but also military resistance against every form of so-called fascist and totalitarian regime, including Islamic State, as the civil war in Syria shows. However, this is perceived as a collective struggle, by the people and for the people. When Joanna Palani demonstrated that she was willing to fight with both YPJ and the Peshmerga and did not comply with the discretion which the politically mobilised Kurds apply, she exposed her individual intent. Her fight was not perceived as being undertaken on behalf of the Kurds, so it is not a Kurdish act. Thus, the activism of Joanna Palani did not prove strong enough to extend the boundaries of being a Kurd in Denmark. For the supporters of the Öcalan movement, it is very important to maintain that Kurdish identity encompasses compliance with the rules. By contrast, young internationalist and socialist activists did not have the same concerns and embraced Tommy Mørck when he was charged with violating the unjust legislation. Even here, Kurdish activists played a very restrained role.

With regard to interaction with the Danish public, I argued that Joanna Palani was adopted by the media as a heroine fighting for Western values, sometimes presented as Danish democratic values, including women's liberation vis-à-vis the totalitarianism of Islamic State. However, when she really needed support, the media adopted the symbol of the Kurdish female fighter rather than that of a woman of flesh and blood. Thus, Joanna Palani's acts in the field and in the courtroom did not manage to transform the ideal of being a Danish woman as the article in the woman's magazine Femina suggested. Instead, she became a somewhat femonational symbol, in keeping with the concept of femonationalism examined by Sarah Farris (2017). Farris describes femonationalism as the convergence of nationalism, feminism and anti-Islam, by which European right-wing politicians and public debaters instrumentalise the migrant and Muslim woman to advance their own objectives. Being a somewhat femonational symbol, Joanna Palani was utilised as a counter-image of the evil-minded male fighter of Islamic State, but without significance of her own.

Joanna Palani's own explanation for the litigations and the lack of support was that she represents a hybrid identity, being both Kurdish and Danish: too Danish for the Kurdish milieu and too Kurdish for the Danish. Most recently, she contributed to the autobiography *Freedom Fighter: My War Against ISIS on the Frontlines of Syria* trying to explain her legacy to an international audience (Palani 2019).

8

THE SUBURB AND THE FIELD: CHARITY WORK

Introduction

Saving Kobane 2014–15

On the outskirts of Næstved, a young man followed the news about the Islamic State attack on Kobane and the refugees arriving in refugee camps in Iraqi Kurdistan. He watched an interview with a local Kurdish girl, who had donated some items to the refugees. Captivated by her desire to devote herself to the needs of the refugees, he immediately decided to do something himself. Working at Bilka, a Danish hypermarket chain, he collected some clothes from the company for charity. He sold the clothes and sent the money to the refugees. He later connected with other young Kurds from around Denmark feeling the same urge to 'do something'. They decided to create the humanitarian organisation Azadi Rekxrawi, which raised money over the next three years that enabled the organisation to help more than 25,000 families from Kobane and Sinjar. At another location, in the suburbs of Odense, volunteers at a newly established humanitarian association, Roj Sor (the Red Sun) collected money and clothes, which they delivered by trucks to Kobane and Sinjar. The first convoy contained 45 tonnes of clothes and necessities. At other places in Denmark, charity dinners were organised by groups of Kurds or by Kurdish organisations. In Ishøj, south of Copenhagen, a group of young Kurds were able to mobilise almost one thousand people, many of whom had never been mobilised before. This was probably the most profitable charity event in autumn 2014 raising 124,000 DKK as people gathered for food, music and sale of donated items and services to raise money for the Kurds in Kobane. In Valby, a suburb of Copenhagen, the auction at a similar charity dinner organised by the Federation of Kurdish Associations in Denmark raised 25,650 DKK. This was the second charity dinner organised by the federation within a short period of time as the federation had held one earlier in 2014 in support of the victims of the Sinjar massacre. All over Denmark, events were dedicated to fundraising for Kobane, including concerts, flea markets and a football tournament. Furthermore, support for the people of Kobane was expressed on social media by Kurds using the hashtag #SaveKobane. The support for Kobane on social media included fundraising campaigns announced by Kurdish humanitarian organisations and challenges mounted by individuals donating specific amounts of money for every like and comment on posts they had written. The humanitarian organisation the Sun of Mesopotamia managed to donate 600,000 DKK to emergency aid for the Kurdish people in 2014.

The battle of Kobane, which lasted from 13 September 2014, when Islamic State initiated the siege of the city, to 27 January 2015, when the city was liberated by Kurdish forces, sparked lots of support initiatives aimed at the city's suffering Kurdish population. Kurds who had not been activists before engaged in humanitarian action both in Denmark and by travelling to conflict areas, and Kurds who were already engaged in humanitarian action became even more involved.

Kurdish activism in the humanitarian arena

This chapter will provide an overview of the various support initiatives that Kurdish activists and groups have launched by collecting and sending money, clothes and other material aid and by offering development assistance to the Kurdish areas in Syria or Kurds from Syria. It will examine the motivation for organising and conducting such activities. I will also discuss the outcome of the support initiatives and how launching them transforms being Kurdish in a Danish setting. While the previous chapters have looked at the Kurdish activism aimed at political and judicial change, this chapter will look at Kurdish humanitarian activism aiming to provide relief and material assistance to the Kurds in need and thereby change the livelihood for the Kurds in the homeland.

Humanitarian action is action intended to 'save lives, alleviate suffering and maintain human dignity during and in the aftermath of man-made crises and natural disasters, as well as to prevent and strengthen preparedness for the occurrence of such situations' (Good Humanitarian Donorship Initiative 2003). This widely adopted characterisation covers a wide range of activities based on the humanitarian principles of humanity: always prioritising human needs; neutrality: refraining from becoming part of the conflicts; impartiality: non-discriminating behaviour in relation to gender, religious belief, political opinion, etc.; and independence: being autonomous in relation to any affiliation (Good Humanitarian Donorship Initiative 2003; OCHA 2012). Humanitarian action encompasses both short- and long-term activities, ranging from immediate emergency aid providing life necessities such as water, food, clothes and shelter; reconstruction activities aiming to rebuild society so that normal life and livelihoods can be restored; and real development assistance with a focus on long-term sustainable development (EUPRHA 2013, p. 8). Humanitarian action also entails providing material aid and contributing with expertise and education. In addition, humanitarian action covers relief related to both man-made crises, such as war and persecution, and natural disasters, such as earthquakes and famine. In line with this, the Kurdish humanitarian actors engage in a variety of humanitarian activities, both emergency aid and development assistance as well as relief related to crises and natural disasters, based on their experience and assessment of the position of the Kurds in the homeland. This chapter will investigate the variety of humanitarian activities related to the crisis in Syria. However, as the mobilisation of the Kurdish diaspora in support of Syria is the main focus of this book, the study of Kurdish humanitarian action will focus on the diasporic donor activities, which aim to provide resources that facilitate humanitarian action in the field. These activities encompass charity dinners, fundraising campaigns and collection of clothes and other necessities. They also include public meetings and information events on the situation in northern Syria, which feature charity and fundraising activities besides preparing the ground for political mobilisation.

Thus, Kurdish humanitarian action creates a humanitarian arena that reaches across the two interlinked sub-arenas, which I will call the 'suburb' and the 'field'. During my fieldwork, it struck me that while political lobbying takes place in the centre of the city around the political institutions, cultural and humanitarian activities most often take place on the periphery of the city, in the suburb far from the Castle and the Square, and far from media attention. The 'suburb' is the place where people live and where pockets of Kurdish space emerge as people engage in Kurdish culture and traditions or gather to discuss issues related to the position of the Kurds in the homeland. As the mobilisation of resources for humanitarian action is mainly directed at the Kurdish diaspora, suburban locations are the natural choice for the humanitarian activists; close to where people live their lives, meet and take action. Thus, humanitarian support activities take place in Kurdish cultural centres, public community centres hired for the events, Kurdish wedding halls, in private homes and on social media among Kurds or in Kurdish forums. The 'field' is the place where the humanitarian action is delivered. For the Kurds, the 'field' is their homeland, to which they are connected through their own personal past and links to family and personal networks. The 'field' is also a place dominated by Kurds, although regional actors try to interfere and obstruct Kurdish humanitarian aid by restricting the access for the Kurdish aid workers.

Humanitarian action is mainly organised by Kurds and for Kurds and unfolds in places free from negotiation with other non-Kurdish actors. However, there is a lot of discussion within the Kurdish community, to which the humanitarian actors have to relate. The main issues being discussed are the humanitarian principles of impartiality, neutrality and independence. In accordance with the theory of strategic interactionism, the rules and regulations of the humanitarian arena are not predefined, but as Hilhorst and Jansen state, humanitarian principles are socially negotiated and acquire meaning in practice (2010). In other words, they are constantly (re)defined through discussion and interaction by the involved actors. For the Kurdish activists, the political impetus is all-pervading but perceived differently by different actors. For some it is inseparable from humanitarian aid; for others political activism is seen as a conflicting mindset of humanitarianism.

Motivation

When asked about their main motivation for becoming involved in humanitarian aid, the Kurdish humanitarian activists give the same explanation as the other Kurdish activists: solidarity with the Kurdish people. As one of my interviewees said, stressing the implications of action, 'You will never forget your people. When our people need our help, then we will do whatever it takes to help them' (F, female, 50s). For some, the solidarity arises from identification with the Kurdish collective and the feeling of injustice because fellow Kurds are suffering. One woman explained, 'for me, Cizre [the Turkish attack on the Kurdish city in south-eastern Turkey in 2015] was the decisive moment. What happened in Cizre made me feel that I had to help. It was so violent and so unjust [. . .] and then there was Kobane' (M, female, 40s). The battle of Kobane proved that not only suffering and suppression but also the resistance and victory of the Kurds could become a motivating factor. Thus, the same woman points to the experience of Kurdish unity as a reason for taking action, fearing that if she did not, she would later regret it. She said, 'Kobane was a very special case, because it was the first time we, the Kurds, experienced that we agreed on something [. . .] and we agreed that Kobane needed to be liberated' (M, female, 40s). However, for most of the humanitarian activists I talked to, the urge to help is motivated by a personal connection to the affected areas or by the personal experience of being a refugee. One interviewee explained that she was motivated by coming from the area, which she considers to be her home even though she was born in Denmark, 'Now, it was my own homeland and my own family that were affected' (I, female, 20s). Others refer to their own refugee background or their family's memories from the time of escape. A young man recounts the story of his family escaping the Iraqi forces in the late 1980s and early 1990s,

> My older brother, he was born in '88. At that time, we were refugees in Kurdistan. I was born in '89, when we were refugees again. My younger brother was born in '91. Again, we were refugees. We were all born during the war. I know what it is like. Of course, I do not remember, but I can tell by looking at my father and my mother what it is like to have been in war, what it is like to have been refugees. When I heard that they needed flour, I thought, what do they use flour for on the mountain? Then my mother said, believe me,

flour is extremely important. She said, I remember when we were refugees and we fled to the mountains on the border with Iran. What we needed the most was flour. In that way, I recognise the story. I can relate to it through my parents and through how I was born and grew up myself. So I think it has something to do with that. (Q, male, 20s)

The decision by young Kurds to take action seems to have forged new intergenerational connections, as the young activists and their parents have apparently come to understand each other better through discussions of matters related to delivering emergency aid or navigating a conflict zone. One of the interviewees mentions daily phone calls with her father while being in the field.

The motivation to help the people in need is also described as a moral obligation fostered by the feeling of luck or gratitude for their own current position in Denmark. One interviewee explains her urge to act by contrasting the experiences of some of her family members with her own situation, having been born to parents who arrived in Denmark before she was born:

I have family members, who have lived in the streets in Italy and have been held back in Bulgaria, and then, after a long journey they have arrived in Germany. It has affected me a lot. I think I felt too lucky [. . .] then I thought, if I do not do this, I am not true to myself. (I, female, 20s)

Another woman points to the political and societal opportunities saying, 'We live in a democratic country, why shouldn't we do something good for them [the Kurds in the Middle East]' (F, female, 50s). The personal gratitude makes yet another interviewee continue, even when he feels exhausted. He says, 'I want to give them just a little of what I have, just a little bit. I think this is what makes me continue' (Q, male, 20s).

Two of the Kurds I interviewed about humanitarian action are medical doctors who engaged in humanitarian action using their professional skills. One acted as a volunteer at a hospital in Rojava; the other was the principal organiser of the network of Kurdish Doctors and Nurses, which organised a collection of hospital equipment. She later initiated a fundraising campaign to finance a Danish mother-and-child hospital in Rojava. Neither of them has done humanitarian work before. Their professional background was an additional mobilising factor as they observed the great need for health care assistance and hospital equipment. One of them explains, 'it is evident that my professional competence has made me feel that I can give something back to my people' (M, female, 40s). The other points to the fact that, when she was 13 years old, she watched a TV show about a Palestinian doctor, who had dedicated his professional life to helping people in need. Inspired by him, she decided to become a doctor herself. While studying at the university, the war in Syria broke out, and her desire to serve people in need merged with her solidarity with the Kurdish people and prompted her to leave for Rojava.

Interestingly, the feeling of restlessness and the urge to act resemble the reasons given by the military fighters joining the Peshmerga or the YPG and YPJ when they witness the atrocities and pressure on their fellow Kurds from a distance. One of the young Kurdish aid workers I interviewed even compared herself to the foreign fighters of Islamic State likening her feelings to their feelings of urgency and obligation to act instead of letting frustration take over. She said,

> I thought, it is now or never. I started to get really restless. I could not even focus on my studies. Well, sometimes when I hear about those young radicalised Muslims who travel and join ISIS because they, too, do not know what to do, but at the same time they feel that there is something down there to do. Some of that resonates with me. (I, female, 20s)

Unsurprisingly, all the activists I talked to during my fieldwork, whether engaged in political lobbyism or humanitarian efforts, stressed the need to act as a means of reaching their goals. The need to act as a way to cope with inner unrest was also widespread among the activists. However, only the military fighters and the humanitarian actors share the inclination to travel to the Kurdish areas and engage in action which directly helps fellow Kurds. The political activists, by contrast, often stress that they are living in Denmark and have an obligation to act there in order to draw the attention of politicians and the public to the situation in the Middle East. The military fighters and political activists resemble each other in another area, though, as both groups perceive their work as contributing to political and ideological goals in the homeland. The humanitarian workers do not agree whether to aim at political goals or not. Some of them deliberately stay away from politics and claim that their humanitarian organisation has no political or religious inclination. They see politics as one of the main causes of conflict and human suffering. The humanitarian workers in Rojava, however, perceive their work as contributing to the liberation of the Kurdish people or even the Rojava revolution, which they support or have come to support by getting involved in humanitarian volunteerism. All the humanitarian workers subscribe to the principles of humanity and impartiality as guidelines for their work among human beings in need, striving to prioritise human needs and refraining from discriminating in any way in terms of ethnicity, political opinion, religion and gender.

Upholding Humanitarian Principles

Upholding the humanitarian principles is not an easy task, though. Driven by the urge to help fellow Kurds in need, some of the activists find themselves in a personal dilemma between pursuing a Kurdish agenda and upholding the universal principles of humanity and impartiality. The humanitarian organisations are also faced with pressure from other diasporic Kurds to position themselves according to the divisions between the Kurdish groupings. The security situation in the field poses a third challenge as executing humanitarian assistance relies on cooperating with local actors, who often are part of the ongoing conflict. This means that the principles of humanity and impartiality and also those of neutrality and independence are challenged in the diaspora as well as in the field.

Personal dilemmas

The personal dilemma between restricting aid to fellow Kurds or embracing all human beings in need presents itself in specific situations when activists are asked to help a non-Kurd. The doctor who volunteered at a hospital in Rojava recalls a specific episode when an Islamic State supporter was brought to the hospital, and her first impulse to earmark aid to the fellow Kurds and refuse to help a wounded enemy was challenged:

> The police brought a member of ISIS to the accident and emergency department, who just had some wounds on his wrist that we had to clean. Most of the nurses would not do it because four weeks earlier, their family members

had been killed by ISIS. But one nurse, who used to wear a T-shirt with her father's blood still on it, helped him. I asked, 'Why are you helping him?'. She replied, 'This is, what separates us from them. I am helping him, even though he wouldn't have helped me. That is the difference between him and me'. I thought this is like something you read about. It is not what you see for real. (I, female, 20s)

The Red Sun organisation also provides aid to Kurdish refugees in Denmark, who receive a residence permit and leave the refugee camps. One of the leading members recalls a situation when a non-Kurdish family asked for help. 'We said yes. We help everyone who needs help. I just said take what you need. The family have got a lot of stuff' (F, female, 50s). Another of the Red Sun leaders added:

> When I say 'our people', I mean everyone. I work with human beings. When I look at the Danes, it is also my people. When I look at the Arabs, the innocent Arabs, in my opinion, they are also my responsibility. I count them as my people. That does not mean that my people are only the Kurds. However, for the moment, the Kurds are most in need of help, because they have been most affected when ISIS captured the area. (G, male, 50s)

In both situations, the Kurdish activists try to overcome the dilemma by referring to a specific and inclusive Kurdish identity that resists the distinctions made by others. In the first situation, the interviewee referred to a colleague, who is presented as a hero, representing what the Islamic State fighter is not. However, she herself was reluctant to help. In the other situation, the interviewee invented a personal understanding of 'my people' being a group of people he feels responsible for. However, he draws a line between the innocent and the guilty. Thus, while a refugee family are considered human beings in need, the status of the Islamic State member is questioned.

Positioning of Kurdish humanitarian organisations

How do the Kurdish humanitarian organisations position themselves vis-à-vis being Kurdish and humanitarian, and how do they respond to questions from potential donors about their religious and political affiliation? During my fieldwork, I talked to the leaders of three Kurdish humanitarian organisations, which offer aid and assistance to people from Syria among others.

These are Roja Sor (the Red Sun), Azadi Rekxrawi (Azadi Humanitarian Organisation) and the Sun of Mesopotamia.

I became familiar with these organisations as they cooperated with the two Kurdish federations FEY-KURD and the Federation of Kurdish Associations in Denmark, channelling funds to and collecting items for people in need in Kobane and Sinjar. I call them Kurdish organisations although they do not label themselves as such. However, they have Kurdish names and symbols, and they are led by Kurds who seem motivated by solidarity with Kurds in the homeland. The Sun of Mesopotamia also points to Kurdistan as its main area of intervention. In their written aims, however, the three organisations stress the universal values and principles aiming to indiscriminately alleviate the suffering of all human beings. The articles of association of the Red Sun explicitly mention that the regulations are inspired by the articles of association of the Danish Red Cross. It also emphasises that the Red Sun is a humanitarian organisation without affiliation to any political party or religion.

The three organisations pursue different strategies to cope with the conflicting pressures of humanitarian principles and Kurdish solidarity. The leaders of Azadi Rekxrawi and the Red Sun vehemently defend their humanitarian purposes when challenged by other Kurdish diaspora members stressing their unwillingness to position themselves according to political and religious segmentations. According to the interviewees, this sometimes causes great suspicion, and they are repeatedly asked which party they support. One interviewee explains, 'They say we are a political organisation [. . .] we do not mind what people say. They can look at our work' (G, male, 50s). When questioned about the often politicised Kurdish identity, he continues, 'We do not care if you are a member of a political party and then become a member of our organisation. But when you join, you must forget all about your party [. . .] That is the way we work. We want to uphold the purpose of our organisation'. They also experience that other Kurds choose to support them precisely because they are impartial and independent and eschew religious and political affiliations. One of the organisations once received a major donation of 300,000 DKK, which allowed them to help 1500 families in a refugee camp in Iraqi Kurdistan, on exactly these grounds.

The Sun of Mesopotamia pursues a different strategy as the organisation resides at the same address as FEY-KURD and the Democratic Kurdish People's

Assembly in Denmark and cooperates very openly with the other elements of the Öcalan movement. There are some divisions of labour between the organisation and the associations, though. Thus, the Sun of Mesopotamia works as the humanitarian branch, while FEY-KURD and the Democratic Kurdish People's Assembly are the political and cultural branches. The Sun of Mesopotamia cooperates with Heyva Sor a Kurdistanê (Kurdistan's Red Crescent, literally Kurdistan's Red Moon), which is a Germany-based humanitarian organisation offering medical aid and relief to the people of Kurdistan and which seems to have inspired the Sun of Mesopotamia with regard to its written purpose. It is clear from the name and symbol that Heyva Sor aspires to be equated with the organisations within the International Committee of the Red Cross. The organisation works within the framework of the Kurdistan National Congress (KNK) (Kurdistan National Congress 2014, October 10) and currently has a substantial presence in the autonomous regions in northern Syria. Because of its clear affiliation with the Öcalan movement, the Sun of Mesopotamia does not attract the same explicit suspicion from diaspora members as it is clear where it stands. Many Kurds, though, support the organisation without necessarily adopting the whole political package of the Öcalan movement, simply because they support the emergency aid and development assistance, for example building medical infrastructure, such as clinics and hospitals.

Navigating in a humanitarian (mine)field

The security situation in the field also plays a major role in determining whether humanitarian organisations are able to uphold the humanitarian principles. When security in an area is threatened, humanitarian actors rely on the will of local power holders, who may or may not be willing to be governed by humanitarian principles. The humanitarian actors must then decide whether they want to fight for their values, compromise or withdraw from the area.

Some of the organisations work very hard to maintain neutrality and independence from Kurdish political actors in the field. When working with local actors, they sometimes have to accept that the local actors themselves are affiliated with political parties, as one of the interviewees said:

> We told them at the beginning that we understand their situation, that they
> have to be members of political parties, otherwise they will not have a good

life. But when they work for us, they must help everybody, whether they are from this or that party, and whether they are Christians or Arabs. They must help human beings. That is our purpose. And they do it. (G, male, 50s)

Another interviewee recounts being threatened while in the field:

When we were on the mountain, we were pulled aside by some of the Kurdish parties in the area, who wanted to know what we were doing. They knew we were a humanitarian organisation. Some said, 'give us the items, we will have it delivered', so that they could have the bonus. We cannot accept that. We cannot tell people that we have given their donation to a Kurdish party, which will have it delivered to get bonus. Regretfully, we have that problem. (Q, male, 20s)

Other Kurdish humanitarian actors accept being affiliated with political power holders or choose this deliberatively as they perceive them to be protectors of humanitarian interests. Thus, emergency aid workers within Rojava have accepted the power of the PYD and the self-determining political entities. This becomes even clearer when launching development initiatives, as the creation of, for example, health care institutions contributes to the societal development of the autonomous region. However, even though the humanitarian actors are in Rojava to support the revolution, some of them experience that their freedom to move around is restricted, officially to guarantee their security. One non-Kurdish development worker openly wondered whether the security guard who was following them was looking after them or monitoring them. The principles of neutrality and independence are clearly more difficult to uphold when the power holders are eager to control a particular area and a particular development.

This touches upon the fierce criticism raised against UN humanitarian aid in Syria during the summer of 2016 (Hearn 2019, p. 132). The criticism was provoked by a report published by the Syrian Campaign, which is an international human rights organisation. The report, 'Taking Sides: The United Nations' Loss of Impartiality, Independence and Neutrality in Syria' (The Syrian Campaign 2016), criticised the UN for having breached the humanitarian principles of impartiality, neutrality and independence. The report claims that the UN had complied with the requirements of the Assad regime, fearing that resisting them would prompt the regime to evict the entire UN mission from Syria. Instead of protecting humanitarian principles, the UN in fact facilitated the regime's starvation and besiegement strategy. I will highlight three arguments in the report that describe the UN's loss of impartiality, independence and neutrality. The report confirms that ninety-six per cent of UN food aid was delivered to regime-controlled areas. It also describes how the regime gained influence over UN strategies by appointing the wife of the Deputy Foreign Minister to high-ranking positions in the Syrian divisions of the UN. In addition, the President's wife, Asma al-Assad, was installed as the head of a local charity organisation, which distributed humanitarian aid funded by the UN (Hopkins and Beals 2016). Finally, the report documents how the UN kept quiet about the government sieges and thereby influenced the conflict dynamics. The world's biggest contributor to humanitarian aid appears to have compromised its universal principles in order to enter the field. While the small humanitarian actors I talked to struggle hard to keep their donors' trust by sticking to their values, the big humanitarian organisations that rely on state support and state donations are apparently willing to compromise.

The Suburb – Mobilising the Donors

While Kurdish political lobbyists and courtroom activists aim to involve politicians and the public as well as members of the Kurdish diaspora, Kurdish humanitarian actors primarily aim to involve members of the Kurdish diaspora, which makes Kurdish humanitarian action primarily a Kurdish enterprise. This section will focus on the challenges and opportunities the humanitarian actors encounter when engaging with potential donors among the Kurdish diaspora members. First, I will examine why the humanitarian actors choose certain support activities. Then, I will investigate their struggle to attract potential donors, and finally, I will investigate the importance of networks in the Danish setting.

Support activities

Three types of initiatives with the aim of mobilising the Kurdish diaspora members are particularly common: charity dinners, clothes collections and fundraising campaigns.

Charity dinners cover a variety of support events, which all feature some kind of cultural or social activities alongside eating Kurdish food and dancing to Kurdish music. As one of the activists said, 'If we do not do anything to attract them, then they will not come. Maybe, 5, 6, 10 will come. But if you say there is music, then they will come. If you say there is good food, then they will come' (G, male, 50s). Besides being cultural events where people socialise and uphold Kurdish cultural traditions, the goal of the charity dinners is of course to collect money for humanitarian aid. Money is raised by selling admission tickets at 100 DKK or by selling the food and beverage or items that people have brought. At one of the most successful support events for Kobane, the organisers were able to mobilise many self-employed Kurds, such as restaurant owners, hairdressers and bakers, who were willing to contribute with large donations or large amounts of money. The wedding hall where the event was held was also free of charge and the musicians played for free. The donated food was sold at a food stall, while the different items and services were sold at an auction. Some credit vouchers were given as gifts in line with the tradition of charity dinners that Kurdish women used to give, one of the organisers told me. At other support events, the organisers invited a Kurdish-Danish politician to act as auctioneer at the auction for donated items and services.

Clothes collections can be either spontaneous or part of a long-term commitment. During the winter of 2014–15 after the Islamic State attack on Mount Sinjar and the battle of Kobane, enormous piles of clothes were collected and shipped to people in need in the homeland. One single man in North Zealand collected clothes and shoes among friends and acquaintances to fill two trucks heading for Kobane. The Federation of Kurdish Associations in Denmark also collected clothes and shoes among its members, resulting in three truckloads, one for Kobane and two for Sinjar. The Red Sun turned clothes collection into a core activity of the organisation. Besides shipping the clothes to Kurdistan, they set up a flea market where they could sell some of the clothes and other items they had collected from people. Clothes tend to be fairly easy to collect, because a lot of people are happy to give away some of their belongings to people in need. As one activist said, 'When it is about money, it is difficult, but if we say that we are collecting clothes, it is much easier and people will come. However, it is also expensive. We cannot do it any more' (G, male, 50s). Thus, collecting clothes and other material objects is both time-consuming and costly as they need to be stored and sorted as well as transported and delivered to the conflict zone.

Fundraising may be the aim of a variety of activities, including those mentioned above. In the following, I will look at efforts to collect money by asking people to donate or become paying members of one of the humanitarian organisations. One of the ways to collect money is through fundraising campaigns. The humanitarian organisations used to place collection boxes in Kurdish-owned shops and pizzerias, but this took a lot of effort as the boxes had to be placed and then collected. Sometimes they were even stolen, despite containing only small amounts of money. Fundraising campaigns on social media with a much wider reach have since taken over. Posts on Facebook complete with photos or videos are better at attracting attention to the aim of the campaign and include information about which bank account or Mobilepay number donors can transfer money to. Social media is also a good way for the organisation to promote itself and document when funds have been delivered to the people in need. The organisations also charge an annual membership fee to ensure a regular minimum income level. All the organisations I talked to bemoaned the lack of strong commitment from the Kurds, however, resulting in membership numbers fluctuating. This is a serious issue for the organisations as an organisation can only be registered as a charity if it meets certain criteria, as per the Tax Assessment Act § 8 A. The criteria include having more than 300 fee-paying members, more than 100 donors donating at least 200 DKK each per year, and an annual income of more than 150,000 DKK (SKAT, n.d.). Being approved as a humanitarian organisation would make donations tax-deductible and place the organisation in a completely different league.

There are other ways of raising money, though. The Rojava Committee deserves special mention as it has experimented with new forms of charity activities to reach a broader audience of both Kurds and non-Kurds. In 2016, in connection with the World Kobane Day on 1 November, the Rojava Committee organised three days of various activities in support of Kobane. The World Kobane Day was launched the year before as an international day of solidarity by the Kobane Canton (The Executive Board of Kobani Canton 2015). The Kobane Days in Copenhagen in 2016 were organised in line with this and also in line with the overall aim of the Rojava Committee, which is 'political lobbyism in support of the revolution in Rojava' (Rojava Komitéen 2016). Thus, most of the activities aimed to mobilise Kurds and non-Kurds politically, focusing specifically on international solidarity with Kobane. The activities included a photo exhibition on the history of the Rojava revolution, a book presentation of Öcalan's pamphlets translated into Danish, a Kurdish theatre play, the showing of a Kurdish film, a panel debate with international supporters of Rojava, a procession through the streets of Copenhagen and, finally, a concert featuring Kurdish musicians. The committee also cooperated with the Red-Green Alliance, who hosted a meeting with the former YPG fighter and UK citizen Macer Gifford. In addition, Kurdish food was sold, as were T-shirts with the logo of the Danish Rojava Committee and various other solidarity accessories (armbands, badges and scarves). The committee also cooperated with the Kurdish Doctors and Nurses and held an art auction of donated valuables and Kurdish art objects. To draw more attention to their humanitarian work, the committee dedicated the revenue from all the activities conducted over the three days to the purchase of medical equipment for a hospital in Rojava. The Kurdish Doctors and Nurses saw the art auction as a way to raise money and at the same time to open the audience's eyes to Kurdish art. In contrast to other humanitarian initiatives, the support activities of the Rojava Committee always merge political mobilisation with humanitarian action and awareness of Kurdish culture. For that reason, the committee is a pioneer within the Öcalan movement, to whom it makes no sense to separate political and humanitarian action as political awareness is considered the basis of all human activity.

The book project 'The Cradle of Eden' (in Danish 'Edens Vugge') also deserves special attention. While the support initiatives of the Rojava Committee go way beyond the Kurdish milieu and reach non-Kurdish political supporters, the Cradle of Eden project is one of the few humanitarian initiatives that reaches beyond both Kurdish circles and circles of political supporters by succeeding in mobilising representatives of the Danish cultural elite. The book is a collection of poems reflecting ambiguous memories from Syria written by the Syrian Kurdish poet Jan Pêt Khorto (Khorto 2016). Khorto writes in Arabic but identifies as Kurdish (Eriksen 2017). The book was published in cooperation with the Danish painter Trine Kandborg, whose expressive paintings of faces from Aleppo are printed alongside the poems. June

Dahy has translated the poems into Danish. All contributors have donated their work so that the revenue from the book sales goes to a school for Syrian refugee children in Mersin, Turkey, run by Syrian refugees. The book and the school project have been presented at various events around the country, including a vernissage held in a gallery in a suburb of Copenhagen. The well-known Danish poet Henrik Nordbrandt was invited to recite some of his poems, one of which, 'King Slurry', satirises Danish antipathy towards foreigners. Besides reaching beyond the Kurdish milieu and circles of political supporters, the project also reflects a new trend involving primarily young Kurds applying their skills to maximise the impact of their humanitarian action. Thus, one of the organisers of the successful charity dinner mentioned in the introduction of this chapter stressed that she and her fellow organisers are experienced strategists and project managers, and all have a higher education in the fields of communication, law and economy, which explains the professional execution of the event.

How to attract donors

When looking closely at the struggle of the humanitarian organisations to attract potential donors, it is evident that in times of conflict or crisis in the homeland, the donations are larger than during more peaceful times. The number of donations and contributions to humanitarian aid among diaspora members seems to correlate with the extent and significance of the conflict or crisis in the homeland. This becomes evident when looking at the donations from the Sun of Mesopotamia to Heyva Sor from 2013 to 2018. According to one of my interviewees (W, male, 30s), the organisation transferred the following amounts of money to the German organisation: 65,000 DKK in 2013, 600,000 DKK in 2014, 600,000 DKK in 2015, 300,000 DKK in 2016, 200,000 DKK in 2017, and 150,000 DKK in 2018 (first half of the year). The Kobane effect – that is, the impact of the battle for Kobane on the will to donate – is clear, peaking during the winter of 2014–15 and then declining. In 2015, the peace process between the Turkish state and the PKK collapsed, and the escalation of the conflict led to major destruction in Kurdish cities, such as Sur and Cizre, which may have affected the level of donations as well. The Turkish invasion of Afrin at the beginning of 2018 is bound to have an effect (of the total amount donated in 2018, 125,000 DKK was collected during the first three months of 2018) like the Turkish invasion of north-eastern Syria in 2019 most likely would.

During my interviews in 2017 and the beginning of 2018, I noticed some frustration among the aid workers. After years of great financial inflow, the income from donations had stagnated, but the humanitarian challenges among the Kurds remained the same. Humanitarian actors struggle for the attention of potential donors, just as political actors vie for attention and political support. One group of rivals to the humanitarian organisations are the families back home. The humanitarian activists are up against the fact that many Kurds in Denmark transfer money abroad to their own families in Turkey or Iraqi Kurdistan. Remittances have become a major source of inflow to the developing countries. In 2016, the World Bank estimated that migrants are sending 441 billion USD to their home countries every year, which is three times the amount of the official development assistance to developing countries (World Bank Group 2016). This explains why some Kurds decline to donate when asked. Many are in fact sending money directly to their families in need. It is difficult to estimate the exact amount of remittances from migrant-receiving countries to Kurds in the homeland. The Kurds being stateless do not appear on any lists by the World Bank or equivalent organisations. However, the major challenge with regard to making a solid estimate of the Kurdish remittance flow is lack of data. As many Kurds do not trust the power holders in the homeland states, they tend to transfer money by means of unofficial channels. The litigation against ROJ TV further complicated the issue as it was a money transfer (to the PKK, however) that represented the core of the case. The coup attempt in 2016 and the Turkish allegations against Gülen supporters, some of whom are Kurds, might also have prompted migrants to take precautions against state interference. This may also partly explain why the remittance inflow to Turkey has halved over the last ten years, according to the World Bank, in contrast to the remittance inflow to almost all other migrant-sending countries (World Bank 2018). As the Kurds make up only a part of the emigrants from Turkey (in Denmark, at least 50 per cent of the migrants from Turkey are Kurdish (Serinci 2011; Mikkelsen 2011, p. 104)), there may be other explanations for the decrease in remittance inflow, such as Turkey's economic growth in the 2000s.

Another group of rivals to the humanitarian organisations in order to attract attention of potential donors are other humanitarian organisations operating in the same conflict areas. Some of the organisation representatives I talked to mention situations where they felt they were being backstabbed by other actors as some of their supporters suddenly turned away. Some Kurds also found it necessary to warn against non-Kurdish organisations, such as VIOMIS, a Danish Muslim humanitarian organisation providing emergency aid to Syria and other Muslim countries, VIOMIS is short for 'Viden Om Islam' (Danish for 'knowledge on Islam'). The Kurds claimed that the organisation spread Salafi ideology while delivering emergency aid to refugees and needy people in war-torn Syria and therefore conflicted with the interests of the Kurds. Many Kurds do, however, support Muslim organisations, and some even adhere to Islamist and Salafi ideology. It is important to note that the income of VIOMIS, including donations, was 2 million DKK in 2014 and 4 million in 2015 (VIOMIS, n.d.), which is a significantly higher amount than the Sun of Mesopotamia was able to raise in the same years. If the Kurdish organisations could attract the donors of VIOMIS, it would be a boost to their aid programmes.

Networking activities

Finally, the importance of networks and allies when organising donation initiatives should not be underestimated. One group of supporters are other activists who donate facilities to host flea markets, provide moving boxes or make transport available to the organisation. The aid workers repeatedly point to the support the organisation receives from kind individuals, Kurds as well as non-Kurds, with whom they have established valuable contact and cooperated with several times. Often this cooperation ensures low costs when donations of money and clothes are handled and sent off. Other groups include relatives who get involved in mobilising their networks to gather as many people as possible. One of the organisers of the main Kobane charity dinner in the autumn of 2014 told me that they knew that mobilising a sizeable group of people was vital for the success of the event. Thus, the organisers asked their mothers to call around, primarily to make people show up at the event, but also to ask people to donate food and items or services for the auction. She assessed this to be the most important explanation for the high number of attendees that paved the way for the major success of the event, which made it possible for the organisers to donate 125,000 DKK.

Some groups tried to establish contact with more established humanitarian organisations. This proved to be troublesome, though. Some have not even thought of the possibility of cooperation. The bottom line is that cooperation between Kurdish humanitarian organisations and Danish humanitarian NGOs is non-existent. However, the Kurdish organisations could benefit from public funding, which is administered by Danish NGOs. A recent report, *Between Aid and Self-Help* (in Danish *Mellem bistand og selvhjælp*) (Sørensen et al. 2018), analyses the involvement of diaspora groups in the Danish development aid programmes. The study focuses on three diaspora groups in Denmark: Somalis, Afghans and Filipinos. The report mentions a number of funds and programmes accessible to diaspora groups who aim to deliver emergency and development aid in their homelands. These are Recycling for Development (in Danish, Genbrug til Syd), the Civic Society Fund (Civilsamfundspuljen), the Danish Emergency Relief Fund (Den Danske Nødhjælpspulje) and the Diaspora Programme (Diasporaprogrammet). The Diaspora Programme is restricted to diaspora groups, and only Somali and Afghan associations. The rest are accessible to all Danish organisations without ethnic and national restrictions. They are all funded by the Danish Ministry of Foreign Affairs but administered by Danish NGOs. Recycling for Development is one of the most popular programmes for small organisations who are not otherwise involved in aid programmes (Sørensen et al. 2018, p. 42). In 2013, Recycling for Development financed 344 container shipments from Denmark to forty different countries. One hundred and forty-two Danish organisations have received funding, translating into 2.4 containers per organisation on average. There are, however, large differences in diaspora involvement in shipments to the various receiving countries. While the diaspora associations are heavily involved in the shipment to Somalia, there is no diaspora involvement in the Moldova shipment at all. Both countries are among the top five receivers of containers funded by Recycling for Development (Sørensen et al. 2018, pp. 43–4). The Danish Emergency Relief Fund was established in 2017 to support emergency aid initiatives. It is accessible to humanitarian organisations that are not otherwise state supported. In 2017, 23 humanitarian initiatives were supported, and half a million people in ten different crisis situations benefitted from the programme (Sørensen et al. 2018, p. 50).

Among the traditional Danish NGOs, which do not administer funds specifically aimed at diaspora groups or invite diaspora associations to apply, the experience of cooperation with diaspora groups is limited and amounts only isolated initiatives. The report argues that this is due to either a lack of knowledge or preconceptions regarding the diaspora groups, which the NGOs suspect have interests that may contradict the humanitarian principles of the Danish humanitarian organisations (Sørensen et al. 2018, p. 114). The motivation of the diaspora associations to seek cooperation with Danish NGOs is high. However, the report also mentions administrative burdens and mental fatigue that prevent the diaspora members from applying the funds. The report argues that the analysis unfortunately indicates that 'primarily, it is the interaction with the Danish funding system that wears down the volunteers' (Sørensen et al. 2018, p. 91).

The report concludes that the Danish emergency and development aid could profit from diaspora groups becoming more involved. The diaspora groups possess invaluable knowledge of the homeland societies as well as Danish society and can therefore mediate between different interaction dynamics. The authors recommend a more ambitious and flexible diaspora policy that recognises diasporic actors as resources.

The position of the Kurds resembles that of the diaspora groups analysed in the report both in terms of the attitude of the Danish humanitarian organisations experienced by the groups and the diaspora groups' own reluctance to cooperate with the Danish humanitarian organisations. When asked about the lack of cooperation with Danish humanitarian NGOs, the Kurdish activists gave a number of explanations. One group tried to cooperate with the Danish Red Cross, but felt their request was not taken seriously, so they withdrew it. Another group was more concerned with their own restrictions and stressed their lack of knowledge about the opportunities for cooperation. This group also launched into explanations about their position as a marginalised group, including lack of language skills and a fear of being dismissed as a non-recognised ethnic group in the homeland. All the groups I talked to regretted their lack of financial weight, which would make them more attractive as collaborators.

The Kurds would definitely benefit from a more flexible diaspora approach within the aid business. First, like many other diaspora groups, Kurdish humanitarian action is based on volunteerism and often relies on a limited number of individuals. Fewer administrative burdens would therefore be appreciated. Second, Danish humanitarian organisations should appreciate the humanitarian attitude and perceive it as genuine. Combined with their knowledge of the homeland and their networks, this attitude makes the Kurds invaluable humanitarian partners. However, the Kurds should learn more about the actual opportunities for funding. Recycling for Development seems like a suitable partner for the Kurds with regard to handling and shipping various equipment for schools and hospitals. The organisation also seems to be a suitable partner regarding its experiences from cooperating with small associations.

The Field – Delivering Humanitarian Aid

This section will focus on the challenges and opportunities humanitarian actors encounter when engaging with the field. First, I will provide a brief overview of the humanitarian activities in the field and the strategies of the humanitarian actors for reaching the people in need by working closely with local actors. Then, I will examine the main obstacles to delivering humanitarian aid, focusing on the response from the main adversaries of the Kurdish aid workers' activities.

Activities

Most of the humanitarian aid delivered from Kurds in Denmark to Kurds in or from Syria is emergency aid. It includes clothes, blankets, sleeping bags, food, cooking stoves and medicine. Some of the deliveries contain items collected in Denmark, while other items have been paid for with money raised by the organisations among diaspora members. Only a few humanitarian initiatives are long-term initiatives aiming at rebuilding damaged societal infrastructures or developing new societal institutions. Prominent examples of this include the delivery of hospital equipment and the financing of a mother and child hospital in Rojava. However, a substantial amount of money has been raised among diaspora groups and international political supporters and channelled to Rojava for political support. Parts of these funds function as development aid as they are used for reconstruction and the development of new political institutions. In 2014, during the siege of Kobane, the Red-Green Alliance raised 30,000 DKK among its members, which was handed over to PYD during PYD chairman Salih Muslim's visit to Denmark. The fund was donated by the Red-Green Alliance to raise awareness of the humanitarian disaster unfolding at the time in northern Syria, but there were no restrictions on how it was to be used (Andersen 2014). As touched upon above, the distinction between humanitarian and political support is not clear when it comes to supporting Rojava. The same applies to long-term development assistance more generally. Thus, development programmes that aim to implement human rights, gender equality and democratic infrastructure may be perceived as universal but they nevertheless represent the ideas of a liberal democratic world order that various donors want to support.

When delivering aid to the people of Kurdistan, the Kurds from Denmark rely on ties to Kurdish actors in the field to reach the people in need. While some of the humanitarian actors draw on personal or family ties, others rely on institutionalised relations. The three humanitarian organisations whose representatives I have interviewed employ three different strategies when cooperating with allies in the field. The Azadi Humanitarian Organisation, a relatively small organisation, ascribes its efficiency to the close relationship with the anchors in Iraqi Kurdistan, who appear to be family members of the prime mover of the organisation. The Red Sun has built up local divisions in both Iraqi and Syrian Kurdistan located in the cities of Dohuk and Qamishlo with whom they cooperate on delivering humanitarian aid. The divisions are recognised by the local authorities and are thus able to work freely in the Kurdish regions. The Sun of Mesopotamia has chosen yet another strategy as the organisation channels its funds to another European organisation, namely the Kurdish-German organisation Heyva Sor, which is present in and works with the autonomous Kurdish entities in northern Syria.

The main obstacles

One of the main obstacles to delivering humanitarian aid to the Syrian Kurds is accessibility. Accessibility relies heavily on local and regional powers, who may or may not allow the delivery to be made. When asked about obstacles to emergency relief, many of my interviewees mentioned a specific episode. At the beginning of 2014, Deniz Celal Kilic, a restaurant owner from Værløse, a town just outside Copenhagen, collected blankets, duvets, clothes and shoes among his fellow townspeople to ship to Kobane. The collection was shipped on a truck registered in Turkey, but when the truck reached the Turkish border on its way to northern Syria, it was refused entry by the Turkish authorities and had to return to Denmark without delivering the emergency aid (Pries 2015). Other trucks were later able to make it all the way, but the event caused a lot of frustration among humanitarian workers as the obstruction by the Turkish state authorities was perceived as a political act to once again suppress the Kurds, this time by preventing Kobane from receiving necessary humanitarian assistance. It is evident that since 2014, the Turkish state has hindered access to the Kurdish areas in northern Syria by closing the border and only arbitrarily allowing aid workers access. From 2015 to 2018, the Turkish state built a border wall in an attempt to isolate the autonomous regions as well as to contain Islamic State. During the same period, the Kurdistan Regional Government also obstructed access to Rojava from the east by alternately allowing and preventing people from crossing the river Tigris as they saw fit. The river represented a major obstacle that only the most dedicated aid workers attempted to cross. Until recently, the only reliable way to enter Rojava was through regime-controlled areas either by plane from Damascus or weekly flights from Beirut to Hassakeh and from there into Kurdish-controlled territory. Access for Kurdish aid workers to Turkey and the Kurdistan Region of Iraq in order to help Syrian Kurdish refugees is much less complicated. However, they are expected to refrain from political activism in support of the PKK and do not interfere in the political decisions on the Syrian Kurdish refugees. Both Turkey and the Kurdistan Region of Iraq each received more than hundred thousand Kurdish refugees from Syria during the battle of Kobane. Thousands of Yezidis from Sinjar also fled to the Kurdistan Region of Iraq during the attack by Islamic State in the summer of 2014.

Expenses and security risks

The expenses and security risks of delivering aid in war torn areas represent yet more major obstacles. As mentioned above, the shipping of clothes and other necessities is expensive. Many of the aid workers I interviewed told me that they have covered their own travel expenses when delivering aid to Kurdish areas in the Middle East in order to maximise the impact of the funds raised. The aid workers also feel obliged to keep the expenses to an absolute minimum as they usually promise their donors that the full amount of their donations will go to emergency aid. It is also worth mentioning that my interviewees are all involved in humanitarian action on a voluntary basis, so they spend all of their spare time campaigning and fundraising when the humanitarian action is running at full throttle.

Some of the Kurdish aid workers also often expose themselves to serious security risks from potential adversaries, such as Islamic State. One aid worker recounts an episode when delivering aid to the Yezidis in Sinjar. Some of the volunteers of his organisation were heading to Sinjar, but the driver took the wrong turn, so they came very close to Islamic State forces. Fortunately, they found the right route and arrived safely in the Kurdish-controlled areas. He explains his motivation to continue despite the danger thus:

> [. . .] it was a really really tough experience. It was not easy. But it was great. When I was there myself and for the first time saw the children and all the people, it was fantastic. Probably, you have seen some photos, when I am on the mountain and take out the stuff and give it to them. It was really really fantastic. (Q, male, 20s)

Other security risks arise when the instructions of the regional powers are transgressed, such as the Turkish and KRG authorities' restrictions on entering Rojava, as mentioned above.

All of the humanitarian activists who personally deliver aid to the Kurdish areas are willing to take enormous personal risks. However, the gratification of being able to meet and support fellow Kurds in real need seems to outweigh the risks.

Outcomes of Kurdish Humanitarian Activism

Alleviating Kurdish suffering

During my fieldwork, I interviewed many immensely dedicated aid workers and witnessed a variety of aid initiatives in support of the Syrian Kurds and other Kurds terrorised by Islamic State. It is hard to measure the overall impact of the aid initiatives as some of the humanitarian actors count the tonnes delivered, others the families they have helped, and yet others total the funds they have been able to transfer. Everybody I met stressed the importance of the Kurdish assistance as it reaches Kurds in serious need or Kurds neglected by other humanitarian actors.

To provide humanitarian aid to the suffering Kurds, the Kurdish activists must possess two main skills: they must be able to mobilise the diaspora and non-Kurdish donors, and they must be able to access the field.

Kurdish activists mainly perform the traditional charity repertoire to reach the diaspora: charity dinners, collecting clothes and fundraising. In times of crisis, many Kurds feel the urge to help their suffering countrymen by donating or contributing to humanitarian relief. However, when the pressure eases or the crisis fades in the eyes of diasporic Kurds, the potential donors no longer feel the same obligation to support, resulting in donations and support initiatives decreasing. This causes frustration among the dedicated Kurdish activists and highlights the financial vulnerability of the Kurdish non-professional humanitarian organisations. Although various Danish governmental aid programmes are available to Kurdish humanitarian activists, the Kurdish organisations do not make use of them to become more resilient to fluctuating resource inflow. This is primarily due to lack of knowledge and lack of confidence in governmental support. The activists seem more willing to try new forms of humanitarian activism to reach non-Kurdish potential donors, including political festivals and fine art projects combining poetry and painting.

In order to reach Kurds in need in areas of the Kurdish homeland, Kurdish activists benefit from access to the transnational Kurdish community. This transnational community is formed and transformed by continual interaction between Kurds who are connected either with family or organisational ties or by political affiliation. This means that the interaction takes place among actors whose relations are built on long-lasting trust rather than ad hoc professional cooperation. This enables the Kurdish humanitarian actors to focus their relief and reach the field quickly, which is a major strength of the Kurdish relief work. The Kurdish activists' transnational networks would clearly be an asset if they were to seek cooperation with other Danish NGOs, but most of the Kurdish activists seem reluctant to partner with more established organisations. Some prefer to work independently as they fear being rejected if they approach the established organisations. Others fear losing their focus on the Kurds or being deprived of the ability to pursue a dynamic approach suitable for a small volunteer association. However, some of the activists are keen to abandon their independence, as they perceive cooperation with Danish humanitarian organisations as a recognition of their non-religious and non-political affiliation.

Kurdish diasporic identities

Another outcome of the Kurdish humanitarian activism is the transformation of Kurdish identities through the processes of interaction and implementation of the humanitarian strategies in support of the Kurds. Most of the Kurdish humanitarian activists I talked to mentioned the immediate feeling of being part of a (transnational) Kurdish community as the main reason for getting involved in relief initiatives. However, becoming an activist and acting in support of fellow Kurds transformed their sense of Kurdish identity into more conscious forms. This is an ongoing dialectical process, which also formed the unreflective sense of belonging to the Kurdish community in the first place (Jenkins 1994).

The Kurdish aid workers' identification as Kurds is transformed by personal reflection and discussions with other Kurds on strategy aimed at Kurds. It is also transformed through interaction with external players, that is, allies and adversaries in Denmark and Kurdistan, who respectively represent opportunities for and constraints on the delivery of the aid. All in all, this is a very complex and dynamic process, which involves the following significant elements.

At the individual level, the Kurds are confronted with their own ambiguity towards helping the Kurds while at the same time upholding the universal principles of humanity and impartiality. Innocent non-Kurds are embraced, while the entitlement of Islamic State members to be helped is questioned.

In in-group discussions among members of the Kurdish transnational community, neutrality and independence as guiding principles of humanitarian action are questioned. Several Kurdish actors both in the Suburb and in the Field demand political commitment from humanitarian activists and organisations. While some Kurdish humanitarian players vehemently reject the demands and gain support by doing so, others perceive humanitarian action as a political act of reversing the unjust committed against the Kurds for decades. Differences also occur when aid workers decide whether non-Kurds should be included in support activities. Most often, the Kurdish humanitarian events and campaigns are enterprises for Kurds only. Some activities do try to mobilise political supporters or humanitarian-minded intellectuals, though.

Interaction with non-Kurdish groupings represents yet another level at which the Kurdish humanitarian action is discussed and the Kurdish identity is formed. In the Danish setting, reaching beyond the Kurdish milieu to political and humanitarian supporters represents opportunities for donations. However, applying for funds or recognition from Danish authorities or non-Kurdish humanitarian NGOs can be a humiliating affair, so Kurdish humanitarian activists often give up on petitioning even before attempting. In the Kurdish setting in the Middle East, the most potent non-Kurdish actors are the adversaries, who seek to obstruct the Kurdish humanitarian action by denying access to the areas hosting the Kurds in need.

All Kurdish humanitarian players will be affected by this. The reaction to both the oppositional positions and encouraging supporters pushes the identity of the Kurdish humanitarian activists in three different directions. Some realise that being Kurdish is a political identity. As one interviewee told me, 'we have reached a point where I do not feel that I can be against the revolution because we have reached a point where it is of immense importance that we as a people are enlightened' (I, female, 20s). Later, she continued, 'When I was younger, I always said that I was from Syria. I never said the Kurdish part of Syria, I just said Syria. But that was before I understood the political aspects.' In other words, her Kurdish identity emerges from political awareness, which took root in her as she became a humanitarian volunteer. Others will identify more with a humanistic non-sectarian position, which perceives Kurdishness as one of many ethnic identities in the human family. Thus, another interviewee concluded, '[w]e will relieve people of their suffering' (G, male, 50s), underscoring the humanitarian rather than the Kurdish aspect of his relief effort. Yet others have their cosmopolitan position confirmed. They perceive being Kurdish as one element among others of their compound identity. One interviewee recounted, '[m]y identity depends on the context. Sometimes I refer to myself as Syrian, sometimes Kurdish and sometimes a Kurd from Syria' (B, male, 20s).

PART IV

FINDINGS AND CONCLUSIONS

9

AMBIGUOUS INTERPLAYS AND REFORMULATIONS OF KURDISH IDENTITIES

The main aim of this book has been to investigate the activism of the Kurdish diaspora in Denmark in support of the Kurds in Syria. I wanted to contribute to the understanding of how a diaspora mobilises and reaffirms its diaspora identity in times of crisis in the homeland. To accomplish this, I investigated how Kurdish support initiatives were launched as a reaction to major events in the homeland. Applying the concept of diaspora and the theory of strategic interactionism to data collected mainly from fieldwork, I analysed how mobilisation took place in various arenas through interaction between Kurdish and other players who supported, accepted or opposed the Kurdish strategies. I also discussed the outcome of the Kurdish activism, meaning the extent to which the Kurdish activists have reached their goals and how identifying as a Kurdish diaspora member has been transformed through activism in support of the homeland. In the following, I will sum up my findings on Kurdish activism and outline and elaborate on the major conclusions with regard to (1) Kurdish diaspora activism in Denmark (the spatial focus of this study) and (2) Kurdish diaspora activism from Kobane to Afrin (the temporal focus of this study). I will argue that Denmark proved to be a 'reluctant host society' for Kurdish activism and that, as a response, the Kurdish players employed a strategy of ambiguous interplay. I will also argue that, in response to Kobane, Kurdish activism generated new ways of identifying as a Kurd. The activism in response to Afrin, on the other hand, revived the more traditional ways of being Kurdish in Denmark.

Findings

This study found that the Kurdish diaspora in Denmark came into being due to the mobilisation of Kurdish refugees and labour migrants who had arrived in Denmark, beginning in the late 1960s. This in turn led to the formation of two main movements, which I have called the Öcalan and the Kurdistan movement, respectively, due to their focal points. These movements reflect the key divisions in the transnational community. The diaspora was dominated by Kurds originating from Turkey, as they made up the largest part of the Kurdish community in Denmark. Syrian Kurds represented only a small part of the diaspora. The Syrian Civil War, when the Syrian Kurds became the main military opponent of Islamic State on the Syrian battle front, provided an opportunity to mobilise for the Kurdish diaspora. The battle of Kobane, especially, provoked a surge of events and initiatives by Kurdish diaspora activists aiming to provide humanitarian relief and political backing to the Kurds of Syria. Thus, this study also found that the war was an opportunity for the Syrian Kurds to step out of the political darkness and become an unavoidable political player in Syria. In the time after the PYD declared the autonomy of the Kurdish areas in Syria, the YPG and the YPJ (in cooperation with the international coalition) conquered around one-third of Syrian territory, including Raqqa, the former capital of Islamic State.

This study identified three main strategies employed by the Kurds in Denmark in support of the Syrian Kurds. These strategies are political activism, courtroom activism and humanitarian action, unfolding in the political, courtroom and humanitarian arenas, respectively.

The main goal of political activism is to pressure political decision-makers to take action in support of the Kurdish cause. This strategy takes the Kurds into two different sub-arenas, which I call 'the castle' and 'the square', as they seek to engage politicians, directly in the political institutions at 'the castle', and indirectly by raising the Danish public's awareness of the Kurdish cause in 'the square'. The outcome has been poor in spite of the fact that the politicians willingly participated in meetings and municipal administrations readily accommodated demonstrations in the public space. However, the study found major differences between the two main Kurdish diaspora movements, who compete against each other for access to and recognition of their respective cause. Analysing their rivalry enabled me to identify four determinants of success: close allies in Parliament, a strong message that appeals to young Kurds, persistent and well-organised members and strong transnational backing. Being in control of these areas gave the Öcalan movement more visibility and bigger influence than the Kurdistan movement.

Courtroom activism was sparked by a few individuals with a desire to combat the injustice they felt was committed by Danish authorities. My analysis focused on the case of Joanna Palani, who decided to have her passport nullification tried in court. She thus pursued a proactive strategy, taking the police to court. When her defence was turned down, she decided to turn the case into a mobilising event. This made the courtroom an arena for judicial interaction and a rostrum for political mobilisation. My study found that both strategies failed as the decision-makers refused to make a distinction between foreign fighters who supported militant Islamism and those who volunteered for Kurdish forces. They maintained that foreign and domestic policies have separate goals. The Danish state cooperated with YPG and YPJ in Syria by participating in the international coalition against Islamic State, while at the same time it criminalised volunteers for YPG and YPJ on par with fighters for Islamic State. Joanna Palani's case was also rejected by the Kurdish diaspora, the political allies of the Öcalan movement and the Danish public. Due to these disappointing experiences with the legal system, the Kurdish diaspora in Denmark is unlikely to resort to courtroom activism in the near future.

While the political lobbyists and courtroom activists took a political stance, humanitarian activists often refused to adopt one. They were more concerned about upholding the universal humanitarian principles and, at the same time, supporting fellow Kurds in need. Most of them pointed out that political division is a source of conflict and distress, and that they had to navigate among Kurdish groups pursuing specific Kurdish interests in both host country and homeland. The present study distinguished between two sub-arenas, 'the suburb' and 'the field', which correspond to two types of humanitarian action. One type of action aims to provide resources and it takes place in the diaspora, primarily in the suburb where the Kurds live.

The other type of action aims to deliver aid and takes place in the field of the homeland. This study identified a widespread desire to support fellow Kurds in a time of crisis. The same applied to the will to donate. However, when the feeling of emergency faded, the funding decreased, even though people were still suffering in the homeland. None of the Kurdish humanitarian organisations I talked to cooperated with non-Kurdish NGOs. This blocked their access to potential funding and organisational support, but also allowed them to maintain their independence. This independence relied on long-lasting relationships with family members or political allies in the field, ensuring that emergency relief was delivered despite security risks and countermeasures by players in the field.

In this book the three strategies which I identified as the main strategies employed by Kurds in Denmark in support of the Syrian Kurds were treated separately. This was done for analytical reasons in order to be able to investigate the interconnectedness of motivations, goals and means as well as the response to Kurdish activism in the various arenas. It was also done because of the way the strategies are employed in the field as, most often, different Kurdish activists are involved in different activities. Thus, the study found that some Kurds engaged in political action, while others engaged in humanitarian action. Few activists chose to engage in military volunteerism and even fewer in courtroom activism in support of the struggle in Syria, in practice just one Kurd. Although the Kurds engaged in different activities, all of the activists I met shared the feeling of urgency and the need to act. Thus, the battle of Kobane spurred all kinds of activism, as did the attack on Afrin. Whether the individual chose one type of action or another seems to reflect what they perceived as the most important goal and the most necessary means to reach this goal in the current crisis. Regarding goals, the political activists and the military fighters shared the goal of political transformation, either indirectly, by persuading Danish decision-makers to engage in the conflict, or directly, by taking up arms to realise a political idea. This was also the case for the courtroom activist who saw her struggle in court as a continuation of the armed struggle, both seen as a struggle for justice. For the humanitarian activists, the relief assistance of the Kurdish people is the most important goal. However, for the humanitarian workers within the Öcalan movement, humanitarian work is perceived as contributing to the political goal of the

Syrian Kurdish struggle, that is, political autonomy. Regarding means, the political activists stressed the obligation to confront Danish politicians. For the activists of the Öcalan movement this means complying with the division of labour prescribed within the movement: every Kurd should work in their respective countries of settlement to avoid allegations of illegal transnational activism. The humanitarian players and the military fighters shared the inclination to travel to Kurdish areas and engage directly in action in support of fellow Kurds. Concrete action, either working with material goods or taking up arms, seems to be the best way for them to cope with the inner turbulence when confronted with the suffering of the Kurdish people.

The study also found that by acting in support of the Kurdish cause, the individual as well as the Kurdish collective maintained a Kurdish identity. Support events and initiatives became mobilising events: opportunities for active diaspora members to invite passive or silent members to join the mobilised community. The events also ensured that already mobilised members maintained and renewed their identification with the Kurdish cause and the Kurdish transnational community through their activism. Both Kurdish movements equated the true Kurd with the political fighter. Some members were therefore nudged into identifying as political fighters which some refused by emphasising the humanitarian aspects of their involvement. Others found their own individual ways of identifying as Kurds. All contributed to the heterogeneity of the Kurdish diaspora identity.

This study introduced the theory of strategic interactionism into Kurdish diaspora studies. Doing so allowed me to investigate diaspora mobilisation as a complex interplay of actors, including various Kurdish players and their opponents and supporters in Denmark and in the homeland. It also allowed me to investigate diaspora mobilisation as a dynamic enterprise of back-and-forth processes through which the diaspora is created anew. Using this approach, the heterogeneity and fluidity of the Kurdish diaspora became evident, manifesting itself in the rivalry between the Öcalan and the Kurdistan movements and in the various ways in which Kurdish activists responded to the Syrian crisis as well as in the transformation of Kurdish identity from Kobane to Afrin. It also brought to light the ambiguous embrace of Kurdish diaspora activism by Danish politicians and authorities, which the Kurdish diaspora seems to accept in order to uphold a desirable room to manoeuvre.

Kurdish Activism in Denmark

This study investigated the mobilisation of the Kurdish diaspora in Denmark as I wanted to shed light on a minor Kurdish community that has not previously been studied very much. I argue that the Kurdish players employ a strategy of ambiguous interplay as a response to the 'reluctant host society' that Denmark proved to be.

Reluctant hosts

In 1985, Jonathan Matthew Schwartz wrote the book *Reluctant Hosts: Denmark's Reception of Guest Workers*. Being a cultural sociologist and an American, he wrote that Denmark had become a reluctant 'host society' by importing 'guest workers' (Schwartz 1985, p. 6) but failing to fulfil the expectations for a welcoming host. The workers were invited for a short period of time between 1967 and 1973 and, like guests, they were supposed to leave again. However, contrary to expectations and intentions, most of them ended up settling in Denmark along with their families. By depicting Denmark as a reluctant host towards these immigrants, Schwartz explained how the Danish self-sufficiency was challenged by the arrival of guest workers. In that way, the Danes were unwillingly dragged into discussions on how to deal with the presence of immigrants in the labour market and in society as a whole.

My analysis showed that the reluctance to recognise the existence of migrants in society prevails, although it has taken new forms. While Danish politicians and researchers in the 1970s were reluctant to recognise that Denmark had become a host society for migrants, as explained by Schwartz, today's Danish politicians and authorities are reluctant to recognise that these migrants have loyalties that reach beyond the borders of Denmark. This manifests itself in the ways in which politicians, public administrations and other authorities deal with loyalty towards the migrants' host countries. I have argued that this is best characterised as an attitude of ambiguous recognition. The diaspora players are free to express their support for the homeland struggle in the castle, in the square, on social media and everywhere else, but their expression of support is most often met with indifference, diversion and silence. The widespread reluctance among Danish decision-makers to react to the agendas of the Kurdish activists becomes evident when compared with Kurdish experiences of inclusion in Sweden and of restrictions in Germany, as shown by Bahar Baser (Baser 2015, pp. 261–5). I have uncovered four instances of ambiguous recognition.

Danish politicians are generally sympathetic towards the Kurdish political struggle in the Middle East against repression and for equal rights. Some also explicitly support the fight for self-determination or independence and call the division of the Middle East by the Great Powers after World War I a historical injustice committed against the Kurdish people. However, when the Kurds call for concrete action, such as financial and military support for YPG, international criticism of the Turkish attack on Afrin or psychological assistance for the Yezidi victims of Sinjar, the broad support evaporates, even among Danish-Kurdish politicians. The only exceptions are politicians from the Red-Green Alliance who are fully committed to the Kurdish cause and have allied with the Öcalan movement. The party has also formed the Kurdistan Solidarity Group, which focuses specifically on political solidarity work in favour of the Kurdish cause, including removing the PKK from the EU list of terrorist organisations.

The ambiguous recognition of the Kurdish cause is also reflected in the attitudes towards volunteering for YPG and YPJ, who constituted the main military force against Islamic State on the Syrian battle front. Members of the Öcalan movement have repeatedly pointed to the inconsistency between Denmark cooperating with the Kurdish forces as a member of the US-led international coalition against Islamic State while at the same time criminalising those who volunteered or intend to volunteer for the very same Kurdish forces. The inconsistency is partly due to conflicting rationales of Danish foreign and domestic policies, as I have argued in a previous chapter. When Danish politicians decided to contribute to the US-led international coalition against Islamic State, the decision was based on a desire to gain international prestige through military action. This, however, left the strategic decisions of 'where, when, and how to fight' (Jakobsen 2016, p. 207) to others. When the US formed a tactical alliance with the Kurdish forces in Syria, Denmark followed suit. The subsequent amendments to the Passport Act and the Criminal Code, which did not distinguish between fighters for Islamic State and their opponents, including the Kurdish militias, were based on the assumption that an individual who had experienced explosions and learned how to handle weapons in a conflict situation would pose a security risk to society when returning. Regardless of the different rationales, this approach is perceived by Kurdish activists and members of the Öcalan movement as an ambiguous attitude towards the Kurdish struggle against a common enemy.

Ambiguous recognition is also seen in the way Danish authorities regulate Kurdish associations. Government subsidies to the diaspora associations depend on the associations' willingness to include integration initiatives. During the 1990s, the public funding available to diaspora associations was increasingly directed at associations engaged in integration initiatives. Diaspora associations which did not actively strive to integrate their members into Danish society had their funding withdrawn (Jørgensen 2009, p. 121). In contrast, Sweden adopted a multicultural policy on funding of cultural initiatives for migrant communities and mother-tongue education of immigrant children, which aimed to preserve and develop the immigration cultures. The argument was that familiarity with their cultural heritage facilitates the immigrants' integration in their host community.

The squares are also a venue for ambiguous recognition. All the Kurdish activists I talked to appreciated their close relationship with the municipal administration and the police. When they apply for permission to demonstrate, their applications are never refused. Only practical obstacles have prevented them from being granted a permit, such as reconstruction on Christiansborg Palace Square and conflicts with existing bookings. However, the accommodating attitude should be seen as a way to favour urban life that has 'an edge' (City of Copenhagen 2015a) rather than as a way to welcome homeland politics in Denmark. When the Kurdish activists occupy the streets and squares of Copenhagen, the City can claim that it follows its own strategy for urban life that requires Copenhageners to spend 20 per cent more time in urban spaces. In addition, freedom of assembly and freedom of speech ensure that the Kurdish activists are allowed to meet and express their sympathy for any organisation, such as, by waving their flags, even those of the banned PKK. I would argue that this is an example of a well-meaning indifference, which becomes clear when contrasted with the tight restrictions on Kurdish demonstrations in Germany. In Germany, the Kurdish demonstrations and marches are redirected to the outskirts and suburbs of the cities to avoid confrontations between Kurds and Turks. The Kurdish activists in Germany are also prohibited from bringing images of Öcalan and waving

PKK flags. The Kurdish activists I have talked to perceive this as a clear rejection of the Kurdish cause.

Ambiguous interplay

Kurdish activists have responded to the Danish decision-makers' reluctance to host Kurdish activism by employing a similarly ambiguous approach. The Kurds have thus turned the interaction between Kurdish activists and Danish authorities into an ambiguous interplay.

All the Kurdish activists I talked to emphasised their good relationship with the authorities when organising events in the public space. In these cases, the authorities refer to the municipal administration, which grants permissions to demonstrate, and to the police, who oversee the demonstrations. For some, it was very important that young demonstrators, some of whom are newcomers to the country, learned the code of conduct for demonstrations in Denmark. Complying with the code of conduct means demonstrating peacefully and refraining from behaving aggressively towards the police or other opponents, such as when demonstrating in front of the Turkish Embassy during the battle of Afrin. The organisers also appointed their own guards to secure peace and order. Similar compliance was demonstrated when interacting with the authorities on other topics related to running an association, for example the regulations governing public subsidies.

For members of the Öcalan movement, the balance between support for the PKK and the freedom to express sympathy towards the party is delicate. While financial support for the PKK is prohibited because it has been categorised as a terrorist organisation, expressions of support are legal, including waving the PKK flag and all other flags related to the organisation. The Kurdish activists desperately wanted to avoid being linked to terrorism as they were during the trials against ROJ TV and the subsequent trial against ten Kurdish men accused of transferring money to the PKK. This also seemed to be the case during the trials against Joanna Palani when the Kurdish activists refrained from supporting her in order to avoid being related to violation of the law. Thus, the ambiguous response of the Kurdish diaspora towards the courtroom activism of Joanna Palani reflects the Kurdish strategy towards the Danish authorities as a whole: observing the rules even when they are perceived to be questionable in order to maintain a convenient space for action.

The Kurdish activists generally chose a non-confrontational approach in compliance with the indifference and ambiguous recognition of the Danish decision-makers and authorities towards their cause. In this way, they managed to maintain a room for manoeuvre in which they could act freely and proclaim their call for support of the Kurdish cause in Syria and in the other parts of Kurdistan. In doing so, they were able to reassert their Kurdish identity as political fighters and mobilise other Kurds at a time of crisis in the homeland.

From Kobane to Afrin

In this section, I will respond to the question of how Kurdish activism and identities transformed during the struggle, in the period between Kobane and Afrin. I have argued that the Kurdish diaspora identity is the outcome of interaction between diaspora members as to which strategies to choose to reach specific goals in support of the Kurdish cause. As the interaction is continuous and involves numerous Kurdish and non-Kurdish players, Kurdish identity is best described as fluid and polyform. In the following, I will point to three main courses of development.

Alter-territorial identification

I will suggest that the Kurdish diaspora's engagement in the battle of Kobane and its support of Kurdish autonomy in Syria paved the way for a type of Kurdish diaspora identity which I call *alter-territorial*. This notion epitomises a certain diaspora inclination towards the homeland that arises from diaspora members' loyalty and political relation to another part of the homeland than the one they are descended from. In connection with the battle of Kobane, Kurds originating from parts of Kurdistan other than Syria joined the Syrian Kurds, celebrating that 'our' people won the victory of Kobane and managed to uphold Kurdish autonomy in the midst of war. As I have argued throughout the book, immense enthusiasm and fierce pride in the achievements of the Syrian Kurds arose among members of the Kurdish diaspora. At an event on the social and political developments in Rojava, which I attended, a panellist spontaneously proclaimed: 'This is my future place of employment'. Even though members of both Kurdish movements praised and identified with the Kurdish struggle in Kobane, only members of the Öcalan movement associated with Rojava as the home of their aspirations. However, during the same period, members of the Kurdistan movement experienced a similar process, associating with the Kurdish territories of Iraq. The alter-territorial identification by members of the Kurdistan movement thus evolved and spread vis-à-vis the independence referendum in Iraqi Kurdistan which was supported and hailed by Kurds from everywhere, not just by Kurds from Iraq. For the Syrian Kurds of the Kurdistan movement, and primarily for the supporters of KDP, alter-territorial identification with the Kurdistan Region of Iraq became a way of expressing a victorious Kurdish identity as mobilising in support of the Kurdish National Council proved to be a complex task due to the domination of the PYD in the Kurdish areas of Syria. Thus, two different alter-territorial movements arose in response to the emergence of two political autonomous regions of Kurdistan: Rojava and Kurdistan-Iraq.

Alter-territorial identification is a political rather than an emotional association. I discovered, as did Minoo Alinia in her study of the Kurds in Gothenburg (Alinia 2004, pp. 322–424) and Ipek Demir in her study of the Kurds in London (Demir 2012), that Kurds in Denmark relate to the homeland in two distinct ways. They relate to their country of origin as the place where they or their parents were born and to which they are tied emotionally. One of my interviewees stressed the emotional connection to places he knows first-hand by saying, 'In my dreams, I am always in Kurdistan. It has become a longing. As soon as I fall asleep, I am there. Scents, colours, mountains and all the places I have been' (R, male, 40s). The Kurds also relate to their country of origin as a battle space, that is, a space where rights and influences are contested, and where they are engaged politically. Another interviewee tried to explain the two ways of relating to the homeland in this way,

> I feel Kurdish and all Kurds are the same for me. They are the same people. However, you care mostly for the area you were born and grew up. Because you have family, you have friends, people you know. You have your old school and so on (F, female, 50s).

Thus, the Syrian Kurds' alter-territorial identification with Iraqi Kurdistan or the Turkish Kurds' alter-territorial identification with Rojava do not erase the emotional ties with their own or their parents' place of birth.

Previously, Kurdish diaspora members have also identified with parts of Kurdistan other than their area of origin, as suggested by the transnational mobilisation in response to the capture and imprisonment of Abdullah Öcalan in 1999 and the defeat of Saddam Hussein's forces in the Kurdistan region of Iraq in 1991. However, the formation of the two rival autonomous Kurdish regions, in Syria and in Iraq, which both claim to be the leading Kurdish political entity, has further politicised the diaspora members' identification with Kurdish regions other than their area of origin.

Return of the Kurdish struggle against Turkey

For the Kurdish transnational community, Kobane represented the beginning of a new and golden era due to the victory of Kurdish forces against the aggressive fighters of the fast-growing Islamic State, while Afrin represented defeat at the hands of one of the Kurds' oldest enemies: the Turkish state.

In 2014, Islamic State besieged the Kurdish city of Kobane. The Kurdish forces were able to resist until the beginning of 2015, when they broke the siege and pushed back the attackers. As I have argued throughout the book, the resistance and victory at Kobane was a major mobilising event among diaspora Kurds. It sparked a range of activism in support of the Syrian Kurds and became a mobilising event in itself (della Porta 2008). Political lobbying was initiated to pressure the public and decision-makers to take action. Humanitarian activities were organised to relieve the suffering of Kurdish victims and support the construction of infrastructure and societal institutions. Courtroom activism was also tested in an attempt to legitimise military volunteerism. The Kurdish activists of the Öcalan movement succeeded in presenting the Kurds as secular, democratic and pro-female liberators, thereby inserting the Kurds in a modern Western tradition in a way that was widely accepted by Danish media. In contrast, members of Islamic State were described as religious fanatics, terrorists, fascists and extremely repressive against women in general, not to mention the enslavement of Yezidi women and children, which became one of the main causes of the Kurdistan movement. At the same time, the US-led coalition against Islamic State initiated cooperation with the YPG and YPJ forces, which in 2015 were formalised as the Syrian Democratic Forces. Although it was a tactical alliance established in response to a common enemy – Islamic State – Kurdish activists perceived the cooperation as recognition of the Kurdish struggle and the fight for autonomy.

However, in January 2018, the cooperation with the coalition proved too weak to protect the Kurdish forces against Turkey. Turkish military forces and Turkish-backed rebels attacked Afrin, the western canton of Rojava, which was taken by the end of March. Yet again, the Kurdish transnational community launched a campaign to appeal for international support from the great powers and from international organisations. In Copenhagen, activists organised demonstrations in front of the American and the Russian embassies, at the UN City, in the streets and in the City Hall Square. The Öcalan movement depicted the enemy, Turkish president Erdoğan and the Turkish state in general, as terrorists and fascists, echoing their depiction of Islamic State. The activists' proclamations in support of the Syrian Kurds against the Turkish invasion also echoed proclamations in support of the Kurdish struggle in Turkey, which has centred on the autocratic development of the Turkish regime since the breakdown of the peace negotiations in 2015. Thus, the struggle of the Syrian Kurds was redirected towards an anti-Erdoğan and anti-Turkish agenda. This was inevitable as the main adversary was replaced. The focus on the Syrian Kurdish struggle diminished, and the Kurdish struggle against Turkey returned as the main cause of the Öcalan movement. The Turkish incursion in October 2019 amplified this shift.

The development was also linked to the hegemonic presence in diaspora politics of Kurds from Turkey, for whom the Kurdish struggle against the Turkish state is well known and well-rehearsed. At the same time, non-Kurdish far-left players increasingly engaged in the development in Rojava, aligning with the revolutionary or anarchist aspects of the development rather than the Kurdish liberation.

The return of the Kurdish struggle against Turkey among the members of the Öcalan movement combined with the alter-territorial identification of the Syrian Kurdish members of the Kurdistan movement forced the Syrian Kurds into political battles that were greater than their own. These are the battle of the Kurds in Turkey and the battle of the Kurds in Iraq.

A diaspora within a diaspora

Besides the tendencies described above, a few young Kurds from various parts of Kurdistan (some of whom were refugees, some children of refugees and still others children of labour migrants) appeared to be different from other mobilised Kurds as they engaged individually in Kurdish questions. Due to some common characteristics, they make up a category of their own. Like members of the two main Kurdish diaspora movements, they mobilised in response to crises in the homeland. However, while other Kurds engaged themselves in collective action supporting either the Öcalan or the Kurdistan movement, this particular group engaged themselves in individual projects pertaining to research, journalism, teaching, human rights, fundraising, media and art, utilising their professional and educational skills. They perceive being Kurdish as an asset, as they speak several languages and understand the social and political dynamics in the Middle East as well as among diaspora Kurds. Thus, being Kurdish is just one element of their identity as they also consider themselves Danish, Turkish or Arab and align with a global class of young educated people. I call them a 'diaspora within a diaspora', drawing on the expression proposed by Jonathan I. Israel (Israel 2002). Israel applies the notion to the Jewish maritime traders who emerged as a distinct class within the Jewish community after the Spanish Expulsion. Their professional skills as traders combined with their Jewish identity (although in disguise) and connections to fellow Jews in North Africa distinguished them from other Jews and Spanish citizens in general. I also want to single out this group as a particularly skilled group of people who dissociate themselves from the traditional Kurdish diaspora movements. Instead, they connect with a global cosmopolitan class of educated people. When crises occur, they mobilise in support of fellow Kurds and become occasional members of the diaspora, however, they continue to act in their own way.

Final Remarks

This book investigated Kurdish activism in Denmark in support of the Kurdish struggle in Syria. It focused on the period between Kobane and Afrin, but also touched upon developments in the Kurdish-held areas of Syria after the capture of Afrin by Turkish and Turkish-backed forces. At the beginning of 2020, the situation in northern Syria remained tense.

After the defeat of Islamic State in the battle of Baghouz in March 2019, which brought the reign of the organisation to an end, new players entered Kurdish-held areas in northern Syria, while others left. In October 2019, the US eventually implemented the decision to pull back its troops from Syria. This left the Kurds with no safeguard against Turkish incursion. On

9 October, Turkey and the Turkish-backed Syrian National Army attacked and subsequently captured the border area from Tell Abyad to Ras al-Ayn, officially to establish a safe zone for Syrian refugees, but covertly to cleanse the region of terrorists who, in their opinion, include the YPG and YPJ militias. Syrian regime forces were called in and were willing to back the Kurdish forces against Turkey, but it seems unlikely that the Syrian regime, supported by Russia, wants to disrupt Syria's unity by accepting autonomy within the borders of the Syrian Arab Republic.

While the Syrian crisis and the international war against Islamic State proved to be an opportunity for the Syrian Kurds to carve out a de facto autonomous region in northern and eastern Syria, the defeat of Islamic State showed that the Kurdish-led autonomy is fragile and depends on the support of strong allies. However, through the eight years of autonomy, the Syrian Kurds have gained a voice that will no longer be quiet. Likewise, the fight for and achievement of autonomy have had a huge impact on the mobilisation of the diaspora. For some, it was the realisation of their ideological vision. For others, it alienated them from their homeland and pushed them into an alter-territorial identification. For still others, it meant temporary action in support of the Syrian Kurds. Nevertheless, the Öcalan movement celebrated Newroz 2020 on a note of hope, inviting members and friends to Christiansborg under the headline 'Newroz Conference 2020: Rojava, the democratic hope of the Middle East'.

APPENDIX

Interviews with Kurdish activists

Code	Gender	Country of origin	Age	Reason for migration	Time of arrival in Denmark	Date of interview
A	F(emale)	Iraq	50s	Political refugee	1980s	Apr 2016
B	M(ale)	Syria	20s	Political refugee	2000s	Aug 2016
C	M	Turkey	50s	Political refugee	1980s	Aug 2016
D	M	Syria	20s	Political refugee	2010s	Sep 2016
E	M	Syria	40s	Political refugee	2010s	Sep 2016
F+G	F+M	Syria and Iraq	50s	Humanitarian refugee and political refugee	1990s	Jan 2017
H	F	Parents from Turkey	20s	Daughter of labour migrants	Born in Denmark	May 2017
I	F	Parents from Syria	20s	Daughter of political refugees	Born in Denmark	Jun 2017
J	Mixed group	Syria	40s	Political refugees	2000s and 2010s	Jun 2017+ Feb 2018
K+L	M+M	Turkey	50s+60s	Political refugees	1980s	Sep 2017
M	F	Turkey	40s	Daughter of labour migrants	1980s	Sep 2017

N+O	M+M	Turkey	50s	Political refugees	1980s	Sep 2017
P	M	Iraq	30s	Son of political refugees	1990s	Nov 2017
Q	M	Iraq	20s	Humanitarian refugee	2000s	Jan 2018
R	M	Turkey	40s	Son of political refugees	1980s	Jan 2018
S	M	Father from Turkey	20s	Son of a political refugee	Born in Denmark	Feb 2018
T	M	Syria	40s	Political refugee	2000s	Mar 2018
U	M	Turkey	40s	Son of labour migrants	1980s	Mar 2018
V	F	Turkey	30s	Daughter of political refugees	1980s	Mar 2018
W	M	Turkey	30s	Son of labour migrants	1980s	Mar 2018
X	M	Syria	20s	Political refugee	2010s	Aug 2018
Y	M	Turkey	50s	Political refugee	1980s	Dec 2018
Z	M	Syria	70s	Student	1970s	Feb 2019

Interviews with Danish politicians and activists

- Three members of parliament (during the summer and autumn of 2017)
- One candidate for parliament, who is also a candidate for the district council of Copenhagen (August 2018)
- Two Danish male activists, one in his 30s and one in his 60s (Autumn 2017)

REFERENCES

Adamson, F. (2013). Mechanisms of Diaspora Mobilization and the Transnationalization of Civil War. In J. T. Checkel (ed.) *Transnational Dynamics of Civil War* (pp. 63–88). Cambridge: Cambridge University Press.

Ahmazahdeh, H. (2003). *Nation and Novel: A Study of Persian and Kurdish Narrative Discourse.* Uppsala: Studia Iranica Upsaliensia.

Al Arabiya (2012, October 10). Assad ordered killing of Kurdish activist Mashaal Tammo: Leaked files. *Al Arabiya* Exclusive. Retrieved from https://english.alarabiya.net/en/2012/10/10/Assad-ordered-killing-of-Kurdish-activist-Mashaal-Tammo-Leaked-files.html

Alinia, M. (2004). *Spaces of Diasporas: Kurdish Identities, Experience of Otherness and Politics of Belonging.* Göteborg Studies in Sociology 22. Department of Sociology. Gothenburg: Gothenburg University. Retrieved from http://hdl.handle.net/2077/16269

Allsopp, H. (2015). *The Kurds of Syria: Political Parties and Identity in the Middle East.* London: I. B. Tauris.

Allsopp, H. (2017). Kurdish Political Parties and the Syrian Uprising. In G. Stansfield and M. Shareef (eds) *The Kurdish Question Revisited* (pp. 298–304). London: Hurst & Company.

Andersen, H. S. (2014, October 3). Enhedslisten sender penge til IS' modstandere i Syrien. *DR.dk.* Retrieved from https://www.dr.dk/nyheder/politik/enhedslisten-sender-penge-til-modstandere-i-syrien

Andersson, A., Høgestøl S. A. E., and Lie, A. C. (2018). Innledning. In A. Andersson, S. A. E. Høgestøl and A. C. Lie (eds) *Fremmedkrigere. Forebygging, strafforfølgning og rehabilitering i Skandinavia* (pp. 9–23). Oslo: Gyldendal.

ARA News (2016, August 14). KNC leader arrested after increasing tensions between rival Kurdish parties in Syria. *Aranews.net*. Retrieved from http://aranews.net/files/2016/08/knc-leader-arrested-increasing-tensions-rival-kurdish-parties-syria/

Ayata, B. (2011). Kurdish transnational politics and Turkey's changing Kurdish policy: the journey of Kurdish broadcasting from Europe to Turkey. *Journal of Contemporary European Studies*, 19(4), 523–33. https://doi.org/10.1080/14782 804.2011.639988

Arendt, H. (1958). *The Human Condition*. Chicago: University of Chicago Press.

B 122 (2014, August). Beslutningsforslag nr. B 122. *Folketinget 2013–14*. Retrieved from https://www.ft.dk/RIpdf/samling/20131/beslutningsforslag/B122/20131_B122_som_fremsat.pdf

B 123 (2014, September). Beslutningsforslag nr. B 123. *Folketinget 2013–14*. Retrieved from http://www.ft.dk/RIpdf/samling/20131/beslutningsforslag/B123/20131_B123_som_fremsat.pdf

B 8 (2015, October). Beslutningsforslag nr. B 8. *Folketinget 2015–16*. Retrieved from http://www.ft.dk/RIpdf/samling/20151/beslutningsforslag/B8/20151_B8_som_fremsat.pdf

B 108 (2016, March). Beslutningsforslag nr. B 108. *Folketinget 2015–16*. Retrieved from http://www.ft.dk/RIpdf/samling/20151/beslutningsforslag/B108/20151_B108_som_fremsat.pdf

B 56 (2017, January). Beslutningsforslag nr. B 56. *Folketinget 2016–17*. Retrieved from http://www.ft.dk/RIpdf/samling/20161/beslutningsforslag/B56/20161_B56_som_fremsat.pdf

Bachmann, U. (2018, March 24). Masseslagsmål efter demonstration: Anholdt bar rundt på kæmpe kødøkse. *Ekstra Bladet*. Retrieved from https://ekstrabladet.dk/112/masseslagsmaal-efter-demonstration-anholdt-bar-rundt-paa-kaempe-koedoekse/7092268

Basch, L., Schiller, N. G., and Blanc, C. S. (1994). *Nations Unbound: Transnational Projects, Postcolonial Predicaments, and Deterritorialized Nation-States*. London: Routledge.

Baser, B. (2015). *Diasporas and Homeland Conflicts: A Comparative Perspective*. Farnham: Ashgate.

Baser, B. (2015b). KOMKAR: The Unheard Voice in the Kurdish Diaspora. In A. Christou and E. Mavroudi (eds) *Dismantling Diasporas: Rethinking the Geographies of Diasporic Identity, Connection and Development* (pp. 113–26). Abingdon: Routledge.

Baser, B., Emanuelsson, A.-C., and Toivanen, M. (2015). (In)visible spaces and tactics of transnational engagement: a multi-dimensional approach to the

Kurdish diaspora. *Kurdish Studies*, 3(2), 128–50. Retrieved from https://www.ceeol.com/search/article-detail?id=476806

Bauböck, R. (2008). Ties across borders: The growing salience of transnationalism and diaspora politics. *IMISCOE Policy Brief 13*.

Bauböck, R. (2010). Cold Constellations and Hot Identities: Political Theory Questions about Transnationalism and Diaspora. In R. Faist and T. Bauböck (eds) *Diaspora and Transnationalism* (pp. 295–322). IMISCOE Research. Amsterdam: Amsterdam University Press. Retrieved from http://cadmus.eui.eu/bitstream/handle/1814/14318/Diaspora_and_Transnationalism.pdf

Bejder, P. (2016). Indvandring til Danmark, efter 1945. *danmarkshistorien.dk*. Aarhus: Aarhus University. Retrieved from https://danmarkshistorien.dk/leksikon-og-kilder/vis/materiale/indvandring-til-danmark-efter-1945/

Bendixen, T., Cordes, S., Winkel, S. E., Olsen, P., Fink, C. K., and Königsfeldt, I. (2015, October 8). Vi hylder 100 danske kvinder som inspirerer os. *Femina*. Copenhagen: Aller Media.

Bendtsen, S., and Sørensen, A. (2015, June 6). Dansk-kurder risikerer terrordom for at gå i krig mod Islamisk Stat. *Berlingske*. Retrieved from https://www.berlingske.dk/politik/dansk-kurder-risikerer-terrordom-for-at-gaa-i-krig-mod-islamisk-stat

Berlingske (2004, May 16). Kemal Koc sagen. *Berlingske*. Retrieved from https://www.berlingske.dk/internationalt/kemal-koc-sagen

Bjerregaard, D., and Kornø, K. (2018, April 5, revised May 2). Ramt af en byge af skud: Så brutal var likvidering af LTF'er. *Ekstra Bladet*. Retrieved from https://ekstrabladet.dk/plus/krimi/ramt-af-en-byge-af-skud-saa-brutal-var-likvidering-af-ltfer/7101405

Blaschke, J. (1991). Die Diaspora der Kurden in der Bundesrepublik Deutschland. *Österreichische Zeitschrift für Zociologie*, 16(3), 85–93.

Blumer, H. (1937). Social Psychology. In P. S. Emerson (ed.) *Man and Society: A Substantive Introduction to the Social Science* (pp. 144–98). New York: Prentice-Hall. Retrieved from https://brocku.ca/MeadProject/Blumer/Blumer_1937.html

Blumer, H. (1962). Society as Symbolic Interaction. In P. Kviesto (ed.) (2011) *Social Theory. Roots and Branches* (4th edn, pp. 242–8). Oxford: Oxford University Press.

Bonnerup, E., Christensen, P. B., Kærgård, N., Matthiessen, P. C., and Torpegaard, J. (2007). *Værdier og normer – blandt udlændinge og danskere*. København: Tænketanken om Udfordringer for Integrationsindsatsen i Danmark.

Boutcher, S. (2011). Mobilizing in the shadow of the law: lesbian and gay rights in the aftermath of Bowers v. Hardwick. *Research in Social Movements. Conflicts and Change*, 31, 175–205

Boutcher, S. (2013). Law and Social Movements: It's More than Just Litigation and Courts. *Mobilizing Ideas*. Retrieved from https://mobilizingideas.wordpress. com/2013/02/18/law-and-social-movements-its-more-than-just-litigation-and-courts/

Brubaker, R. (2005). The 'diaspora' diaspora. *Ethnic and Racial Studies*, 28(1), 1–19. Retrieved from https://doi.org/10.1080/0141987042000289997

Brubaker, R. (2017). Revisiting 'The "diaspora" diaspora'. *Ethnic and Racial Studies*, 40(9), 1556–61. https://doi.org/10.1080/01419870.2017.1308533

Bruinessen, M. v. (1978). *Agha, Shaikh and State: On the Social and Political Organization of Kurdistan*. Utrecht: Rijksuniversiteit te Utrecht.

Bruinessen, M. v. (1999). The Kurds in movement: migrations, mobilisations, communications and the globalisation of the Kurdish question. Working Paper, 14. Islamic Area Studies Project. Tokyo, Japan.

Bruinessen, M. v. (2014). Kurdish studies in Western and Central Europe. *Weiner Jahrbuch für Kurdische Studien*, 18–96.

Carnegie Middle East Center (2012, February 15). The Kurdish National Council in Syria. In A. Lund (ed.) *Syria in Crisis*. Middle East Insights from Carnegie. Carnegie Middle East Center. Retrieved from http://carnegie-mec.org/diwan/48502?lang=en

Carnegie Middle East Center (2012, April 1). The Damascus Spring. In A. Lund (ed.) *Syria in Crisis*. Middle East Insights from Carnegie. Carnegie Middle East Center. Retrieved from http://carnegie-mec.org/diwan/48516?lang=en

Casier, M. (2011). The Kurdish nationalist movement (in-)between Turkey and Europe. Transnational political activism and transformation of home through the EU. PhD dissertation, Ghent University. Retrieved from https://biblio. ugent.be/publication/4132140/file/4335485.pdf

Christiansen, C. C. (2008). Hometown associations and solidarities in Kurdish transnational villages: the migration–development nexus in a European context. *The European Journal of Development Research*, 2(1), 88–103.

Christiansen, T. (2017). Spaniensfrivillige. *Den Store Danske*. Gyldendal. Retrieved from http://denstoredanske.dk/index.php?sideId=162851

City of Copenhagen (2009). *A Metropolis for People*. The Technical and Environmental Administration. City of Copenhagen. Retrieved from https://international. kk.dk/artikel/creating-liveable-city

City of Copenhagen (2015a). *Co-Create Copenhagen.* The Technical and Environmental Administration. City of Copenhagen. Retrieved from https://urbandevelopmentcph.kk.dk/artikel/co-create-copenhagen

City of Copenhagen (2015b). *Urban Life Account.* The Technical and Environmental Administration. City of Copenhagen. Retrieved from https://international.kk.dk/artikel/creating-liveable-city

Cohen, R. (2008). *Global Diasporas: An Introduction.* 2nd edn. London: Routledge.

Collet, B. A. (2008). Confronting the insider-outsider polemic in conducting research with diasporic Communities: towards a community based approach. *Refuge*, 25(1), 77–83.

Crone, Mani (2016). Radicalization revisited: violence, politics and the skills of the body. *International Affairs*, 92(3), 587–604.

Danmarks Statistik (2019). *Indvandrere i Danmark.* København: Danmarks Statistik. Retrieved from https://www.dst.dk/da/Statistik/Publikationer/VisPub?cid=29446

Damsgård, Puk (2017, September 18). DR i Raqqa: Ari fra Danmark kæmper for koalitionen men bryder dansk lov. *DR.dk.* Retrieved from https://www.dr.dk/nyheder/udland/dr-i-raqqa-ari-fra-danmark-kaemper-koalitionen-men-bryder-dansk-lov

Degner, V., Diehl, J., Höhne, V., Peters, D., and Ziegler, J.-P. (2018, March 12). Anschläge auf Türkische Einrichtungen in Deutschland: Die Luft schmeckt nach Asche. *Spiegel Online.* Retrieved from http://www.spiegel.de/panorama/justiz/anschlaege-auf-tuerkische-einrichtungen-was-die-ermittler-vermuten-a-1197624.html

della Porta, D. (2008). Eventful Protest, Global Conflicts. *Scandinavian Journal of Social Theory*, 9(2). 27–8. https://doi.org/10.1080/1600910X.2008.9672963

della Porta, D. (2013). Repertoires of Contention. In D. A. Snow, D. della Porta, B. Klandermans and D. McAdam. *The Wiley-Blackwell Encyclopedia of Social and Political Movements. Volume III. Pe–Z* (pp. 1081–3). Chichester: Wiley-Blackwell.

della Porta, D. (2014a). In-depth Interview. In D. della Porta (ed.) *Methodological Practices in Social Movement Research* (pp. 228–61). Oxford: Oxford University Press.

della Porta, D. (2014b). Life histories. In D. della Porta (ed.) *Methodological Practices in Social Movement Research* (pp. 262–88). Oxford: Oxford University Press.

Demir, I. (2012). Battling with *Memleket* in London: the Kurdish diaspora's engagement with Turkey. *Journal of Ethnic and Migration Studies*, 38(5), 815–31. https://doi.org/10.1080/1369183X.2012.667996

Demir, I. (2015). Battlespace diaspora: How the Kurds of Turkey revive, construct and translate the Kurdish struggle in London. In A. Christou and E. Mavroudi (eds) *Dismantling Diasporas: Rethinking the Geographies of Diasporic Identity, Connection and Development* (pp. 71–84). Abingdon: Routledge.

Demir, I. (2017). Shedding an Ethnic Identity in Diaspora: De-Turkification and the Transnational Discursive Struggles of the Kurdish Diaspora. *Critical Discourse Studies,* 14(3), 276–91. https://doi-org.ep.fjernadgang.kb.dk/10.1080/174059 04.2017.1284686

Doherty, B., and Hayes, G. (2012). Having your day in court: judicial opportunity and tactical choice in anti-GMO campaigns in France and the United Kingdom. *Comparative Political Studies*, 47(1), 3–29.

Duzel, E. (2018). Fragile goddesses: moral subjectivity and militarized agencies in female guerrilla diaries and memoirs. *International Feminist Journal of Politics.* https://doi.org/10.1080/14616742.2017.1419823

Duyvendak, J. W., and Fillieule, O. (2014). Patterned Fluidity: An Interactionist Perspective as a Tool for Exploring Contentious Politics. In J. M. Jasper and J. W. Duyvendak (eds) *Players and Arenas: The Interactive Dynamics of Protest* (pp. 295–318). Amsterdam: Amsterdam University Press.

Duyvendak, J. W., and Jasper, J. M. (eds) (2015). *Breaking Down the State: Protestors Engaged.* Amsterdam: Amsterdam University Press.

Dürr, H. (2018, January 23). Syriske demonstranter blev provokeret af flag. *Jydske Vestkysten.* Retrieved from https://www.jv.dk/aabenraa/Syriske-demonstranter-blev-provokeret-af-flag/artikel/2579620

Eccarius-Kelly, E. (2002). From Terrorism to Political Activism in Europe: The Transformation of the Kurdish Diaspora to a Transnational Challenger Community. PhD dissertation, The Fletcher Law and Diplomacy School. Tufts University.

Eccarius-Kelly, V. (2011). *Militant Kurds. A Dual Strategy for Freedom.* Santa Barbara, CA: Praeger.

Eccarius-Kelly, V. (2017). Modern Turkey: opportunities and challenges. The Kurdish diaspora and Europe's gatekeeping after Kobane. *The Copernicus Journal of Political Studies,* 1, 39–53. http://dx.doi.org/10.12775/CJPS.2017.003

Eisinger, P. K. (1973). The conditions of protest behavior in American cities. *The American Political Science Review,* 67(1), 11–28.

Eliassi, B. (2013). *Contesting Kurdish Identities in Sweden: Quest for Belonging Among Middle Eastern Youth.* London: Palgrave Macmillan.

Eliassi, B. (2018). Political Islam among Kurds. *The Kurdish Studies Summer School,* Institut Kurde de Paris, 3–6 September 2018. Unpublished presentation.

Elkjær, S. F. (2019, August 27). Højesteret har talt: Tommy skal et halvt år i fængsel for at kæmpe mod Islamisk Stat i Syrien. *DR.dk*. Retrieved from https://www. dr.dk/nyheder/regionale/oestjylland/hoejesteret-har-talt-tommy-skal-et-halvt-aar-i-faengsel-kaempe-mod

Eltard-Sørensen, R. (2014, October 7). Kurdere i aktion: Frygter massakre i Kobane. *Modkraft*. Retrieved from http://modkraft.dk/artikel/kurdere-i-aktion-frygter-massakre-i-kobane

Embassy Copenhagen (2006, May 26). Denmark looking to strengthen case against pro-PKK ROJ-TV. *Wikileaks*. Wikileaks Cable: 09COPENHAGEN241_a Retrieved from https://wikileaks.org/plusd/cables/09COPENHAGEN241_a. html

Emanuelsson, A.-C. (2005). *Diaspora Global Politics: Kurdish Transnational Networks and Accommodation of Nationalism*. Department of Peace and Development Research. Gothenburg University.

Enab Baladi (2017). The Kurdish political movement in Syria. *Enab Baladi English*. Retrieved from http://english.enabbaladi.net/archives/2017/05/kurdish-political-movement-syria/

Enhedslisten (2014, August 28). Støtte til kurdernes kamp mod ISIS. *Enhedslisten*. Retrieved from https://org.enhedslisten.dk/artikel/stoette-til-kurdernes-kamp-mod-isis-73157

Enhedslisten. Internationalt Udvalg (n.d.). Kurdistan-solidaritetsgruppe etableret. *Enhedslisten*. Retrieved from http://iu.enhedslisten.dj/node/21558

Erdoğan, R. T. (2019, January 7). Trump is right on Syria: Turkey can get the job done. *The New York Times*. Retrieved from https://www.nytimes.com/2019/01/07/opinion/erdogan-turkey-syria.html

Eriksen, M. N. (2017). *100% Foreign?* Metropolis/Copenhagen International Theatre. Retrieved from https://100pctfremmed.dk/interview/jeg-levede-allerede-i-eksil-saa-ideen-om-at-vende-hjem-giver-ikke-mening-for-mig/

Eskesen, A. H. (2015, March 31). Dansk familiefar i krig i Syrien: Det er skræmmende let at slå IS ihjel. *Euroman*. Retrieved from https://www.euroman.dk/mennesker/dansker-i-kamp-i-syrien-det-er-skrammende-let-at-sla-is-ihjel

EUPRHA (2013). *State of the Art of Humanitarian Action*. European Universities on Professionalization on Humanitarian Action. Retrieved from http://euhap.eu/upload/2014/09/the-state-of-art-of-humanitarian-action-2013.pdf

Faist, T. (2010). Diaspora and transnationalism: what kind of dance partners? In R. Bauböck and T. Faist (eds) *Diaspora and Transnationalism* (pp. 9–34). IMISCOE Research. Amsterdam: Amsterdam University Press. Retrieved from http://cadmus.eui.eu/bitstream/handle/1814/14318/Diaspora_and_Transnationalism.pdf

Farris, Sara (2017). *In the Name of Women's Rights*. Durham, NC: Duke University Press.

Fenger-Grøndahl, M. (2016, June 1). Yari-tilhængere vil anerkendes i Danmark. *Kristeligt Dagblad*. Retrieved from https://www.kristeligt-dagblad.dk/kirke-tro/yari-tilhaengere-vil-anerkendes-i-danmark

Féron, E. and Lefort, B. (2018). Diasporas and conflicts: understanding the nexus. *Diaspora Studies*. https://doi.org/10.1080/09739572.2018.1538687

Folketinget (n.d.). The Foreign Affairs Committee. *Folketinget*. Retrieved from https://thedanishparliament.dk/en/committees/committees/uru

Folketinget Nyheder (2017, July 4). Permanent sikring af Christiansborg Slotsplads på vej. *Folketinget*. Retrieved from http://www.ft.dk/da/aktuelt/nyheder/2017/07/slotspladsen

Folketingets Administration (n.d.). Brug af Folketingets lokaler. *Folketinget*. Retrieved from https://www.ft.dk/organisation/brug-af-folketingets-lokaler

Fominaya, C. F. (2014). *Social Movements and Globalization: How Protest, Occupations and Uprisings Are Changing the World*. London: Palgrave Macmillan.

Galanter, M. (1974). Why the 'haves' come out ahead: speculations on the limits of legal change. *Law and Society Review*, 9, 95–160.

Gambetti, Z. (2013, October 31). The politics of visibility. *Cultural Anthropology Website*. Retrieved from: https://culanth.org/fieldsights/401-the-politics-of-visibility

Global Security (n.d.). Kurdish People's Protection Unit YPG. *GlobalSecurity.org*. Retrieved from http://www.globalsecurity.org/military/world/para/ypg.htm

Gloppen, S. (2013). Social movement activism and the courts. *Mobilizing Ideas*. Retrieved from https://mobilizingideas.wordpress.com/2013/02/04/social-movement-activism-and-the-courts/#more-4550

Good Humanitarian Donorship Initiative (2003). *Principles and Good Practice of Humanitarian Donorship*. Good Humanitarian Donorship Initiative. Retrieved from https://www.ghdinitiative.org/ghd/gns/principles-good-practice-of-ghd/principles-good-practice-ghd.html

Goodwin, J., and Jasper, J. M. (2009). *The Social Movement Reader: Cases and Concepts*, 2nd edn. Chichester: Wiley-Blackwell.

Gordon, M. R., and Schmitt, E. (2017, May 9). Trump to arm Syrian Kurds, even as Turkey strongly objects. *The New York Times*. Retrieved from https://www.nytimes.com/2017/05/09/us/politics/trump-kurds-syria-army.html

Greenwood, M. T. (2018). Becoming a Foreign Fighter: The Ethics and Agency of Fighting Jihad. PhD dissertation, Copenhagen: Department of Political Science.

Grojean, O. (2011). Bringing the organization back in. In M. Casier and J. Jongerden (eds) *Nationalisms and Politics in Turkey: Political Islam, Kemalism and the Kurdish Issue* (pp. 182–99). London: Routledge.

Gude, H. (2017, March 10). De Maizière verbietet Öcalan-Porträts. *Spiegel Online*. Retrieved from http://www.spiegel.de/politik/deutschland/thomas-de-maiziere-verbietet-portraets-von-pkk-anfuehrer-abdullah-oecalan-a-1138207.html

Gunes, C. (2012). *The Kurdish National Movement in Turkey: From Protest to Resistance*. London: Routledge.

Gunes, C., and Lowe, R. (2015). The Impact of the Syrian War on Kurdish Politics Across the Middle East. Research Paper. Chatham House. Retrieved from https://syria.chathamhouse.org/assets/documents/20150723SyriaKurdsGunesLowe.pdf

Gunter, M. M. (2014). *Out of Nowhere: The Kurds in Syria in Peace and War*. London: Hurst.

Gürbüz, M. (2016). *Rival Kurdish Movements in Turkey: Transforming Ethnic Conflict*. Amsterdam: Amsterdam University Press

Gustafsson, L., and Ranstorp, M. (2017). *Swedish Foreign Fighters in Syria and Iraq*. Stockholm: Swedish Defence University.

Gökalp, D. (2017). Review: Rival Kurdish movements in Turkey: transforming ethnic conflict. *Contemporary Sociology*, 46(6), 674–77. https://doi.org/10.1177/0094306117734868n

Hall, J. (2015). Dispaoras and civil war. In T. G. Jakobsen (ed.) *War: An Introduction to Theories and Research on Collective Violence*, 2nd edn (pp. 217–35). Hauppauge, NY: Nova Publishers.

Harlow, C., and Rawlings, R. (1992). *Pressure Through Law*. London: Routledge.

Hassanpour, A. (2003). Diasporas, homeland and communication technologies. In K. H. Karim (ed.) *The Media of Diaspora* (pp. 76–88). London: Routledge.

Hassanpour, A., and Mojab, S. (2005). Kurdish diaspora. In M. Ember, C. R. Ember, and I. Skoggard (eds) *Encyclopedia of Diasporas: Immigrant and Refugee Cultures Around the World. Volume I: Overviews and Topics* (pp. 214–24). Boston, MA: Springer. https://doi.org/10.1007/978-0-387-29904-4

Hearn, R. (2019). Humanitarian aid to a Middle East in crisis. In A. Jagerskog, M. Schulz and A. Swain (eds) *Routledge Handbook on Middle East Security* (pp. 127–40). Abingdon: Routledge.

Hertoft, M. (2019, September). Frihedskæmper skal i fængsel – selvom han kæmpede mod terroristerne. *Enhedslisten.dk*. Retrieved from http://org.enhedslisten.

dk/medlemsblad/frihedskaemper-skal-i-faengsel-selvom-han-kaempede-mod-terroristerne

Hilhorst, D., and Jansen, B. J. (2010). Humanitarian spaces as arena: a perspective on the everyday politics of aid. *Development and Change*, 41(6), 1117–39.

Hilson, C. (2013). The Courts and social movements: two literatures and two methodologies. *Mobilizing Ideas*. Retrieved from https://mobilizingideas.wordpress.com/2013/02/18/the-courts-and-social-movements-two-literatures-and-two-methodologies/

Hjarnø, J. (1988). *Indvandrere fra Tyrkiet i Stockholm og København*. Esbjerg: Sydjysk Universitetsforlag.

Hjarnø, J. (1991). *Kurdiske indvandrere*. Esbjerg: Sydjysk Universitetsforslag.

Hopkins, N., and Beals, E. (2016, August 29). UN pays tens of millions to Assad regime under Syria aid programme. *The Guardian*. Retrieved from https://www.theguardian.com/world/2016/aug/29/un-pays-tens-of-millions-to-assad-regime-syria-aid-programme-contracts

Human Rights Watch (1993). *Genocide in Iraq: The Anfal Campaign Against the Kurds. A Middle East Watch Report*. Human Rights Watch. Retrieved from https://www.hrw.org/legacy/reports/1993/iraqanfal/

IISS (2016). Chapter seven: Middle East and North Africa. *The Military Balance* 116(1), 307–64.

Institut Kurde de Paris (2016). Kurdish diaspora. *Institut Kurde de Paris*. Retrieved from https://www.institutkurde.org/en/info/kurdish-diaspora-1232550988

International Crisis Group (2013, January 22). Syria's Kurds: a struggle within a struggle. *Report 136. Middle East & North Africa*. Retrieved from https://www.crisisgroup.org/middle-east-north-africa/eastern-mediterranean/syria/syria-s-kurds-struggle-within-struggle

Israel, J. I. (2002). *Diasporas within a Diaspora: Jews, Crypto-Jews, and the World Maritime Empires (1540–1740)*. Leiden: Brill.

Jakobsen, P. V. (2016). The Danish Libya campaign: out in front in pursuit of pride, praise, and position. In D. Henriksen and A. K. Larssen (eds) *Political Rationale and International Consequences of the War in Libya* (pp. 192–208). Oxford: Oxford University Press.

Jakobsen, P. V., and Møller, C. (2012). Good news: Libya and the Danish way of war. In N. Hvidt and H. Mouritzen (eds) *Danish Foreign Policy Yearbook 2012* (pp. 106–21). Copenhagen: Danish Institute for International Studies. Retrieved from https://www.diis.dk/files/media/documents/publications/000.yearbook_2012_web.pdf

Jakobsen, P. V., Ringsmose, J., and Saxi (2018). Prestige-seeking small states: Danish and Norwegian military contributions to US-led operations. *European Journal of International Security,* 3(2), 256–77. https://doi.org/10.1017/eis.2017.20

James, W. (2018, January 22). United States concerned by 'Turkish incident' in northern Syria, Tillerson says. Reuters. Retrieved from https://www.reuters.com/article/us-mideast-crisis-syria-turkey-usa/united-states-concerned-by-turkish-incident-in-northern-syria-tillerson-says-idUSKBN1FB1OJ

Jasper, J. M. (2006). *Getting Your Way: Strategic Dilemmas in the Real World.* Chicago: University of Chicago Press.

Jasper, J. M. (2014a). *Protest: A Cultural Introduction to Social Movements.* Malden, MA: Polity Press.

Jasper, J. M. (2014b). Playing the game. In J. M. Jasper and J. W. Duyvendak (eds) *Players and Arenas: The Interactive Dynamic of Protest* (pp. 9–32). Amsterdam: Amsterdam University Press.

Jasper, J. (2015). Introduction: players and arenas formerly known as the state. In J. W. Duyvendak and J. M. Jasper (eds) *Breaking Down the State: Protesters Engaged* (pp. 9–24). Amsterdam: Amsterdam University Press.

Jasper, J. M., and Duyvendak, J. W. (eds) (2014). *Players and Arenas: The Interactive Dynamic of Protest.* Amsterdam: Amsterdam University Press.

Jasper, J. M., Tramontano, M., and McGarry, A. (2015). Scholarly research on collective identities. In A. McGarry and J. M. Jasper (eds) *The Identity Dilemma: Social Movements and Collective Identity* (pp. 18–42). Philadelphia, PA: Temple University Press.

Jenkins, R. (1994). Rethinking ethnicity: identity, categorization and power. *Ethnic and Racial Studies,* 17(2), 197–223. https://doi.org/10.1080/01419870.1994.9993821

Jenkins, R. (2014). *Social Identity,* 4th edn. London: Routledge.

Jensen, J. D. (2010). Kurdiske asylansøgere fra Syrien afbryder sultestrejke. *sameksistens.dk.* Retrieved from https://www.sameksistens.dk/nyhed/article/kurdiske-asylansoegere-fra-syrien-afbryder-sultestrejke/

Jensen, H., and Sørensen, A. (2015, August 30). Syrienkriger-loven rammer skævt. *Berlingske.* Retrieved from https://www.b.dk/politiko/syrienkriger-loven-rammer-skaevt

Jongerden, J. (2007). *The Settlement Issue in Turkey and the Kurds: An Analysis of Spatical Policies, Modernity and War.* Leiden: Brill.

Jørgensen, M. B. (2009). *National and Transnational Identities: Turkish Organising Processes and Identity Construction in Denmark, Sweden and Germany.* Aalborg

University: Institut for Historie, Internationale Studier og Samfundsforhold, Aalborg Universitet. Spirit PhD Series, No. 19. Retrieved from http://vbn.aau.dk/files/18624296/spirit_phd_series_19_jorgensen.pdf

Kajjo, S and Sinclair, C. (2011, August 31). The evolution of Kurdish politics in Syria. *MERIP*. Retrieved from http://www.merip.org/mero/mero083111

Kardaş, K. and Yesiltaş, M. (2017) Rethinking Kurdish geopolitical space: the politics of image, insecurity and gender. *Cambridge Review of International Affairs* (30)2–3, 256–82. https://doi.org/10.1080/09557571.2017.1410098

KB (2011). Azadî Friday: from Qamişlo to Houran. *Kurdistan Commentary*. Retrieved from https://kurdistancommentary.wordpress.com/2011/05/19/azadi-friday-from-qamislo-to-houran/

Keles, J. Y. (2015). *Media, Diaspora and Conflict: Nationalism and Identity amongst Turkish and Kurdish Migrants in Europe*. London: I. B. Tauris.

Khalaf, R. (2016). Governing Rojava: layers of legitimacy in Syria. *Middle East and North Africa Programme, Dec. 2016*. Chatham House. Retrieved from https://syria.chathamhouse.org/assets/documents/2016-12-08-governing-rojava-khalaf.pdf

Khayati, K. (2008). From Victim Diaspora to Transborder Citizenship? Diaspora formation and transnational relations among Kurds in France and Sweden. Linköping Studies in Arts and Sciences. PhD dissertation, Linköping University. Retrieved from https://www.mah.se/upload/forskningscentrum/mim/2009%20seminars/khalid%20khayati%2011%20mars.pdf

Khayati, K. (2012). Sweden as a gravitation center for the Kurds: diaspora formation and transnational relations. Retrieved from http://www.diva-portal.org/smash/get/diva2:646036/FULLTEXT01.pdfKhalid

Khorto, J. P. (2016). *Edens vugge – Hviskende skæbner fra Syrien*. Vejle: Baskerville & Co.

Klitgaard, L. K. et al. (planner) (2017, October 26). *Forbryder eller frihedskæmper* (in English: Criminal or Freedom Fighter). Denmark: DR and Pipeline Production. Accessible at https://www.dr.dk/tv/se/forbryder-eller-frihedskaemper/forbryder-eller-frihedskaemper-2/forbryder-eller-frihedskaemper#!/43:44

Knapp, M., and Jongerden, J. (2016). Communal democracy: The social contract and confederalism in Rojava. *Comparative Islamic Studies*, 10(1), 87–109. https://doi.org/10.1558/cis.29642

Koinova, M. (2018). *Diaspora mobilizations for conflict. Beyond amplification and reduction*. In: R. Cohen and C. Fischer (eds) *Handbook of Diaspora Studies*. (pp. 311–19). London: Routledge.

Kongstad, J., and Kaae, M. (2014, September 27). Danske piloter, fly og bomber i kamp mod Islamisk Stat. *Berlingske*. Retrieved from https://jyllands-posten.dk/protected/premium/indland/article7058848.ece/

Kühle, L., and Larsen, M. (2017). *Moskeér i Danmark II: En ny kortlægning af danske moskeér og muslimske bedesteder*. Aarhus: Aarhus University. Retrieved from http://ebooks.au.dk/index.php/aul/catalog/book/239

Kurdisk Forum (2010). *Vedtægter for Kurdisk Forum*. Kurdisk Forum.

Kurdistan National Congress (2014, October 10). *KNK Appeal for Kobane*. Retrieved from https://peaceinkurdistancampaign.com/2014/10/10/knk-appeal-for-kobane/

Kurdistan National Congress (2017). Members of the Kurdistan National Congress KNK, 17th General Congress. *KNK*. Retrieved from http://www.kongrakurdistan.net/en/members/

KurdWatch (2010). Stateless Kurds in Syria: illegal invaders or victims of a nationalistic policy? *KurdWatch Report 5*. Retrieved from http://www.kurdwatch.org/pdf/kurdwatch_staatenlose_en.pdf

Kurzman, C. (2004). The poststructuralist consensus in social movement theory. In J. Goodwin and J. M. Jasper (eds) *Rethinking Social Movements: Structure, Meaning, and Emotion* (pp. 111–20). Lanham, MD: Rowan and Littlefield Publishers.

L 92 (2020, January). Lovforslag nr. L 92. *Folketinget 2019–20*. Retrieved from https://www.ft.dk/samling/20191/lovforslag/L92/som_fremsat.htm

L 99 (2014, December). Lovforslag nr. L 99. *Folketinget 2014–15*. Retrieved from https://www.ft.dk/ripdf/samling/20141/lovforslag/l99/20141_l99_som_fremsat.pdf

L 99 – Questions (2015). Lovforslag nr. 99. Udvalgsbehandling. *Folketinget 2014–15*. Retrieved from https://www.ft.dk/samling/20141/lovforslag/L99/spm.htm

L 99 – Voting (2015). Lovforslag nr. 99. Afstemning. *Folketinget 2014–15*. Retrieved from https://www.ft.dk/samling/20141/lovforslag/L99/57/afstemninger.htm

L 187 (2016, May). Lovforslag nr. L 187. *Folketinget 2015–16*. Retrieved from https://www.ft.dk/ripdf/samling/20151/lovforslag/l187/20151_l187_som_fremsat.pdf

L 187 – Debate (2016). Lovforslag nr. L 187. 1. Behandling. *Folketinget 2015–16*. Retrieved from https://www.ft.dk/samling/20151/lovforslag/L187/BEH1-91/forhandling.htm

Ladefoged, A., and Sørensen, A. (planners) (2015, June 6). *Dokumentar. Joanna – en dansker i krig* (in English: Documentary: Joanna – a Dane in war). Berlingske. Retrieved from https://www.berlingske.dk/internationalt/dokumentar-joanna-en-dansker-i-krig

Landsbcrg, A. (2004). *Prosthetic Memory: The Transformation of American Remembrance in the Age of Mass Culture*. New York: Columbia University Press.

Levitt, P. (2001). *The Transnational Villagers*. Berkeley: University of California Press.

Levitt, P., and Nyberg-Sørensen, N. (2004). The transnational turn in migration studies. *Global Migration Perspectives,* 6. Retrieved from https://www.refworld.org/docid/42ce48754.html

Lilleør, K. (2016, February 12). Heltinden Joanna. *Berlingske*. Retrieved from https://www.berlingske.dk/kommentatorer/heltinden-joanna

Lindhardt, J. M., Westphal, K., and Falther, M. B. (2016, February 17). Martins krig. *Ugeavisen Esbjerg*. Retrieved from https://danskemedier.dk/wp-content/uploads/red.ideer-soelv-ugeavisen-esbjerg-83-4.pdf

Mahmod, J. (2016). *Kurdish Diaspora Online: From Imagined Community to Managing Communities*. London: Palgrave Macmillan.

Mannheim, K. (1923). From 'The Sociological Problem of Generations'. In J. K. Olick, V. Vinitzky-Seroussi and D. Levy (eds) (2011). *The Collective Memory Reader* (pp. 92–8). Oxford: Oxford University Press.

Martin, G. (2015). *Understanding Social Movements*. London: Routledge.

McAdam, D. (1982). *Political Process and the Development of Black Insurgency, 1930–1970*. Chicago: University of Chicago Press.

McAdam, D., Tarrow, S., and Tilly, C. (2001). *Dynamics of Contention*. Cambridge: Cambridge University Press.

McCarthy, J. D., and Zald, M. N. (1973). Resource mobilization and social movements: a partial theory. *American Journal of Sociology,* 82(6), 1212–41.

McDowall, D. (2004). *A Modern History of The Kurds*. 3rd revised edn. London: I. B. Tauris.

McGarry, A., Davidson, R. J., Accornero, G., Jasper, J. M., and Duyvendak, J. W. (2016). Players and arenas: strategic interactionism in social movements studies. *Social Movement Studies,* 15(6), 634–42. https://doi.org/10.1080/1474 2837.2016.1199320

Mchangama, J. (2015, November 24). 5 principper for ny terrorlovgivning. *Blog: Retsstaten*. Berlingske. Retrieved from https://mchangama.blogs.berlingske.dk/2015/11/24/5-principper-for-ny-terrorlovgivning/

Mchangama, J. (2015, June 8). Terrorist eller frihedskæmper: skal de behandles ens? (in English: Terrorist or freedom fighter: shall they be treated alike?). *Blog: Retsstaten*. Berlingske. Retrieved from https://mchangama.blogs.berlingske.dk/2015/06/08/terrorist-eller-frihedskaemper-skal-de-behandles-ens/

Mchangama, J., and Prener, C. (2014). *Væsentlige retssikkerhedsmæssige udfordringer – Analyse om lovudkast om ændring af paslov*. Copenhagen: Justitia. Retrieved from http://justitia-int.org/wp-content/uploads/2014/12/Analyse_V%C3%A6sentlige-retssikkerhedsm%C3%A6ssige-udfordringer_Lovudkast-om-%C3%A6ndring-af-paslov-mm_Dec14.pdf

Melucci, A. (1989). *Nomads of the Present: Social Movements and Individual Needs in Contemporary Society*. London: Hutchinson Radius.

Melucci, A. (1996). *Challenging Codes: Collective Action in the Information Age*. Cambridge: Cambridge University Press.

Mikkelsen, F. (2011). *Transnational identitet under forandring – indvandrernes sociale, religiøse og politiske mobilisering i Danmark 1965–2010*. Migration and integration, nr. 4. Copenhagen: Museum Tusculanums Forlag.

Ministry of Immigration and Integration (2020, January 1). Administrativ fratagelse af dansk statsborgerskab. *Ministry of Immigration and Integration*. Retrieved from https://uim.dk/arbejdsomrader/statsborgerskab/danske-statsborgere/administrativ-fratagelse-af-dansk-statsborgerskab

Ministry of Justice (2016, September 28). Bekendtgørelse om forbud mod indrejse eller ophold i visse konfliktområder. Ministry of Justice.

Ministry of Justice (2016, July 1). Information om indrejseforbud. Justitsministeriet. Retrieved from http://www.justitsministeriet.dk/nyt-og-presse/pressemeddele-lser/2016/information-om-indrejseforbud

Ministry of Justice (2019, April 26). Regeringen vil opdatere forbudszoner i Syrien og Irak. *Ministry of Justice*. Retrieved from https://www.justitsministeriet.dk/nyt-og-presse/pressemeddelelser/2019/regeringen-vil-opdatere-forbudszoner-i-syrien-og-irak

Mische, A. (2014). Fractal arenas: dilemmas of style and strategy in a Brazilian student congress. In J. M. Jasper and J. W. Duyvendak (eds) *Players and Arenas: The Interactive Dynamic of Protest* (pp. 55–78). Amsterdam: Amsterdam University Press.

Moestrup, J. H. R., and Vesterlund, P. (2017, March 2). Far leder efter døtre i Tyrkiet: Datter var selv med til at radikalisere andre. *TV2/Nyheder*. Retrieved from http://nyheder.tv2.dk/2017-03-02-far-leder-efter-doetre-i-tyrkiet-datter-var-selv-med-til-at-radikalisere-andre

Mosca, L. (2014). Methodological practices in social movement online research. In D. della Porta (ed.) *Methodological Practices in Social Movement Research* (pp. 397–417). Oxford: Oxford University Press.

Montgomery, H. (2005). *The Kurds of Syria: An Existence Denied*. Berlin: Europäisches Zentrum für Kurdische Studien.

Mügge, L. (2010). *Beyond Dutch Borders: Transnational Politics Among Colonial Migrants, Guest Workers and the Second Generation.* (IMISCOE Research). Amsterdam: Amsterdam University Press.

Necef, M. Ü. (2018). Kurdish overrepresentation among Danish Islamic State warriors. *News Analysis.* The Centre for Contemporary Middle East Studies. Retrieved from https://portal.findresearcher.sdu.dk/en/publications/kurdisk-overrepr%C3%A6entation-blandt-danke-islamisk-stat-krigere

NeJaime, D. (2011). Winning through losing. *Iowa Law Review,* 96, 941–1012.

Nicolai, J. (2015). *Heval. En dansk soldats autentiske beretning fra krigen mod Islamisk Stat.* Copenhagen: Jørgen Nicolai.

Nielsen, B. (2019, September 9). Advokat til syriens-kriger efter dom: Gå hjem, spis chili con carne og drik en bajer. *JydskeVestkysten.*

Obama, B. (2014, September 10). *Statement by the President on ISIL.* Retrieved from https://obamawhitehouse.archives.gov/the-press-office/2014/09/10/statement-president-isil-1

Öcalan, A. (2013). *Democratic Confederalism,* 3rd edn. Cologne: International Initiative 'Freedom for Abdullah Öcalan – Peace in Kurdistan'.

OCHA (2012). *What are Humanitarian Principles?* The United Nations Office for the Coordination of Humanitarian Affairs (OCHA). Retrieved from https://www.unocha.org/sites/dms/Documents/OOM-humanitarianprinciples_eng_June12.pdf

O'Grady, S. (2019, October 9). Turkey plans a Syrian 'safe zone.' Advocates fear a 'death trap'. *The Washington Post.* Retrieved from https://www.washingtonpost.com/world/2019/10/09/turkey-plans-syrian-safe-zone-advocates-fear-death-trap/

Palani, J. (2019). *Freedom Fighter: My War Against ISIS on the Frontlines of Syria.* Ghostwritten by Lara Whyte. London: Atlantic Books

Peace in Kurdistan (2015, February 19). Establishing Kobane Reconstruction Board. *Peace in Kurdistan.* Retrieved from https://peaceinkurdistancampaign.com/2015/02/19/establishing-kobane-reconstruction-board/

Pedersen, R. B. (2018). Bandwagon for status: changing patterns in the Nordic States status-seeking strategies? *International Peacekeeping,* 25(2). 217–41. https://doi.org/10.1080/13533312.2017.1394792

Pelling, L. (2013). Post-Remittances? On Transnational Ties and Migration between the Kurdistan Region in Iraq and Sweden. PhD dissertation, University of Wien. Retrieved from http://othes.univie.ac.at/29379/1/2013-03-12_0647588.pdf

Petersen, M. (2011). Mobilitet, barrierer and muligheder Et studie af unge flygtninges tilhørsforhold og Positioneringer. PhD dissertation, Institut for Sociologi, Socialt arbejde og Organisation, Aalborg Universitet. Retrieved from https://www.

ucviden.dk/portal/files/29250321/Ph_d_afhandling_Mimi_Petersen_november_2010.pdf

Polletta, F., and Kretschmer, K. (2014). Movement factions: players and processes. In J. M. Jasper and J. W. Duyvendak (eds) *Players and Arenas: The Interactive Dynamic of Protest* (pp. 35–54). Amsterdam: Amsterdam University Press.

Pries, J. (2015, April 20). Afvist nødhjælp fra Furesø må returnere fra Tyrkiet. *DR.dk*. Retrieved from https://www.dr.dk/nyheder/regionale/hovedstadsomraadet/afvist-noedhjaelp-fra-furesoe-maa-returnere-fra-tyrkiet

Research Turkey (2014, June 27). Interview with Dr. Bahar Başer on her book: Turkish – Kurdish Question in the Diaspora, Second-generation Turkish and Kurdish Diasporas in Sweden and Germany. *Research Turkey. Centre for Policy Analysis and Research on Turkey*. Retrieved from http://researchturkey.org/interview-with-dr-bahar-baser-on-her-book-turkish-kurdish-question-in-the-diaspora-second-generation-turkish-and-kurdish-diasporas-in-sweden-and-germany/

Reuters (2019, November 26). Denmark offers to lead NATO training mission in Iraq from 2021. Reuters. Retrieved from https://www.reuters.com/article/us-nato-summit-denmark-iraq/denmark-offers-to-lead-nato-training-mission-in-iraq-from-2021-idUSKBN1Y01DK

Ritzau (2017, November 14). Højesteret tager passet fra dansk-tyrkisk syrienkriger. *Politiken*. Retrieved from https://politiken.dk/indland/art6205180/H%C3%B8jesteret-tager-passet-fra-dansk-tyrkisk-syrienkriger

Ritzau (2018, March 26). Fire unge er fængslet for angreb mod Tyrkiets ambassade. *Ekstra Bladet*. Retrieved from https://ekstrabladet.dk/112/fire-unge-er-faengslet-for-angreb-mod-tyrkiets-ambassade/7093922

Ritzau (2019, June 26). Kvinde vinder sag mod politiet om pas og udrejse. *Politiken.dk*. Retrieved from https://politiken.dk/indland/art7272128/Kvinde-vinder-sag-mod-politiet-om-pas-og-udrejse

Rojava Komitéen (2016). *@Rojava_Komiteen*. Retrieved from https://twitter.com/Rojava_Komiteen

Romano, D. (2006). *The Kurdish Nationalist Movement*. Cambridge: Cambridge University Press.

Rosenberg, G. N. (1991). *The Hollow Hope: Can Courts Bring About Social Change?* Chicago: University of Chicago Press.

Rudaw (2013, November 14). Kurdish declaration of autonomy in Syria rejected by Turkey. *Rudaw.net*. Retrieved from http://www.rudaw.net/english/middleeast/syria/14112013

Rudaw (2014, April 4). Four Syrian Kurdish groups aim to merge into one party. *Rudaw.net*. Retrieved from http://www.rudaw.net/english/middleeast/syria/04042014

Rudaw (2016, August 16). KNC denounces PYD's intimidation of critics in Rojava. *Rudaw.net*. Retrieved from http://www.rudaw.net/english/middleeast/syria/160820161

Rudaw (2017, January 17). Turkey invites three Kurdish leaders to Astana peace talks. *Rudaw.net*. Retrieved from http://www.rudaw.net/english/kurdistan/170120171

Rudaw (2017, March 27). Kurdish delegates in Geneva fail to raise Kurdish question. *Rudaw.net*. Retrieved from http://www.rudaw.net/english/middleeast/syria/27032017

Rudaw (2018, January 28). KNC not invited to Sochi for calling on Kurdish cause to be part of agenda. *Rudaw.net*. Retrieved from http://www.rudaw.net/english/middleeast/syria/280120183

Safran, W. (1991). Diasporas in modern societies: myths of homeland and return. *Diaspora: A Journal of Transnational Studies*, 1(1), 83–99. https://doi.org/10.1353/dsp.1991.0004

Savelsberg, E. (2016). The PKK as the lesser of two evils? Kurds, Islamists and the battle for Kobani. In M. M. Gunter (ed.). *Kurdish Issues. Essays in Honor of Robert W. Olson* (pp. 221–34). Costa Mesa, CA: Mazda Publishers.

Saxtorph-Poulsen, J., and Underbjerg, L. P. (2017, March 22). 19-årig dansker ville bekæmpe Islamisk Stat – men så kom der kampklædte betjente. *TV2/Nyheder*. Retrieved from http://nyheder.tv2.dk/udland/2017-03-22-19-aarig-dansker-ville-bekaempe-islamisk-stat-men-saa-kom-der-kampklaedte-betjente

Scheingold, S. A. (2004). *The Politics of Rights: Lawyers, Public Policy, and Political Change*. 2nd edn. Ann Arbor: University of Michigan Press.

Schmidinger, T. (2013). The Kurdish Spring in disapora? Austria and its Kurds. In M. M. A. Ahmed and M. M. Gunter (eds) *The Kurdish Spring. Geopolitical Changes and the Kurds* (pp. 308–38). Costa Mesa, CA: Mazda Publishers.

Schmidinger, T. (2018). *Rojava: Revolution, War, and the Future of Syria's Kurds*. London: Pluto Press.

Schuetze, C. F. (2018, July 23). Mesut Ozil's exit from German soccer team stokes debate on integration. *The New York Times*. Retrieved from https://www.nytimes.com/2018/07/23/world/europe/mesut-ozil-germany-soccer.html

Schwartz, J. M. (1985). *Reluctant Hosts: Denmark's Reception of Guest Workers*. Kultursociologiske Skrifter 1. Copenhagen: University of Copenhagen.

Schøtt, A. S. (2014). *Berbernes kamp for anerkendelse i Libyen efter Gaddafi*. Unpublished Master's thesis, Department of Cross Cultural and Regional Studies. University of Copenhagen.

Schøtt, A. S. (2017). The Kurds of Syria: from the forgotten people to world state actors. *Brief, Royal Danish Defence College*. Retrieved from https://pure.fak.dk/files/7248264/The_Kurds_of_Syria.pdf

Self-Rule in Rojava (2014). The social contract. *Peace in Kurdistan*. Retrieved from https://peaceinkurdistancampaign.com/charter-of-the-social-contract/

Serinci, D. B. (2011, October 11). Hvor mange kurdere bor der i Danmark? *Jiyan. dk*. Retrieved from https://jiyan.dk/2011/10/hvor-mange-kurdere-bor-der-i-danmark/

Serinci, D. B. (2014, October 13). Hundreds of European Kurds join Peshmerga and YPG. *Rudaw.net*. Retrieved from http://www.rudaw.net/english/world/13102014

Serinci, D. B. (2015, November 4). 30-årsdag for drab på kendt PKK-kritiker i Brøndby. Jiyan.dk. Retrieved from https://jiyan.dk/2015/11/30-aarsdag-for-drab-paa-kendt-pkk-kritiker-i-broendby/

Serinci, D. B. (2015). *Terrorens kalifat – et indblik i Islamisk Stat*. Frederiksberg: Frydelund.

Serinci, D. (2016, July 3). Danske muslimer kæmper mod IS. *Jyllands-Posten*.

Serinci, D., and Villemoes, S. K. (2017, January 27). Kurder mod Kurder. *Weekendavisen*.

Shain, Y., and A. Barth (2003). Diasporas and International Relations Theory. *International Organization*, 57(3), 449–79. https://doi.org/10.1017/S0020818303573015

Sheffer, G. (2003). *Diaspora Politics: At Home Abroad*. Cambridge: Cambridge University Press.

Sheikh, Jakob (2015). *Danmarks børn i hellig krig*. Copenhagen: Lindhardt og Ringhof Forlag.

Sheikhmous, O. (2013). *United in Disunity – The Fractious Character of Kurdish Politics in Syria*. Paper for the Conference 'Governing Diversity: The Kurds in a New Middle East', Iraq Institute for Strategic Studies, November 28–30 2013, Beirut.

Sheikhmous, O. (2018). *Future Options for the Kurds in Syria – Rojava*. Paper for the International Conference 'Future Options of the Kurds', University of Sulaimani, October 9–19 2018.

Sheikhmous, O. (2019). *The Essence of Kurdish National Identity – The Role of Kurdish Nationalist Movements in its Formation and its impact on the 'New Order in the Middle East'*. Draft Paper presented to the International Conference: 'New Order of the Middle East and National Kurdish Identity', University of Sulaimani.

Sheyholislami, J. (2011). *Kurdish Identity, Discourse and the New Media*. London: Palgrave Macmillan.

Shino, Z. (2018, March 11). Germany eases up on PYD, YPG bans. *Rudaw.net*. Retrieved from http://www.rudaw.net/english/world/11032018

Sinclair, C. (2010). Syrian Kurds in Europe 2010: migration, asylum, and deportation. *Kurdistan Commentary*. Retrieved from https://kurdistancommentary.

wordpress.com/2010/12/19/syrian-kurds-in-europe-2010-migration-asylum-and-deportation/

Sirkeci, I. (2006). *The Environment of Insecurity in Turkey and the Emigration of Turkish Kurds to Germany*. New York: Edwin Mellen Press.

SKAT (n.d.). Godkendelse til at modtage gaver. *Foreninger*. Retrieved from https://skat.dk/skat.aspx?oid=2234905

Skjoldager, M. (2014, October 20). Dansk-kurdisk kvinde: Hellere dø i kamp end på flugt. *Politiken*. Retrieved from https://politiken.dk/magasinet/interview/art5548898/Dansk-kurdisk-kvinde-Hellere-d%C3%B8-i-kamp-end-p%C3%A5-flugt

Snow, D. A., and Benford, R. D. (1988). Ideology, frame resonance, and participant mobilization. *International Social Movement Research*, 1, 197–217.

Snow, D. A., and Benford, R. D. (2000). Framing processes and social movements: an overview and assessment. *Annual Review of Sociology*, 26, 611–39.

Snow, D. A., Soule, S. A., and Kriesi, H. (eds) (2007). *The Blackwell Companion to Social Movements*. Malden, MA: Blackwell Publishing.

Sökefeld, M. (2006). Mobilizing in transnational space: a social movement approach to the formation of diaspora. *Global Networks*, 6(3), 265–84.

Staghøj, M. (2017, March 1). Tommy var lokal leder i Alternativet. Så tog han i krig mod Islamisk Stat i Syrien. *Zetland*. Retrieved from https://www.zetland.dk/historie/s8qDREyN-ae6XddvA-1b3ce

Staghøj, M. (2018, January 29). Hvem blinker først? Hvorfor Trump og Erdoğan har blikket stift rettet mod samme sted. *Zetland*. Retrieved from https://www.zetland.dk/historie/s8x7WPbj-ae6XddvA-2aea3

Statistics Denmark (2020a). RAS308: Employed (end November) by country of origin, industry (DB07), socioeconomic status, age and sex. Copenhagen: Statistics Denmark. Retrieved from http://www.statistikbanken.dk/RAS308

Statistics Denmark (2020b). VAN66: Residence permits (year) by type of residence permit and citizenship. Copenhagen: Statistics Denmark. Retrieved from http://www.statistikbanken.dk/10026

Stewart, P. (2017, May 10). U.S. to arm Syrian Kurds fighting Islamic State despite Turkey's ire. *Reuters*. Retrieved from http://www.reuters.com/article/us-mideast-crisis-usa-kurds-idUSKBN18525V

Søndergaard, S. (1997). Den kurdiske fjende I Europa. In L. Budtz, G. Petersen, V. Sigurdsson, K. Slavensky, and S. Søndergaard (eds) *De uønskede. Kurdernes situation i Europa og Mellemøsten*. Copenhagen: Gyldendal.

Sørensen, N. N., Vammen, I. M. S., and Kleist, N. (2018). Mellem bistand og selvhjælp. Nye perspektiver på diasporagruppers engagement i dansk udviklingsbistand. *DIIS*

Report 2018(05). Retrieved from https://www.diis.dk/publikationer/danmark-brug-ambitioes-fleksibel-diasporapolitik

Tejel, J. (2009). *Syria's Kurds: History, Politics and Society*. London: Routledge.

Tejel, J. (2012, October 6). Syria's Kurds: troubled past, uncertain future. *Carnegie Europe*. Retrieved from http://carnegieeurope.eu/2012/10/16/syria-s-kurds-troubled-past-uncertain-future-pub-49703

Tejel, J. (2011). Scholarship on the Kurds in Syria: a history and state of the art assessment. *Syrian Studies Association Newsletter* 16(1). Retrieved from https://kurdistancommentary.files.wordpress.com/2011/05/ssanewlettersp2011_kurds.pdf

Tejel, J. (2014). Toward a generational rupture within the Kurdish movement in Syria? In O. Bengio (ed.) *Kurdish Awakening. Nation Building in a Fragmented Homeland*. Austin: University of Texas Press.

The Center for Terror Analysis (2016). *Assessment of the Terror Threat against Denmark*. The Danish Security and Intelligence Service (PET). Retrieved from https://www.pet.dk/English/~/media/VTD%202016/20160428VTDengelsk-pdf.ashx

The Center for Terror Analysis (2018). *Assessment of the Terror Threat against Denmark*. The Danish Security and Intelligence Service (PET). Retrieved from https://www.pet.dk/English/Center%20for%20Terror%20Analysis/~/media/VTD%202018/VTD2018ENGpdf.ashx

The City Court of Copenhagen (2016, February 4). Copenhagen Police v. Joanna Palani. *SS 2-30641/2015*.

The City Court of Copenhagen (2017a, October 26). Copenhagen Police v. Joanna Palani. *SS 3-2721/2017*.

The City Court of Copenhagen (2017b, November 22). The Prosecution Service v. Joanna Palani. *SS 1-12074/2017*.

The Democratic Kurdish People's Assembly in Denmark (2016, March 22). 'Dansk-Kurdisk Kulturcenter' bliver ændret til 'Den Demokratiske Kurdiske Folke-forsamling i Danmark'. *Kurder.dk*. Retrieved from http://www.kurder.dk/nuce/2016/03/dansk-kurdisk-kulturcenter-bliver-aendret-til-den-demokra-tiske-kurdiske-folkeforsamling-i-danmark/

The District Court of Esbjerg (2016, December 12). South Jutland Police v. Martin Leth Jakobsen. *31-2931, 1201,6*.

The European Court of Human Rights (2011, January 27). *Aydin v. Germany, no. 16637/07*. Retrieved from http://echr.dk/aydin-mod-tyskland-sagsnum-mer-1663707/

The Executive Board of Kobani Canton (2015, November 1). *A Call for an International Solidarity Day with Kobani*. Retrieved from https://peaceinkurdistancampaign.com/2015/10/29/executive-board-of-kobane-canton-calls-for-international-solidarity-on-1-november/#more-4709

The High Court of Eastern Denmark (2018, August 16). The Prosecution Service v. Joanna Palani. *S-2948-18*.

The High Court of Western Denmark (2017, June 22). The Prosecution Service v. Martin Leth Jakobsen. *V.L. S–2522–16*.

The Supreme Court (2017). Frakendelse af dansk indfødsret og udvisning. *Højesteret*. Retrieved from http://www.hoejesteret.dk/hoejesteret/nyheder/Afgorelser/Pages/Frakendelseafdanskindfoedsretogudvisning.aspx

The Syria Campaign (2016). Taking sides: The United Nations' loss of impartiality, independence and neutrality in Syria. The Syria Campaign. Retrieved from http://takingsides.thesyriacampaign.org/

The Syrian Observer (2014, January 17). Who's who: Abdulhamid Darwish. *The Syrian Observer*. Retrieved from https://syrianobserver.com/EN/who/33709/whos_who_abdulhamid_darwish.html

Tilly, C. (1986). *The Contentious French*. Belknap Press. Cambridge, MA: Harvard University Press

Tilly, C. (1998). Social movements and (all sorts of) other political interactions – local, national, and international – including identities. *Theory and Society*, 27(4). 453–80.

Toivanen, M. (2014). Negotiating Home and Belonging: Young Kurds in Finland. PhD dissertation, Faculty of Social Sciences. Department of Social Research. Division of Sociology. University of Turku. Retrieved from http://www.utupub.fi/bitstream/handle/10024/98544/Annales%20B%20389%20Toivanen%20DISS.pdf

Toivanen, M. (forthcoming). *A Comparative Study of Kurdish Diaspora Mobilisation: The Kobane Generation?* Helsinki: Helsinki University Press.

Toivanen, M., and Baser, B. (2016). Gender in the representations of an armed conflict: female Kurdish combatants in French and British media. *Middle East Journal of Culture and Communication*, 9, 294–314.

Toivanen, M. and Baser, B. (2019). Introduction. Methodological approaches in Kurdish studies: politics of fieldwork, positionality, and challenges ahead. In B. Baser, M. Toivanen, B. Zorlu and Y. Duman (eds) *Methodological Approaches in Kurdish Studies: Theoretical and Practical Insights from the Field*. London: Lexington Books.

Toksvig, M. L., Yasar, N., and Bjerregaard, D. (2018, April 8). Et skuddrab. Et voldsomt røveri. Og trusler, der ikke var ulovlige. *Politiradio*. Denmark: 25syv. Accessible at https://www.24syv.dk/programmer/politiradio/27036557/et-skud-drab-et-voldsomt-roveri-og-trusler-der-ikke

Tölölyan, K. (1991). The Nation-State and Its Others: In Lieu of a Preface. *Diaspora: A Journal of Transnational Studies*, 1(1), 3–7. https://doi.org/10.353/dsp.1991.0008

Udenrigsudvalget (2018, March 1). Udenrigsudvalget TV. *Folketinget*. Retrieved from https://www.ft.dk/da/udvalg/udvalgene/uru/tv?s=20171&m=td.1465267&as=1#player

Udenrigsudvalget (n.d.). Udenrigsudvalgets kalender. *Folketinget*. Retrieved from https://www.ft.dk/da/udvalg/udvalgene/uru/kalender

UNAMI (2016). *A Call for Accountability and Protection: Yezidi Survivors of Atrocities Committed by ISIL*. United Nations Assistance Mission for Iraq – Human Rights Office. Retrieved from https://www.ohchr.org/Documents/Countries/IQ/UNAMIReport12Aug2016_en.pdf

UNSCR 2178 (2014). *United Nations Security Council Resolution 2178. Threats to international peace and security caused by terrorist acts*. UNSCR. Retrieved from http://unscr.com/en/resolutions/doc/2178

Vanhala, L. (2009). Anti-discrimination policy actors and their use of litigation strategies: the influence of identity politics. *Journal of European Public Policy*, 16(5), 738–54. https://doi.org/10.1080/13501760902983473

Vanly, I. C. (1968a). *The Kurdish Problem in Syria: Plans for the Genocide of a National Minority*. Amsterdam: Committee for the Defense of the Kurdish People's Rights.

Vanly, I. C. (1968b). *The Persecution of the Kurdish People by the Baath Dictatorship in Syria: The Syrian 'Mein Kampf' against the Kurds*. Amsterdam: Committee for the Defense of the Kurdish People's Rights.

Vanly, I. C. (1992). The Kurds in Syria and Lebanon. In P. G. Kreyenbroek and S. Spearl (eds) *The Kurds. A Contemporary Overview* (pp. 143–70). London: Routledge.

Vestergaard, J. (2016). Internationale, europæiske og danske regler om fremmed-krigere i terroristers tjeneste. In H. M. Motzfeldt, S. Schaumburg-Müller, R. Gottrup and K. Østergaard (eds) *Mod og mening. Hyldestskrift til Frederik Harhoff*. Copenhagen: Jurist- og Økonomforbundets Forlag, 527–54.

Vesterlund, P. (2020, January 23). Faderen til to kvinder fra Brøndby Strand har hentet sine døtre ud af fangenskab i Syrien. De befinder sig nu i Tyrkiet. *TV2*. Retrieved from https://nyheder.tv2.dk/samfund/2020-01-23-is-kvinder-fra-broendby-strand-hentet-ud-af-syrien

VIOMIS (n.d.). Årsrapport for perioden 01. januar 2015 – 31. december 2015. *Audit and Accounting Service*. Retrieved from http://www.indsamlingsnae-vnet.dk/~/media/_raw_indsam/Regnskaber%20I/V_Regnskaber/Viomis_IN_00170_aarsregnskab_2015.ashx

Vittus, C. (2016, February 4). Shaho og Alan frygter at blive straffet for at kæmpe mod IS. *DR.dk*. Retrieved from https://www.dr.dk/nyheder/indland/shaho-og-alan-frygter-blive-straffet-kaempe-mod

Vittus, C. (planner) (2016). De skandinaviske krigere 2:3. *DR P1*. (radio programme)

Wahlbeck, Ö. (1999). *Kurdish Diasporas: A Comparative Study of Kurdish Refugee Communities*. London: Macmillan.

Wahlbeck, Ö. (2017). Keynote lecture: the future of the Kurdish diaspora. *Kurdish Migration Conference 2017*. Middlesex University, London.

Wahlbeck, Ö. (2019). The Future of the Kurdish Diaspora. In M. Gunter (ed.) *Routledge Handbook on the Kurds*. London: Routledge, 413–24.

Wedeen, L. (1999). *The Ambiguity of Domination: Politics, Rhetoric, and Symbols in Contemporary Syria*. Chicago: University of Chicago Press.

Weinstein, Jeremy (2007). *Inside Rebellion*. Cambridge: Cambridge University Press.

Weiss, N. (2018). De gode radikale I krig mot 'Den Islamiske Stat'. In A. Andersson, S. A. E. Høgestøl and A. C. Lie (eds) *Fremmedkrigere. Forebygging, strafforfølgning og rehabilitering i Skandinavia* (pp. 407–31). Oslo: Gyldendal.

Wodak, R. (2009). *The Discourse of Politics in Action. Politics as Usual*. London: Palgrave Macmillan.

World Bank (2018). Remittances data inflows. Migration and Remittances Data. Retrieved from http://www.worldbank.org/en/topic/migrationremittancesdia-sporaissues/brief/migration-remittances-data

World Bank Group (2016). *Migration and Remittances Factbook*. The Global Knowl-edge Partnership on Migration and Development. Retrieved from http://sit-eresources.worldbank.org/INTPROSPECTS/Resources/334934-119980790 8806/4549025-1450455807487/Factbookpart1.pdf

Wæver, O. (2016). Danmark i krig, igen og igen. In P. V. Kessing, and A. Laursen (eds) *Robust Mandat – juridiske udfordringer ved danske militære missioner i det 21. århundrede* (pp. 19–42). Copenhagen: Jurist- og Økonomforbundets Forlag.

Yildiz, K. (2005). *The Kurds in Syria: The Forgotten People*. London: Pluto Press.

Zettervall, C. (2013). *Reluctant Victims into Challengers – Narratives of a Kurdish Political Generation in Diaspora in Sweden*. Lund Dissertations in Sociology 103. Lund: University of Lund. Retrieved from https://lup.lub.lu.se/search/ws/files/5278945/3737392.pdf

Zisser, E. (2014). The Kurds in Syria: caught between the struggle for civil equality and the search for national identity. In O. Bengio (ed.) *Kurdish Awakening: Nation Building in a Fragmented Homeland.* Austin: University of Texas Press.

Østergaard-Nielsen, E. (2003). *Transnational Politics: Turks and Kurds in Germany.* London: Routledge.

@realDonaldTrump (2018, December 19). We have defeated ISIS in Syria. . . . Twitter. Retrieved from https://twitter.com/realDonaldTrump/status/1075397 797929775105

@SalehMaslem (2018, March 12). To all Kurdish activists and friends . . . Twitter. Retrieved from https://twitter.com/SalehMaslem/status/972983080561586178

INDEX